Study Guide and Working Papers

for use with

Modern Advanced Accounting

Tenth Edition

E. John Larsen
University of Southern California

 **McGraw-Hill**
Irwin

Boston   Burr Ridge, IL   Dubuque, IA   Madison, WI   New York   San Francisco   St. Louis
Bangkok   Bogotá   Caracas   Kuala Lumpur   Lisbon   London   Madrid   Mexico City
Milan   Montreal   New Delhi   Santiago   Seoul   Singapore   Sydney   Taipei   Toronto

**McGraw-Hill
Irwin**

Study Guide and Working Papers for use with
MODERN ADVANCED ACCOUNTING
E. John Larsen

Published by McGraw-Hill/Irwin, an imprint of The McGraw-Hill Companies, Inc., 1221 Avenue of the Americas, New York, NY 10020. Copyright © 2006, 2003, 2000, 1997 by The McGraw-Hill Companies, Inc. All rights reserved.

2 3 4 5 6 7 8 9 0 BKM/BKM 0 9 8 7 6 5

ISBN 0-07-299116-X

www.mhhe.com

The McGraw-Hill Companies

TABLE OF CONTENTS

STUDY GUIDE

WORKING PAPERS

TO THE STUDENT

This **Study Guide** has been prepared to accompany the tenth edition of **Modern Advanced Accounting** by E. John Larsen. However, it may be used with other advanced accounting texts. The main purposes of this **Study Guide** are to help you:

1.   **Master the material** as you study each chapter.

2.   **Summarize the essential points** in each chapter and **test your knowledge** with objective questions, short exercises, and cases, thus making it possible for you to **review the material quickly** from time to time, particularly before examinations.

3.   Make the study of accounting **more enjoyable and less tedious.** This is accomplished by presenting an informal and concise summary of each chapter, followed by three groups of objective questions, short exercises, and a case that requires an "essay" answer.

The answers to the questions, short exercises, and cases are provided at the end of each chapter of the **Study Guide to give you immediate feedback and point out the concepts that need additional attention.**

The manner in which students use this **Study Guide** may differ; however, I recommend the following approach:

1.   Study the chapter in the textbook.

2.   Read the **"Highlights of the Chapter"** section of the **Study Guide.** If you note any statements that you do not understand, refer to the textbook for a more detailed discussion of the topic or specific point covered.

3.   Prepare solutions for the questions, short exercises, and cases in the **Study Guide,** and compare your solutions with those provided at the end of each chapter. This will show you how well you understand the material contained in the related chapter of the textbook. Again, if you find something you do not understand, refer to the textbook for a more detailed discussion of the specific subject matter covered in the question, short exercise, or case. Of course, your answers to cases may differ from those provided in the **Study Guide** if you took a different approach or position.

4.   Prepare solutions for the exercises, cases, and problems in the textbook assigned by your instructor.

Once you have mastered the material in this manner, reading the **"Highlights of the Chapter"** section in the **Study Guide** again may provide a quick and effective way of reviewing the material before examinations. Of course, no study technique is equally effective for all students. You may modify the approach suggested above to suit your specific needs and study habits.

E. JOHN LARSEN

CHAPTER 1
ETHICAL ISSUES IN ADVANCED ACCOUNTING

Highlights of the Chapter

1. In recent years, critics have alleged that ethical standards of accountants have deteriorated, resulting in "cute accounting" and "cooking the books" by accountants.

2. Until recently, most efforts to develop ethical standards for accountants have focused on CPAs in the practice of public accounting—primarily auditing. However both the Institute of Management Accountants (IMA) and the Financial Executives International (FEI) promulgated standards of ethical conduct for their members in the 1980s.

3. Despite the AICPA's contention that the primary responsibility for financial statements and financial reporting rests with enterprise management, there has been a long-held view that the first line of defense against improper financial reporting was independent auditors.

4. An early effort to establish ethical standards for preparers of financial statements was a criticism of the lack of a code of ethics for members of the FEI, by participants in the 1970 Seaview Symposium.

5. The Equity Funding fraud, discovered in 1973 after a duration of about nine years, involved at least 10 executives of Equity, many of whom were CPAs with public accounting experience.

6. The Institute of Management Accountants (IMA) **Standards of Ethical Conduct for Members** cover the management accountant's obligations as to competence, confidentiality, integrity, and objectivity, and provide guidance for resolutions of ethical conflict.

7. Although briefer than the IMA standards described in paragraph **6,** the FEI's **Code of Ethics** covers essentially the same areas of professional conduct as the IMA standards.

8. The Treadway Commission made 49 recommendations for curbing fraudulent financial reporting, which is defined as "intentional or misleading conduct, whether act or omission, that results in materially misleading financial statements." The recommendations dealt with public companies; independent public accountants; the SEC, financial institution regulators, and state boards of accountancy; and education. One recommendation was that public companies should maintain accounting functions that are designed to meet their financial reporting obligations.

9. In 1988, the members of the AICPA approved a revised **Code of Professional Conduct,** which included several Rules of Professional Conduct that apply to AICPA members not practicing in a CPA firm.

10. Common requirements of the IMA, FEI, and AICPA ethics pronouncements are for competence, integrity, and objectivity; confidentiality of sensitive information; avoidance of discreditable acts; and avoidance of conflicts of interest. The IMA standards and FEI code specifically require communication of complete information to users of their members' reports; AICPA members indirectly are comparably obligated. Only the AICPA code requires compliance with generally accepted accounting principles.

11. A **conflict of interest** results when an individual reaps an inappropriate personal benefit from his or her acts in an official capacity. **Insider trading** of a publicly owned enterprise's securities is a form of conflict of interest.

12. Data provided by the Treadway Commission indicate that "cooking the books" episodes do not evidence a wholesale breakdown of ethical conduct by management accountants and financial executives of business enterprises. However, an important question is whether the codes of conduct for management accountants and financial executives recently established or revised by the IMA, the FEI, and the AICPA may help those key players in corporate financial reporting to resist pressures to falsify financial statements and financial reports.

Questions

True or False

For each of the following statements, circle the **T** or the **F** to indicate whether the statement is true or false.

T   F   1. **Standards of Ethical Conduct for Members** were issued by the Financial Executives International.

T   F   2. The Code of Ethics of the Financial Executives International specifically prohibits conflicts of interest.

T   F   3. A member of the AICPA not in public practice need not comply with Rule 101 Independence of the AICPA's Rules of Professional Conduct.

T   F   4. "Cooking the books" refers to stretching the form of accounting standards to the limit, regardless of the underlying substance of the business transactions or events.

T   F   5. The AICPA holds that independent auditors are primarily responsible for the integrity of financial statements and financial reports.

T   F   6. Members of the IMA are obligated not to condone violations of **Standards of Ethical Conduct for Members** by others in the organization.

T   F   7. Rule 203 Accounting Principles of the AICPA Code of Professional Conduct has no counterpart in the ethics codes of either the IMA or the FEI.

T   F   8. SEC enforcement actions against accountants, reported in **AAERs,** have involved CPAs in private industry as well as in public accounting practice.

T   F   9. The SEC accepts the "good soldier" defense of unethical conduct by accountants for business enterprises.

Completion Statements

Fill in the necessary words to complete the following statements.

1. A term used to describe fraudulent financial reporting is _____ _____ _____.

2. Ethical standards issued by the Institute of Management Accountants apply to _____ _____ _____.

3. According to the Treadway Commission, the responsibility for reliable financial reporting resides first and foremost at the _____ _____.

4. _____ (number) rules of the AICPA's Rules of Professional Conduct apply to all AICPA members, including those in private industry, governmental entities, and nonprofit organizations.

5. The IMA's Standards of Ethical Conduct for Members cover the management accountant's obligations as to _____, _____, _____, and _____.

6. The Code of Professional Conduct of the AICPA consists of _____ sections: the _____ and the _____.

Multiple Choice

Choose the best answer for each of the following questions and enter the identifying letter in the space provided.

_____ 1. Which of the following organizations did not participate in the Seaview Symposium of 1970?
   a. AICPA
   b. FEI
   c. IMA
   d. None of the foregoing

_____ 2. The Treadway Commission's 49 recommendations did not include any directed to:
   a. The Commodity Futures Trading Commission
   b. The Securities and Exchange Commission
   c. Financial institution regulators
   d. State boards of accountancy

_____ 3. The 1988 revision of the AICPA Code of Professional Conduct was triggered by the report of the:
   a. Anderson Committee
   b. Treadway Commission
   c. Seaview Symposium
   d. Cohen Commission

_____ 4. Compliance with generally accepted accounting principles is required specifically by the ethics code of:
   a. The IMA
   b. The FEI
   c. The AICPA
   d. All the foregoing

_____ 5. According to the AICPA's **Rules of Professional Conduct**, the interests of clients and employers of AICPA members are best served when the members fulfill their responsibility to:
   a. Clients and employers
   b. The AICPA
   c. The SEC
   d. The public

_____ 6.   Do the AICPA's **Rules of Professional Conduct** require members not in public practice of
            accounting to maintain:

	Independence?	Objectivity?
a.	Yes	Yes
b.	No	Yes
c.	Yes	No
d.	No	No

Case

Mary Sullivan, CPA, an AICPA member who presently is an audit manager with a local CPA firm, is interviewing for the position of controller of Ace Industries, Inc., a publicly owned company that is subject to the jurisdiction of the Securities and Exchange Commission despite its common stock's being traded over the counter. During her interview with Charles Crampton, chief executive officer of Ace, Sullivan learns that Ace does not have an audit committee of its five-person board of directors. Sullivan knows that one of the recommendations of the National Commission on Fraudulent Financial Reporting (Treadway Commission) was that all publicly owned enterprises should have an audit committee composed of independent (nonmanagement) directors. In response to her question as to why Ace has no audit committee, Crampton states that Ace is too small to attract "outside" directors and has always had a board of directors composed of officers of the company. Apart from Ace's lack of an audit committee, Sullivan considers the job opportunity at Ace an attractive one.

In her decision whether to accept employment as controller of Ace Industries, Inc., what weight—if any—should Mary Sullivan give to the lack of an audit committee of Ace's board of directors? Explain.

Solutions to Questions and Case: Chapter 1

Questions

True or False

1. F 2. T 3. T 4. F 5. F 6. T 7. T 8. T 9. F

Completion Statements

1. Cooking the books. 2. Accountants in industry. 3. Corporate level. 4. Six. 5. Competence, confidentiality, integrity, objectivity. 6. Two, principles, rules.

Multiple Choice

1. c 2. a 3. a 4. c 5. d 6. b

Case

Given the importance attached to independent audit committees by the Treadway Commission, the Institute of Management Accountants, and the Sarbanes-Oxley Act of 2002, Mary Sullivan might consider the consequences of the lack of an audit committee if she were to encounter an ethical dilemma as controller of Ace Industries, Inc. The absence of an audit committee constitutes a potentially significant weakness in the internal control structure of Ace—a weakness compounded by a board of directors composed solely of officers of Ace. Sullivan might explore further the backgrounds of the Ace director-officers and attempt to determine their ethical postures before deciding to accept the controllership of Ace.

CHAPTER 2
PARTNERSHIPS: ORGANIZATION AND OPERATION

HIGHLIGHTS OF THE CHAPTER

1. The Uniform Partnership Act defines a **partnership** as "an association of two or more persons to carry on, as co-owners, a business for profit." Although a partnership may be formed without a written contract, a carefully prepared written contract is desirable. Today, the limited liability partnership (LLP) has supplanted the general partnership as the primary form of partnership organization.

2. The basic characteristics of the limited liability partnership form of business organization are:
    a. **Ease of formation** A limited liability partnership may be created by written agreement or may be implied by the conduct of two or more persons.
    b. **Limited life** A partnership may be ended by the death, retirement, bankruptcy, or incapacity of any partner.
    c. **Mutual agency** Each partner has the authority to act for the partnership.
    d. **Co-ownership of partnership assets and earnings** Partners have an equity in the net assets and earnings of the partnership; individual partners do not own specific assets of the partnership.

3. The income tax status of a business enterprise and its owners should be considered before choosing between the corporate and the partnership forms of organization. Unlike a corporation, a partnership is not a taxable entity. A partnership is required to file an **information return** showing the computation of net income and the allocation of the net income among the partners.

4. A **Subchapter S corporation** may elect to be treated as a partnership for income tax purposes.

5. For financial accounting, a limited liability partnership is considered to be a **separate entity,** despite the fact that a partnership legally is an **association of individuals.** A limited liability partnership also is a separate legal entity because it may own property, be sued, or bring suit against others. In the fields of law, medicine, and public accounting, the limited liability partnership currently is the usual form of organization.

6. Among the points to be covered by a **partnership contract** are the following:
    a. The date of formation and the planned duration of the partnership, the names of the partners, and the name and business activities of the partnership
    b. The assets to be invested by each partner, the procedures for valuing noncash investments, and the penalties for a partner's failure to invest and maintain the agreed amount of capital
    c. The authority of each partner and the rights and duties of each
    d. The accounting period to be used, the nature of accounting records, financial statements, and audits by independent public accountants
    e. The plan for sharing net income or losses
    f. The drawings allowed to partners and the penalties, if any, for excessive withdrawals
    g. Insurance on the lives of partners, with the partnership or surviving partners named as beneficiaries
    h. Provision for arbitration of disputes and liquidation of the partnership

7. Three types of ledger accounts generally are maintained for each partner: (a) **capital** accounts, (b) **drawing** or **personal** accounts, and (c) accounts for **loans** to or from partners. Subsequent to the original investment, partners' equities are **increased** by net income; partners' equities are **decreased** by withdrawals and by a share of net losses incurred by the partnership.

8. Periodic drawings are recognized by debits to the partners' drawing accounts. At the end of an accounting period the net income or loss is transferred to the partners' capital ledger accounts in the income-sharing ratio, and the debit balances in the drawing accounts are closed to the partners' respective capital accounts.

9. When a partnership receives a loan from a partner, the Loans Payable to Partners ledger account is credited; when a partnership makes a loan to a partner, the Loans Receivable from Partners account is debited.

10. Noncash assets invested in a partnership should be appraised and recognized at their current fair values at the time the assets are invested. Any gain or loss on the disposal of noncash assets invested by the partners is divided among the partners in the income-sharing ratio.

11. Partners may agree on any type of income-sharing plan; however, if partners do not formulate an explicit plan for sharing net income or losses, the Uniform Partnership Act requires that net income or losses be shared equally among the partners. Some possible plans for sharing net income or losses are:

    a. Equally, or in some other ratio

    b. In the ratio of the partners' capital account balances on a particular date, or in the ratio of average capital account balances during the year

    c. Allowing interest on partners' capital account balances and dividing the remaining net income or loss in a specified ratio

    d. Allowing salaries to partners and dividing the resultant net income or loss in a specified ratio

    e. Bonus to managing partner based on income

    f. Allowing salaries and interest on capital account balances, and dividing the remaining net income or loss in a specified ratio

12. When average capital account balances are used as a basis for income sharing, or as the basis for interest computations, debits to the partners' drawing accounts generally are not considered in the computation of the average capital account balances, because these changes are considered to be withdrawals of current earnings. The partnership contract should specify the items to be included in the computation of the average capital account balances. Computation of the average capital account balance for partner Clark is illustrated as follows:

Clark, Capital

Apr. 1	12,000	Jan 1 bal.	60,000
		Aug. 31	15,000

Capital account balance	Fraction of year unchanged	
$60,000	1/4	$15,000
48,000	5/12	20,000
63,000	1/3	21,000
Average capital account balance		$56,000

13. If a partnership contract includes interest on capital and/or salaries in the division of net income or loss, interest and salaries are provided in full even if the partnership incurs a net loss (before allowances for interest and salaries). A partnership contract that permits partners to make regular drawings should specify whether such drawings are intended to be a factor in the division of net income or loss.

©The McGraw-Hill Companies, Inc., 2006

14. A partner acting as manager of a partnership may be allowed a bonus, based on either income **before** or income **after** the bonus. If income before the bonus is $22,000, a bonus of 10% of income after the bonus would be $2,000 ($22,000 x 1/11 = $2,000).

15. After each partner's share (including bonus, interest, salary, and any balance) of net income is computed, the credit balance of the Income Summary ledger account is closed to the partners' capital accounts. Each partner's share of net income or loss may be displayed in the partnership income statement or in a separate exhibit accompanying the income statement. If salaries allowed to partners are included in operating expenses, the amount of such salaries should be disclosed.

16. A **statement of partners' capital** is a financial statement prepared for a partnership at the end of the accounting period. It shows for each partner the beginning capital, additional investments or withdrawals of a permanent nature, share of net income or loss for the period, regular drawings, and the ending capital. In addition, a Combined column is used to show totals of all items included in the statement.

17. Errors in the measurements of partnership net income or loss for prior accounting periods should be analyzed carefully when the income-sharing ratio is changed or when changes in membership of a partnership take place. Each partner's capital should be restated based on that partner's share of the adjustment to net income or loss for each prior period.

18. The operation of a limited liability partnership generally is not interrupted by a change in the membership of the partnership. Legally, a change in membership terminates the existing partnership and creates a new partnership. Changes in membership result when a partner is admitted to the firm, retires, or dies.

19. Before admission of a new partner is recorded, the partnership accounting records should be brought up to date. Current fair values of assets should be considered in setting the amount to be invested by the incoming partner for a share of the net assets of the partnership. The admission of a new partner may take place in one of two ways: (a) through the **acquisition of all or part of the interest** of one or more of the existing partners or (b) through the **investment of assets in the partnership** by the new partner.

20. If the new partner acquires an ownership interest from one or more of the existing partners, the transaction is recorded by a debit to the capital account of each selling partner and a credit to the capital account of the new partner. For example, if Young has a capital account balance of $10,000 representing a 20% equity in a partnership, and Young sells the entire equity directly to Zeno for $15,000, the transaction is recorded in the partnership accounting records as follows:

Young, Capital	10,000	
Zeno, Capital		10,000

To record transfer to Young's interest in partnership to Zeno.

The amount paid by Young to Zeno is not entered in the partnership accounting records because no assets are received by the partnership.

21. When a new partner **makes an investment** in a limited liability partnership, the following three situations may be encountered:

   a. The new partner's capital account is credited for the **current fair value** of the assets he or she is investing, and the capital accounts of the existing partners remain unchanged.

   b. The new partner may invest an amount that is larger than his or her percentage share of the net assets, thus potentially requiring the recognition of a **bonus or goodwill to the existing partners.**

   c. The new partner may invest an amount that is less than his or her percentage share of net assets, thus potentially requiring the recognition of a **bonus or goodwill to the new partner.**

22. When the net assets (assets less liabilities) of the limited liability partnership are fairly stated in the accounting records, the bonus and goodwill methods of recording the admission of a new partner are illustrated by the following examples:

Assume that Ames and Borg, partners of Ames & Borg LLP, have capital account balances of $80,000 and $100,000, respectively, and that they share net income or losses equally. Chun is to be admitted as a new partner for an investment of the net assets specified in (1) and (2) below of a single proprietorship for a 25% interest in the net assets of the partnership. Chun is to have a 30% interest in net income or losses, and Ames and Borg each will have a 35% interest.

Net Assets Invested by New Partner in a Limited Liability Partnership

Type of solution	(1) $50,000 (bonus or goodwill to new partner)			(2) $70,000 (bonus or goodwill to existing partners)		
Bonus	Net Assets	50,000		Net Assets	70,000	
	Ames, Capital	3,750		Ames, Capital		3,750
	Borg, Capital	3,750		Borg, Capital		3,750
	Chun, Capital		57,500	Chun, Capital		62,500
	New total capital: $180,000 + $50,000 = $230,000. Bonus to Chun: ($230,000 x 0.25) − $50,000 = $7,500, divided equally between Ames and Borg.			New total capital: $180,000 + $70,000 = $250,000 Bonus to Ames and Borg: $70,000 − ($250,000 x 0.25) = $7,500, divided equally between Ames and Borg.		
Goodwill	Net Assets	50,000		Net Assets	70,000	
	Goodwill	10,000		Goodwill	30,000	
	Chun, Capital		60,000	Ames Capital		15,000
				Borg, Capital		15,000
				Chun, Capital		70,000
	Capitalize existing partners' investment ($180,000 ÷ 3/4 = $240,000). $240,000 x 1/4 = $60,000. Goodwill to Chun: $60,000 − $50,000 = $10,000			Capitalize Chun's investment ($70,000 ÷ 1/4 = $280,000). Goodwill to Ames and Borg: $280,000 − $250,000 = $30,000, divided equally between Ames and Borg.		

23.   A new partner may invest an amount that involves the recognition of a **bonus or goodwill to existing partners** for the privilege of becoming a member of a limited liability partnership with high earning power. In contrast, existing partners may allow a **bonus or goodwill to the new partner** when he or she has unusual ability or invests the net assets of a business enterprise of superior earning power in the partnership.

24.   When a new partner invests an amount of cash larger than the carrying amount of the interest in net assets that he or she acquires, the transaction should be recorded by the bonus method. Recording the implied goodwill in such situations is not acceptable (in the opinion of the author) **because the implied goodwill has not been acquired by the partnership**.

25.   The restatement of partnership assets to current fair values before a new partner is admitted to a limited liability partnership may be the most convenient method of achieving equity among the partners.

26.   A retiring partner may receive an amount in settlement for his or her equity from the partnership or may sell his or her equity, either to an existing partner or to an outsider. A settlement price to be paid from partnership assets should be determined pursuant to the partnership contract. In most cases, the equity of the retiring partner is based on the current fair values for all partnership

assets. The current fair values may or may not be entered in the accounting records of the partnership.

27. If the amount paid to a retiring partner differs from the carrying amount of his or her equity, the difference should be recorded as a bonus to the retiring partner or a bonus to the continuing partners. Goodwill should not be recognized by the partnership when the amount paid to the retiring partner exceeds the carrying amount of the partner's equity.

28. The final settlement with a retiring partner often is deferred for some time after withdrawal to permit the measurement of net income or loss to date of withdrawal and the accumulation of sufficient cash to pay the retiring partner.

29. Terms of settlement with the estate of a deceased partner generally are specified in the partnership contract. The journal entries to record payments to a deceased partner's estate are similar to journal entries to record the settlement with a retiring partner.

30. Legal provisions governing limited partnerships are provided by the Uniform Limited Partnership Act. Limited partnerships differ in several respects from limited liability partnerships, especially with respect to the rights and obligations of limited partners.

31. The formation of a limited partnership is evidenced by a **certificate** filed with the county recorder, which includes a number of items in addition to those found in the typical partnership contract of a limited liability partnership.

32. The membership **units** offered to prospective limited partners are subject to the Securities Act of 1933, which may require registration of the units with the Securities and Exchange Commission.

33. The SEC has provided standards for financial statements of limited partnerships subject to the SEC's jurisdiction. A significant requirement is the disclosure of **per-unit** information in the income statements and balance sheets of limited partnerships.

Questions

True or False

For each of the following statements, circle the **T** or the **F** to indicate whether the statement is true or false.

T   F   1. The creation of a limited liability partnership requires a written contract and approval by the state in which the partnership is organized.

T   F   2. The admission of a new member to an existing limited liability partnership, or the death or bankruptcy of a partner, legally ends the partnership.

T   F   3. Each partner has the authority to negotiate contracts on behalf of the limited liability partnership.

T   F   4. If a judgment is entered against a limited liability partnership by a court, each partner is liable for the full amount of the judgment, and the creditor may collect from any of the partners.

T   F   5. A partnership is not a taxable entity; however, a partnership may elect to be taxed as a corporation.

T   F   6. A limited liability partnership is not considered a separate entity, for either financial accounting or legal purposes.

T F   7. The display of salaries to partners among expenses in a limited liability partnership income statement tends to distort the net income or loss of the partnership and makes comparisons with similar business enterprises operating as corporations less meaningful.

T F   8. Disputes arising among partners that cannot be resolved by reference to the limited liability partnership contract may be settled by the managing partner of the partnership.

T F   9. Debit balances of partners' drawing ledger accounts are closed to the Income Summary account at the end of the accounting period.

T F 10. Noncash assets invested in a limited liability partnership are recognized at current fair values rather than at the carrying amounts in the accounting records of the investing partner.

T F 11. A partner may be entitled to receive a larger share of net income than of net assets of the limited liability partnership.

T F 12. If a partner receives a bonus of 10% of income after the bonus, and if the income before the bonus amounts to $44,550, the amount of the bonus is $4,050.

T F 13. The main purpose of allowing partners salaries and interest on their capital account balances is to achieve a more equitable distribution of partnership net income.

T F 14. Xeno & Yang LLP had income of $10,000 for 2005 before salaries to partners. Yang's share of net income would be the same whether Yang was allowed a salary of $12,000 or guaranteed a minimum of $12,000 as a share of partnership net income.

T F 15. Corrections to net income or losses of prior years should be displayed in the income statement of a limited liability partnership as extraordinary items.

T F 16. If after the death of a partner the surviving partners decide to continue as a new partnership, creditors of the former limited liability partnership also are creditors of the new partnership.

T F 17. If after the death of a partner the surviving partners of a limited liability partnership fail to reach settlement with the estate of the deceased partner, the estate may have the value of the deceased partner's interest determined as of the date of death and may recover this amount from the new partnership.

T F 18. The acquisition of an interest by a new partner from an existing partner in a private transaction does not require a journal entry in the accounting records of a limited liability partnership.

T F 19. It is preferable not to recognize in the accounting records any goodwill allowed to the existing partners on admission of a new partner, and goodwill to the new partner should be recognized only when the new partner invests a highly profitable business enterprise in the limited liability partnership.

T F 20. A **limited liability partnership** is a special form of **limited partnership.**

T F 21. The legal requirements for organizing a limited partnership are the same as the legal requirements for organizing a limited liability partnership.

T F 22. Limited partners may not provide services as their investment in a limited partnership.

Completion Statements

Fill in the necessary words or amounts to complete the following statements.

1. If a law firm is incorporated, the organization would be known as a _____ _____.

2. The three types of limited liability partners' ledger accounts are _____, _____, (or _____), and _____ to or from partners.

3. If limited liability partners do not agree on a plan for sharing net income or losses, the presumption is that they intended to share _____.

4. A limited liability partnership is _____ by the retirement or death of one of the partners.

5. Partners Ang and Bon share net income or losses in a 3:2 ratio and have capital account balances of $18,000 and $17,000, respectively. If Clay invests the identifiable net assets of a business enterprise with a current fair value of $15,000 for a 25% equity in the net assets of the limited liability partnership, a bonus is allowed to the (new or existing) _____ partner(s).

6. Assuming that the bonus method is used to record the admission of Clay as described in question **5,** the ending balances of the partners' capital ledger accounts are as follows: **(a)** Partner Ang $_____, **(b)** Partner Bon $_____, and **(c)** Partner Clay $_____.

7. The _____ method generally is not acceptable for recording the withdrawal of a partner from a limited liability partnership.

8. The formation of a limited partnership is evidenced by a _____ filed with the county recorder of the principal place of business of the limited partnership.

9. Membership in a limited partnership is offered to prospective limited partners in _____.

Multiple Choice

Choose the best answer for each of the following questions and enter the identifying letter in the space provided.

_____ 1. A limited liability partnership is considered an accounting entity separate from the individual partners for purposes of:
a. Both financial accounting and federal income taxes
b. Federal income taxes but not financial accounting
c. Financial accounting but not federal income taxes
d. Neither financial accounting nor federal income taxes

____ 2. Alex and Bame, partners of Alex & Bame LLP, share net income or losses in a 2:1 ratio, respectively. Each partner receives an annual salary allowance of $6,000. If the salaries are recognized as an expense rather than as a means for division of net income, the total amount allocated to each partner for salaries and net income will be:
   a. Less for both Alex and Bame
   b. Unchanged for both Alex and Bame
   c. More for Alex and less for Bame
   d. More for Bame and less for Alex

____ 3. Mason & Nelson LLP was formed on February 28. On that date, the following assets were invested (at current fair values):

	Mason	**Nelson**
Cash	$25,000	$ 35,000
Inventories		55,000
Building		100,000
Equipment	15,000	

The building was subject to a mortgage note payable of $30,000 that was to be assumed by the partnership. The partnership contract provided that Mason and Nelson were to share net income or losses 25% and 75% respectively. Nelson's capital account balance on February 28 is:
   a. $190,000
   b. $160,000
   c. $172,500
   d. $150,000
   e. Some other amount

____ 4. Based on the same facts as in question **3,** if the partnership contract provides that the partners initially should have an equal interest in partnership capital with no investment of intangible assets. Mason's capital account balance on February 28 is:
   a. $100,000
   b. $115,000
   c. $200,000
   d. $230,000
   e. Some other amount

____ 5. Evans, Farmer, and Grove invested $40,000, $30,000, and $25,000, respectively, in Evans, Farmer & Grove LLP on June 30, 2005. They agreed to divide income or losses as follows:
   (1) Salaries of $10,000, $8,000, and $6,000, respectively, to Evans, Farmer, and Grove
   (2) Interest of 10% on beginning capital account balances
   (3) Remaining net income or loss divided equally
   (4) A minimum of $15,000 of income guaranteed to Grove

If the income of the partnership for the fiscal year ended June 30, 2006, before salaries and interest allowances to partners, was $44,000, the amount of income credited to Evans is:
   a. $17,500
   b. $16,000
   c. $14,667
   d. $14,000
   e. Some other amount

_____ 6. The admission of a new partner for a 20% interest in a partnership for an investment of $18,000 cash, with total capital to be $75,000, results in the recognition of:
   a. Goodwill to the existing partners
   b. Goodwill to the new partner
   c. A bonus to the existing partners
   d. A bonus to the new partner

_____ 7. If E is the total capital of a limited liability partnership before the admission of a new partner, F is the total capital of the partnership after the admission of the new partner, G is the amount of the new partner's investment, and H is the amount of capital credited to the new partner, there is:
   a. Goodwill to the new partner if $F >$ (is larger than) $(E + G)$ and $H <$ (is less than) G
   b. Goodwill to the exiting partners if $F = E + G$ and $H > G$
   c. A bonus to the new partner if $F = E + G$ and $H > G$
   d. Neither a bonus nor goodwill if $F > (E + G)$ and $H > G$

_____ 8. The total of partners' capital account balances of a limited liability partnership was $105,000, excluding goodwill. A partner whose share of net income or losses was 20% decided to withdraw from the partnership. The withdrawing partner was paid $37,000 by the partnership in final settlement. The withdrawal was improperly recorded by the goodwill method. The continuing partners' capital account balances, excluding their share of the goodwill, totaled $80,000 after withdrawal. The improperly imputed goodwill of the partnership was:
   a. $125,000
   b. $80,000
   c. $70,000
   d. $60,000
   e. Some other amount

_____ 9. On July 1, 2005, Ann Moore and Grace Pulis formed Moore & Pulis LLP, agreeing to share net income and losses in a 2:3 ratio, respectively. Moore invested land with a current fair value of $50,000 that had cost her $25,000. Pulis invested $50,000 cash. The land was disposed of for $52,100 on July 5, 2005. The amount to be recorded in Moore's capital account on formation of the partnership is:
   a. $10,000
   b. $20,000
   c. $25,000
   d. $50,000
   e. $52,100

_____ 10. Cicero and Dino, partners of Cicero & Dino LLP, shared net income and losses in the ratio 7:3, respectively. On May 5, 2005, their capital account balances were as follows:
   Cicero $35,000
   Dino   30,000

   On May 5, 2005, the partners agreed to admit Estes as a partner with a one-third interest in the partnership capital and net income or losses for an investment of $25,000. The new limited liability partnership was to begin with total capital of $90,000. Immediately after Estes's admission, the capital account balances of Cicero, Dino, and Estes, respectively, were:
   a. $30,000; $30,000; $30,000
   b. $31,500; $28,500; $30,000
   c. $31,667; $28,333; $30,000
   d. $35,000; $30,000; $25,000

11. The income-sharing provision of the contract that established Koo & Lee LLP provided that Koo was to receive a bonus of 20% of income after deduction of the bonus, with the remaining income or losses distributed 40% to Koo and 60% to Lee. If the income of the partnership before the bonus was $240,000 for the current year, the capital accounts of Koo and Lee would be credited, respectively, in the amounts of:
   a. $120,000 and $120,000
   b. $124,800 and $115,200
   c. $96,000 and $144,000
   d. $163,200 and $76,800
   e. Some other amounts

SHORT EXERCISES

1. Martha Fong was admitted to Fong & Wick LLP by investing the following net assets:

	Carrying amounts to Fong	Current fair values
Building	$64,000	$48,000
Accumulated depreciation	(12,000)	
Land	15,000	35,000
Unexpired insurance	120	120
Mortgage note payable	(22,390)	(22,390)
Accrued interest on mortgage note payable	(95)	(95)
Net investment by Martha Fong	$44,635	$60,635

In the following form, prepare a journal entry to record the admission of Martha Fong to Fong & Wick LLP.

Fong & Wick LLP
Journal Entry

2. Activity in the capital ledger accounts for Alan and Boone, partners of Alan & Boone LLP, was as follows:

	Alan	Boone
Balances, Jan. 1, 2005	$40,000	$80,000
Investment, Mar. 1, 2005	20,000	
Withdrawal, Dec. 1, 2005		40,000

Net income of Alan & Boone LLP for 2006 amounted to $48,000 (before interest or salary allowances to partners).

In the space below, enter the amount of the net income that each partner would receive under each of the following assumptions:

a. The partnership contract is silent as to sharing of net income or losses.

b. Net income or losses are divided on the basis of the weighted-average capital account balances (not including the income or loss for the current year).

c. Net income or losses are divided on the basis of beginning capital account balances.

d. Net income or losses are divided on the basis of ending capital account balances (not including the income or loss for the current year).

e. Salaries of $12,000 and $6,000 are allowed to Alan and Boone, respectively; interest of 10% is allowed on weighted-average capital account balances as computed in **b;** and the remainder is divided equally.

	Net income to Alan	Net income to Boone	Total net income
a.	$_____	$_____	$48,000
b.	$_____	$_____	$48,000
c.	$_____	$_____	$48,000
d.	$_____	$_____	$48,000
e.	$_____	$_____	$48,000

3. The partners of Lee & Moye LLP shared net income or losses in a 3:2 ratio in 2004 and in a 2:1 ratio in 2005. On January 2, 2006, they discovered the following errors and ask you to prepare an appropriate journal entry to correct the partnership's accounting records.

	Dec. 31, 2004	Dec. 31, 2005
Inventories overstated	$5,000	$7,400
Accrued liabilities understated	600	450
Allowance for doubtful accounts understated	300	750
Unexpired insurance understated	200	350

a. Complete the analysis below to compute the net increase or decrease in the net income of Lee & Moye LLP for 2004 and 2005:

	Increase or (decrease) in net income	
	2004	2005
Inventories overstated, Dec. 31:		
2004	$	$
2005		
Accrued liabilities understated, Dec. 31:		
2004		
2005		
Allowance for doubtful accounts understated, Dec. 31:		
2004		
2005		
Unexpired insurance understated, Dec. 31:		
2004		
2005		
Net increase or (decrease) in net income	$	$

b. In the space below, prepare a journal entry on January 2, 2006, to correct the accounting records of Lee & Moye LLP.

Lee & Moye LLP
Journal Entry

2006			
Jan. 2			

4. Current capital ledger account balances of the partners of Bora, Cali & Duva LLP are as follows:

Bora, capital	$45,000
Cali, capital	36,000
Duva, capital	9,000

Enns is admitted as a partner to Bora, Cali & Duva LLP, agreeing to invest $10,000 cash in the partnership and, in addition, to pay directly to the other partners (in proportion to their capital account balances) an amount sufficient to give Enns a 20% equity in the net assets of the partnership.

In the space below, prepare a journal entry to record Enns's admission to Bora, Cali, Duva & Enns LLP.

Bora, Cali, Duva & Enns, LLP
Journal Entry

	Cash	10,000	

5. The partners of Moye, Nobe & Ord LLP share net income and losses in a 5:2:1 ratio and have combined capital account balances of $42,000. Pard is admitted to Moye, Nobe & Ord LLP with an investment of identifiable net assets of a single proprietorship having a current fair value of $18,000, and is given a one-third interest in assets and a 20% share of net income or losses of the partnership, the other partners to share in the remaining net income or losses in the original ratio.

   a. In the spaces below, enter the new income-sharing ratio for each partner:

   Moye _____   Ord _____

   Nobe _____   Pard _____

   b. In the spaces below, prepare journal entries to record the admission of Pard to Moye, Nobe & Ord LLP under (1) the bonus method and (2) the goodwill method.

Moye, Nobe, Ord & Pard LLP
Journal Entry

(1)	Bonus method:		
	Identifiable Net Assets	18,000	

Moye, Nobe, Ord & Pard LLP
Journal Entry

(2)	Goodwill method:		
	Identifiable Net Assets	18,000	

CASE

Pamela Cross is negotiating with the partners of Lawes, Moon & Norris LLP the terms of her admission to the partnership. Cross points out that her cash resources are limited at present; she requests permission to invest $10,000 cash and a $40,000, two-year, 10% promissory note in Lawes, Moon & Norris LLP, in exchange for a $50,000 capital account balance. Cross points out that her expected share (20%) of partnership net income would be adequate to provide both her living expenses and the $48,000 maturity value of the note on its due date.

Should Lawes, Moon, and Norris agree to the proposal of Pamela Cross? Explain.

SOLUTIONS TO QUESTIONS, SHORT EXERCISES, AND CASE: CHAPTER 2

QUESTIONS

True or False

1. F   2. T   3. T   4. F   5. F   6. F   7. F   8. F   9. F   10. T   11. T   12. T   13. T   14. F   15. F   16. T   17. T   18. F   19. T   20. F   21. F   22. T

Completion Statements

1. Professional corporation.   2. Capital, drawing (or personal), loans.   3. Equally.   4. Dissolved. 5. Existing.   6. a. $19,500;   b. $18,000;   c. $12,500.   7. Goodwill.   8. Certificate.   9. Units.

Multiple Choice

1. c   2. b   3. b ($35,000 + $55,000 + $100,000 − $30,000 = $160,000)   4. a [($160,000 + $25,000 + $15,000) ÷ 2 = $100,000]   5. b ($4,000 + $10,000 + 3,500 − $1,500 = $16,000)   6. c   7. c

8. d [$\dfrac{\$37,000 - (\$105,000 - \$80,000)}{0.20} = \$60,000$]

9. d   10. b   11. a

SHORT EXERCISES

1.
Fong & Wick LLP
Journal Entry

	Buildings	48,000	
	Land	35,000	
	Unexpired Insurance	120	
	Mortgage Note Payable		22,390
	Interest Payable		95
	Martha Fong, Capital		60,635
	To record admission of Martha Fong to the partnership.		

2.

	Net income to Alan	Net income to Boone	Total net income
a. Equally (in absence of agreement)	$24,000	$24,000	$48,000
b. 42.5% to Alan and 57.5% to Boone (on basis of weighted-average capital account balances*)	$20,400	$27,600	$48,000
c. In 40:80 ratio (on basis of beginning capital account balances)	$16,000	$32,000	$48,000
d. In 60:40 ratio (on basis of ending capital account balances)	$28,800	$19,200	$48,000
e. Salaries	$12,000	$ 6,000	$18,000
Interest at 10% of weighted-average capital account balances*	5,667	7,667	13,334
Remainder of $16,666 equally	8,333	8,333	16,666
Totals	$26,000	$22,000	$48,000

*Weighted-average capital account balances:

Alan: ($40,000 x 1/6) + ($60,000 x 5/6)	$ 56,667	(42.5%)
Boone: ($80,000 x 11/12) + ($40,000 x 1/12)	76,667	(57.5%)
Totals	$133,334	(100%)

3. a.

	Increase or (decrease) in net income	
	2004	2005
Inventories overstated, Dec. 31:		
2004	$(5,000)	$5,000
2005		(7,400)
Accrued liabilities understated, Dec. 31:		
2004	(600)	600
2005		(450)
Allowance for doubtful accounts understated, Dec. 31:		
2004	(300)	300
2005		(750)
Unexpired insurance understated, Dec. 31:		
2004	200	(200)
2005		350
Net (decrease) in net income	$(5,700)	$(2,550)

b.

Lee & Moye LLP
Journal Entry

2006			
Jan. 2	Unexpired Insurance	350	
	Lee, Capital	5,120	
	Moye, Capital	3,130	
	Inventories		7,400
	Accrued Liabilities Payable		450
	Allowance for Doubtful Accounts		750
	To correct accounting records for misstatement of net income in		
	2004 and 2005. The debits to partners' capital account balances		
	are computed as follows:		
		2004 2005	
	Net decrease of $5,700 in net income for 2004,		
	divided in 3:2 ratio	$3,420 $2,280	
	Net decrease of $2,550 in net income for 2005,		
	divided in 2:1 ratio	1,700 850	
	Totals	$5,120 $3,130	

4.

Bora, Cali, Duva & Enns LLP
Journal Entry

	Cash	10,000	
	Bora, Capital	5,000	
	Cali, Capital	4,000	
	Duva , Capital	1,000	
	Enns, Capital		20,000
	To record admission of Enns to the partnership. Enns invested		
	$10,000 cash in the partnership and paid $10,000 cash directly to		
	Bora, Cali, and Duva (divided in ratio of capital account		
	balances) to obtain a 20% equity in the net assets of $100,000.		

5. a.

Moye	50%	(80% x 5/8)
Nobe	20	(80% x 2/8)
Ord	10	(80% x 1/8)
Pard	20	
Total	100%	

b. (1)

Moye, Nobe, Ord & Pard LLP
Journal Entry

Bonus method:			
Identifiable Net Assets		18,000	
Moye, Capital		1,250	
Nobe, Capital		500	
Ord, Capital		250	
Pard, Capital			20,000
To record admission of Pard. One-third of ($42,000 + $18,000) =			
$20,000; therefore, the bonus to Pard equals $2,000 ($20,000 –			
$18,000 = $2,000).			

(2)

Moye, Nobe, Ord & Pard LLP
Journal Entry

Goodwill method:			
Identifiable Net Assets		18,000	
Goodwill		3,000	
Pard, Capital			21,000
To record admission of Pard. Existing capital of $42,000 equals			
two-thirds of implied value of partnership; therefore, goodwill			
equals $3,000 ($42,000 + $21,000 – $60,000 = $3,000).			

CASE

Lawes, Moon, and Norris should not agree to the terms proposed by Pamela Cross for her admission to Lawes, Moon & Norris LLP. Her capital account should be credited for only $10,000, the amount of her cash investment. The promissory note she proposes to invest is essentially a piece of paper rather than an asset; given her admitted shortage of cash resources, it is doubtful that a bank would accept the note for discounting by the partnership.

Perhaps Cross might agree to reinvest in the partnership a portion of her anticipated share of partnership net income, rather than withdrawing all of it (assuming such withdrawal would be sanctioned by the partnership contract). Such a course would decrease the total interest to be paid on the promissory note and would increase Cross's capital account balance long before the maturity date of the proposed note.

CHAPTER 3
PARTNERSHIP LIQUIDATION AND
INCORPORATION; JOINT VENTURES

HIGHLIGHTS OF THE CHAPTER

1. The **liquidation** of a limited liability partnership means winding up the partnership by realizing the noncash assets, paying the liabilities, and distributing the remaining cash to the partners. Liquidation may be completed quickly, or it may require several months. The term **realization** means the conversion of assets to cash.

2. When partners decide to liquidate their limited liability partnership, the partnership's accounting records are adjusted, and the net income or loss for the final period of operations is entered in the partners' capital accounts. Gains or losses on the realization of assets, divided among the partners in the income-sharing ratio, also are entered in the partners' capital accounts.

3. After all noncash assets are realized and partnership creditors are paid, partners receive cash payments equal to the balances of their capital accounts. If the cash generated from the realization of noncash assets is insufficient to pay the liabilities, unpaid partnership creditors may collect unpaid liabilities from the personal assets of any solvent partner whose actions caused the partnership's insolvency, even from partners who have debit balances in their capital accounts.

4. If the realization of assets is completed before any cash is paid to the partners, the final gain or loss on the realization of assets is known and is allocated to partners' capital accounts. In such cases, the available cash is paid to creditors and then to partners according to the balances of their capital accounts. Deficits in the capital accounts of any of the partners must be eliminated through additional investments by the affected partners. However, if a deficit partner is insolvent, the deficit must be absorbed by the other partners in their income-sharing ratio.

5. If the realization of assets has not been completed, and the final gain or loss on realization of assets is not known, cash may be distributed to partners in installments as long as sufficient cash is withheld to cover any unpaid liabilities and possible costs of liquidation. The amount of cash that may be paid to partners at various stages of liquidation is determined by preparation of an exhibit in which partners' capital accounts are charged for the maximum possible loss (including liquidation costs) that may be incurred in winding up the limited liability partnership.

6. In the course of liquidation, partners may withdraw assets **in kind.** No distribution of cash or other assets should be made to partners until after all possible losses and liquidation costs have been considered. Each interim payment of cash to partners is made on the assumption that it may be the last, that is, that no additional cash will be available for partners.

7. Although partners' loans to the partnership theoretically should be repaid before partners' capitals, the **right of offset** requires that loan balances be added to the capital account balances for liquidation purposes. The fact that a partner has made a loan to the partnership does not mean that the partner will receive cash any sooner on liquidation. Thus, in a statement of realization and liquidation, loan and capital account balances may be combined for each partner. However, loan and capital account balances are not combined in the partnership ledger.

8. The income-sharing ratio used during the operation of a limited liability partnership also is generally applicable to the gains and losses during liquidation. However, the partners may agree to distribute liquidation gains and losses in a different ratio. When all liquidation gains and losses are allocated to the partners' capital accounts, the amount of cash available (after payment of liabilities) is equal to the total of the balances of the partners' capital and loan accounts. Cash then is distributed to the partners in amounts equal to the total amount of each partner's capital and loan accounts.

9. In an insolvent limited liability partnership, at least one partner has a capital deficit. At this point in the liquidation process, partnership creditors may demand payment from any solvent partner whose actions caused the partnership's insolvency. Payments to partnership creditors by a partner from personal funds are recorded by debits to partnership liability accounts and a credit to the partner's capital account. If the partner with the capital deficit pays the required amount, sufficient cash will be available to pay the partnership creditors in full.

10. When both a limited liability partnership and some of the partners are insolvent, the legal rule of **marshaling of assets** is applied. This rule states that creditors of each partner have first claim on his or her personal assets, and partnership creditors have first claim on partnership assets. Any amounts payable to creditors of an insolvent limited liability partnership that has no assets may be obtained from **one** or **any combination** of the solvent partners whose actions caused the partnership's insolvency. Any partner who is forced to invest in the partnership more than originally agreed on has a right to collect from the other partners. However, if the other partners were insolvent, this would be a meaningless right. The creditors of an insolvent partner may claim only that partner's equity interest, if any, in the partnership.

11. To illustrate the marshaling of assets, assume that, after the realization of all the noncash assets of Apto, Bart & Capp LLP, liabilities of $15,000 remain unpaid. Assume the following financial status for each partner:

	Partnership capital (deficit)	Net personal assets (deficit)
Partner Apto	$15,000	$30,000
Partner Bart	(12,500)	5,000
Partner Capp	(17,500)	(2,500)

The partnership creditors can recover the entire $15,000 from Apto only if Apto's actions caused the partnership's insolvency. If Bart was the cause, partnership creditors would receive only $5,000 of their $15,000 total claims. The personal creditors of Capp could not proceed against the personal assets of either Apto or Bart, and they would not receive anything from the partnership because Capp has a capital deficit.

12. When the liquidation of a limited liability partnership is expected to extend over several months, partners usually will want to receive cash (or other assets) as soon as possible. Installment payments to partners may be made if precautions are taken to **ensure that all creditors are paid in full and that no partner is paid prematurely.**

13. In installment liquidations, the liquidator must not authorize distributions to partners that may have to be returned by the partners if large liquidation losses cause deficits in their partnership equity (capital plus loan accounts). Installment distributions of cash or other assets to partners are determined as follows:

   a. Assume a total loss on the realization of all remaining noncash assets.

   b. Assume that any partner with a potential capital deficit will be unable to pay anything to the partnership from personal assets.

   To implement these assumptions, installment cash payments to partners are made as if no more cash would become available, either from the realization of assets or from the collection of any potential capital deficits.

14. When installment distributions to partners are made according to the rules listed in paragraph **13,** the effect will be to bring the partners' equities to the income-sharing ratio as quickly as possible. After installment distributions to partners have reduced the partners' equities to the income-sharing ratio, subsequent distributions of cash or other assets to partners may be made in the income-sharing ratio.

15. A complete cash distribution program may be prepared before liquidation starts. The procedures to be followed in the preparation of such a program are as follows:

a. Ascertain the **equity** (capital, plus any loan to the partnership, less any loan from the partnership) for each partner.

b. Divide the equity of each partner by each partner's income-sharing ratio to determine the **capital per unit of income sharing** for each partner.

c. The partner with the largest capital per unit of income sharing is entitled to receive enough cash to reduce his or her capital per unit of income sharing to the capital of the partner with the second highest amount. The amount of cash to be paid at this point is computed by multiplying the required reduction in the capital per unit of income sharing of the highest-ranking partner by that partner's income-sharing ratio.

d. The process described in **c** is continued until the capital per unit of income-sharing amounts for all partners are equal. Additional cash distributions then may be made in the income-sharing ratio.

16. Partners Ray, Sam, and Tom share net income and losses in the ratio of 4:3:2, and have total equities in the limited liability partnership as follows: Ray, $16,000; Sam, $10,500; and Tom, $6,020. How should cash or other assets be paid to the partners (after all liabilities have been paid) as they become available in the course of liquidation? The answer may be developed as follows:

	Ray	Sam	Tom
Capital balances (equities) before liquidation	$16,000	$10,500	$6,020
Income-sharing ratio	4	3	2
Capital per unit of income sharing	$ 4,000	$ 3,500	$3,010
First cash of $2,000 ($500 x 4 = $2,000) to Ray	(500)		
Capital per unit of income sharing	$ 3,500	$ 3,500	$3,010
Next $3,430 to Ray and Sam: $490 x 4 or $1,960 to Ray, and $490 x 3 or $1,470 to Sam	(490)	(490)	
Capital per unit of income sharing	$ 3,010	$ 3,010	$3,010
Any cash in excess of $5,430 may be paid to Ray, Sam, and Tom in the 4:3:2 ratio.			

After cash or other assets of $5,430 are distributed to the partners as computed above, the **actual** capital account balances would be in the income-sharing ratio of 4:3:2, as follows: Ray, $12,040; Sam, $9,030; and Tom, $6,020.

17. In some cases, the liquidator may elect to set aside cash to pay any remaining liabilities and potential liquidation costs and distribute any residual cash to partners according to the program described in paragraph **15**.

18. The Uniform Limited Partnership Act provides that after outside creditors of a liquidating limited partnership have been paid, the equities of the limited partners must be paid before the general partner or partners may receive any cash. Also, the limited partners may agree that one or more of them may have priority over the others regarding payments in liquidation of the limited partnership.

19. If a limited liability partnership is incorporated, the net assets of the partnership must be restated to current fair values before they are transferred to the corporation. This assures that the capital stock of the corporation will be distributed to the partners in the ratio of their respective equities in the partnership. The accounting records of the partnership may be modified and continued in use by the corporation, but usually a new set of accounting records is established for the corporation.

20. A **joint venture** differs from a limited liability partnership in that it generally is limited to carrying out a single project. Joint ventures may be created for such purposes as to develop a tract of land, sell agricultural products, explore for natural resources, or undertake construction projects.

21. A **corporate joint venture** is a corporation owned and operated by a small group of joint venturers as a separate business enterprise. The investment in the common stock of a corporate joint venture is accounted for by the **equity method** of accounting. Supplementary disclosure of assets, liabilities, and results of operations of the corporate joint venture is made in a note to the financial statements of each venturer if the investment in the venture is material.

22. Either the **equity method** of accounting or the **proportionate share method** of accounting may be used for an investment in an **unincorporated joint venture.** In the proportionate share method of accounting, the investor recognizes in its accounting records its share of each asset, liability, revenue, and expense of the joint venture.

QUESTIONS

True or False

For each of the following statements, circle the **T** or the **F** to indicate whether the statement is true or false.

T F 1. The terms **liquidation** and **realization** may be used interchangeably.

T F 2. A loan from a partner to a limited liability partnership is treated as a liability when the partnership is in liquidation.

T F 3. Gains and losses on the realization of noncash assets during liquidation of a limited liability partnership are divided in the ratio of the partners' capital account balances, in the absence of a specific agreement for sharing such gains and losses.

T F 4. A partnership's loan receivable from a partner should be deducted from his or her capital account balance in the preparation of a program of cash distributions to partners prior to liquidation.

T F 5. Separate ledger accounts for each partner's capital and for any loan to the partnership should be maintained to provide a record of the terms under which funds were invested by the partners.

T F 6. If a partner is unable to pay a capital deficit, the deficit must be absorbed by all partners, including the partner with the capital deficit, in the income-sharing ratio.

T F 7. After the realization of all noncash assets and the distribution of all available cash to creditors, Rye & Spa LLP still owes $10,000 to creditors. If Rye has a capital account balance of $4,000, Spa has a capital deficit of $14,000.

T F 8. In the process of liquidation, partners may receive cash from a limited liability partnership before creditors do if all the assets of the partnership are noncash assets that are expected to be realized for more than carrying amount.

T F 9. If the partners' capital account balances of a liquidating limited liability partnership have been reduced to the income-sharing ratio, subsequent cash payments to partners may be made in the income-sharing ratio.

T F 10. A solvent limited liability partnership is liquidated in a manner different from the liquidation of a general partnership.

T F 11. If the carrying amount of partnership net assets is equal to current fair value, the conversion of a limited liability partnership to a corporation may be recorded by debiting the partners' capital accounts and crediting the Common Stock and Paid-in Capital in Excess of Par ledger accounts.

T F 12. A corporate joint venture is a partnership of short duration owned by two or more corporations.

T F 13. Investments in both unincorporated joint ventures and corporate joint ventures generally are maintained by the cost method of accounting.

Completion Statements

Fill in the necessary words or amounts to complete the following statements.

1.   The term _____ means the payment of liabilities; the term _____ means the disposal of assets for cash.

2.   The gains and losses from the realization of noncash assets of a liquidating partnership are divided among the partners in the _____ ratio; cash or other assets are distributed to the partnership on liquidation according to balances in the partners' _____ ledger accounts and _____ ledger accounts.

3.   Combining partners' loan and capital ledger account balances is required under the doctrine known as the _____ _____ _____. However, loan and capital balances should not be combined in the_____ _____.

4.   A debit balance in the capital account of partner who is solvent is recognized as a _____ in the balance sheet of a limited liability partnership in liquidation. If a partner is unable to pay a capital deficit, the deficit is written off against the _____ _____ of the other partners.

5.   Personal creditors of a partner are paid from _____ assets; any remaining unpaid claims are paid from _____ assets if the partner has a positive _____ in the solvent limited liability partnership.

6.   The partners of Ham, Iago & Job LLP share net income and losses in a 2:1:1 ratio and have equities in the partnership of $42,000, $23,000, and $15,000, respectively, The first $_____ cash available for distribution to partners in the course of liquidation would be paid to Partner _____, and the next $_____ would be paid to Partners _____ _____ _____ in a _____ ratio.

7.   The _____ method of accounting generally is used for investments in the common stock of corporate joint ventures.

8.   In the _____ _____ method of accounting for an investment in an unincorporated joint venture, the investor recognizes a portion of each asset, liability, revenue, and expense of the joint venture.

Multiple Choice

Choose the best answer for each of the following questions and enter the identifying letter in the space provided.

_____ 1. In a limited liability partnership liquidation, the final cash distribution to partners is made in accordance with the:
- a. Partners' income-sharing ratio
- b. Balances of partners' capital accounts
- c. Ratio of original investments by partners
- d. Ratio of original investments less withdrawals by partners

_____ 2. The partners of Dawes & Epps LLP share net income and losses equally. Both Dawes and Epps are insolvent. At the time they decided to liquidate the limited liability partnership, its balance sheet included the following: cash, $1,000; other assets, $19,000; liabilities, $8,000; Dawes capital, $3,000; and Epps capital, $9,000. The other assets realized $12,000 and the liabilities were paid. The amount Epps received from the liquidation of the partnership was:
- a. $6,500
- b. $5,500
- c. $5,000
- d. $2,500
- e. Some other amount

_____ 3. On January 1, 2005, the partners of Snell & Thomas LLP had capital account balances of $40,000 and $20,000, respectively. They shared net income and losses equally, and the partnership had a net income of $10,000 during 2005. On December 31, 2005, the partnership was liquidated. If, after realization of noncash assets and payment of liabilities, $30,000 remained for distribution to the partnership, Snell received:
- a. $15,000
- b. $20,000
- c. $25,000
- d. $30,000
- e. Some other amount

_____ 4. After realization of a portion of the noncash assets of Saul, Tapp & Uris LLP, which is being liquidated, the capital account balances were Saul, $35,000; Tapp, $40,000; and Uris, $43,000. Cash of $42,000 and other assets with a carrying amount of $78,000 were on hand. Creditors' claims totaled $2,000. The partners shared net income and losses equally. The cash that may be paid to Uris at this time is:
- a. $43,000
- b. $17,000
- c. $14,000
- d. $13,333
- e. Some other amount

_____ 5. The partners of Lon & Mab LLP share net income and losses equally. After the realization of all noncash assets and payment of all liabilities, Lon had a capital account balance of $3,800, and Mab had a capital deficit of $3,800. Lon has personal assets of $30,000 and personal liabilities of $35,000; Mab has personal assets of $20,000 and personal liabilities of $18,000. The total amount that personal creditors of Lon should expect to receive after marshaling of assets is:

    a. $35,000
    b. $33,800
    c. $32,000
    d. $30,000
    e. Some other amount

_____ 6. The partners of Cey, Doy & Ebb LLP had capital account balances of $40,000, $50,000, and $18,000, respectively, and an income-sharing ratio of 4:2:1, respectively. If Cey received only $8,000 on the liquidation of the partnership, the total amount received by all the partners on liquidation was:

    a. $108,000
    b. $56,000
    c. $52,000
    d. $24,000
    e. Some other amount

_____ 7. Assume the same facts as in question **6,** except that Cey received $26,000 on liquidation. How much cash did Ebb receive from the liquidation?

    a. $26,000
    b. $18,000
    c. $14,500
    d. $14,000
    e. Some other amount

_____ 8. Clark Corporation invested $100,000 in a real estate corporate joint venture on January 2, 2005. During 2005, Clark received dividends of $9,500 from the joint venture, and its share of joint venture net income (after depreciation) was $12,000. The depreciation expense applicable to Clark's share of net income was $4,000. Clark values its joint-venture investment in its December 31, 2005, balance sheet (under the equity method of accounting) at:

    a. $116,000
    b. $112,000
    c. $102,500
    d. $100,000
    e. Some other amount

_____ 9. On January 2, 2005, Bur, Cam & Dee LLP was organized, with Cam and Dee each investing $100,000 cash and Bur investing $75,000 cash, with a commitment to invest an additional $25,000 cash on January 2, 2007. However, on December 31, 2005, the partners agreed to liquidate the insolvent limited liability partnership, which had liabilities totaling $410,000 on that date but assets at current fair value, including a $25,000 loan receivable from Bur, of only $200,000. Bur has a personal net worth of $750,000, but Cam and Dee are both insolvent. Because Bur is the partner responsible for the partnership's insolvency, Bur's maximum liability for unpaid partnership liabilities is:
   a. $95,000
   b. $185,000
   c. $210,000
   d. $235,000
   e. Some other amount

_____ 10. Refer to the facts in question **9.** If Bur were a limited partner, Bur's maximum obligation for unpaid limited partnership liabilities would be:
   a. $0
   b. $25,000
   c. $210,000
   d. $235,000
   e. Some other amount

_____ 11. The following balance sheet was prepared for Adams, Barnes & Clason LLP, whose partners share net income and losses in the ratio of 3:1:1, respectively:

Cash	$ 40,000
Other assets	140,000
Total	$180,000
Liabilities	$ 70,000
Adams, capital	50,000
Barnes, capital	50,000
Clason, capital	10,000
Total	$180,000

The partners agreed to liquidate the partnership after realization of the other assets. How much will each partner receive at this time if the other assets realize $80,000?

	Adams	**Barnes**	**Clason**
a.	$12,500	$37,500	$0
b.	$13,000	$37,000	$0
c.	$14,000	$38,000	$2,000
d.	$50,000	$50,000	$10,000
e.	Some other amounts		

SHORT EXERCISES

1. Cate, Dean & Etts LLP is unable to pay all its creditors; furthermore, two partners are insolvent. The partners share net income and losses in the ratio of 4:3:2, respectively. The balance sheet of the partnership of March 31, 2005, is shown on page 30.

CATE, DEAN & ETTS LLP
Balance Sheet
March 31, 2005

Cash	$ 1,000	Trade accounts payable	$ 74,000
Other assets	$121,000		
		Partners' capital:	
		Cate, Capital	20,000
		Dean, Capital	12,000
		Etts, Capital	16,000
Total	$122,000	Total	$122,000

The personal financial position of the partners is as follows:

	Current fair values of personal assets	Personal liabilities
Cate	$62,000	$40,000
Dean	18,900	23,800
Etts	8,000	10,000

a. Assuming that the other assets realized $67,000 cash, complete the statement of realization and liquidation below.

CATE, DEAN & ETTS LLP
Statement of Realization and Liquidation
March 31, 2005

	Assets		Liabilities	Partners' capital		
	Cash	Other		Cate (4)	Dean (3)	Etts (2)
Balances before liquidation	$1,000	$121,000	$74,000	$20,000	$12,000	$16,000
Realization of other assets at a loss of $_____						
Balances	$		$	$	$	$
Payment to creditors						
Balances	$		$	$	$	$
Additional loss because of insolvency of Partner Dean						
Balances	$		$	$		$
Additional investment by Partner Cate						
Settlement with creditors and Partner Etts						

b. In the space below, compute the minimum amount that must be realized from the other assets so that Dean's creditors would receive full payment on their claims.

Computations:

2. The partners of Aba, Bepp, Carp & Dino LLP shared net income and losses in a 5:3:2:1 ratio, respectively. They decided to liquidate the limited liability partnership by realizing noncash assets gradually to minimize losses. The trial balance for the partnership on October 1, 2005, the date liquidation commenced, is as follows:

	Debit	Credit
Cash	$ 1,000	
Trade accounts receivable (net)	30,000	
Inventories	32,000	
Equipment (net)	70,000	
Trade accounts payable		$ 18,000
Loan payable to Aba		2,500
Loan payable to Bepp		13,000
Aba, capital		37,500
Bepp, capital		20,000
Carp, capital		30,000
Dino, capital		12,000
Totals	$133,000	$133,000

Complete the working paper below as of October 1, 2005, showing how cash should be distributed among the partners in installments as it becomes available during liquidation.

ABA, BEPP, CARP & DINO LLP
Working Paper for Cash Distributions to Partners during Liquidation
October 1, 2005

	Aba	Bepp	Carp	Dino
Capital balances before liquidation (including loans)				
Income-sharing ratio				

3. The balance sheet for Allen & Barr LLP is presented below.

ALLEN & BARR LLP
Balance Sheet
March 31, 2005

Cash	$19,500	Trade accounts payable	$15,500
Trade accounts receivable	20,000	Allen, capital	38,300
Inventories	50,000	Barr, capital	36,200
Short-term prepayments	500		
Total	$90,000	Total	$90,000

Allen and Barr shared net income and losses equally. On March 31, 2005, the partnership was reorganized as a corporation (Alba, Inc.), as follows:

(1) Barr's capital account was credited for $1,000, representing reimbursement of costs incurred by Barr in organizing Alba, Inc.

(2) Goodwill of $9,000 was recognized by the partnership, and patents with a current fair value of $15,000 were invested in the partnership by Allen.

©The McGraw-Hill Companies, Inc., 2006

(3) Ten thousand shares of $1 par common stock of Alba, Inc., were issued to Allen and Barr in proportion to the balances of their capital accounts.

    a. In the space below, prepare journal entries to bring the partnership accounting records up to date and to transfer the net assets of the partnership to Alba, Inc. Do not record the receipt of shares of common stock from Alba, Inc., in the accounting records of the partnership.

Allen & Barr LLP
Journal Entries

2005			
Mar. 31	(1)		
31	(2)		
31	(3)		

b. In the space below, prepare a journal entry for Alba, Inc.

Alba, Inc.
Journal Entry

2005			
Mar. 31			

CASE

Alan Rath and Kyle Stern, partners of Rath & Stern LLP, have been discussing incorporation of the partnership with an attorney. They ask you, as accountant for the partnership and a CPA who is a member of the IMA, FEI, and AICPA (see Chapter 1 of the textbook), whether the undistributed earnings of the partnership, computed as the excess of net income over net losses and partners' drawings during the partnership's existence, might be allocated to the Retained Earnings ledger account in the opening journal entry for the corporation.

After considering the ethics or professional conduct codes of the IMA, FEI, and AICPA in the appendixes of Chapter 1 of the textbook, prepare an answer to the partners' question.

SOLUTIONS TO QUESTIONS, SHORT EXERCISES, AND CASE: CHAPTER 3

QUESTIONS

True or False

1. F 2. F 3. F 4. T 5. T 6. F 7. T 8. F 9. T 10. F 11. T 12. F 13. F

Completion Statements

1. Liquidation, realization. 2. Income-sharing, loan, capital. 3. Right of offset, partnership ledger.
4. Receivable, capital accounts. 5. Personal, partnership, equity. 6. $2,000, Iago, $18,000, Ham and Iago, 2:1. 7. Equity. 8. Proportionate share.

Multiple Choice

1. b 2. c ($9,000 – $3,500 – $500 = $5,000) 3. c ($40,000 + $5,000 – $20,000 = $25,000) 4. b
($43,000 – $26,000 = $17,000) 5. c ($30,000 + $2,000 = $32,000) 6. c ($108,000 – $56,000 = $52,000) 7. c ($18,000 – $3,500 = $14,500) 8. c ($100,000 + $12,000 - $9,500 = $102,500) 9. d
[$410,000 – ($200,000 – $25,000) = $235,000] 10. b 11. a

SHORT EXERCISES

1. a.

CATE, DEAN & ETTS LLP
Statement of Realization and Liquidation
March 31, 2005

	Assets		Liabilities	Partners' capital		
	Cash	**Other**		**Cate (4)**	**Dean (3)**	**Ette (2)**
Balances before liquidation	$ 1,000	$121,000	$74,000	$20,000	$12,000	$16,000
Realization of other assets at loss of $54,000	$67,000	(121,000)		(24,000)	(18,000)	(12,000)
Balances	$68,000		$74,000	$(4,000)	$(6,000)	$ 4,000
Payment to creditors	(68,000)		(68,000)			
Balances	$ -0-		$ 6,000	$(4,000)	$(6,000)	$ 4,000
Additional loss because of insolvency of Partner Dean				(4,000)	6,000	(2,000)
Balances	$ -0-		$ 6,000	$(8,000)		$ 2,000
Additional investment by Partner Cate	8,000			8,000		
Settlement with creditors and Partner Etts	(8,000)		(6,000)			(2,000)

b.

Dean's capital in partnership	$ 12,000
Less: Amount Dean must receive from partnership interest to satisfy personal creditors ($23,800 – $18,900)	4,900
Maximum loss that may be charged to Dean	$ 7,100
Carrying amount of assets other than cash	$121,000
Less: Loss on realization that would reduce Dean's capital to $4,900: ($7,100 ÷ 3/9 = $21,300)	21,300
Amount on realization of other assets permitting a cash payment to Dean that would satisfy personal creditors in full	$ 99,700

2.

ABA, BEPP, CARP & DINO LLP
Working Paper for Cash Distributions to Partners during Liquidation
October 1, 2005

	Aba	Bepp	Carp	Dino
Capital balances before liquidation (including loans)	$40,000	$33,000	$30,000	$12,000
Income-sharing ratio	5	3	2	1
Capital per unit of income sharing	$ 8,000	$11,000	$15,000	$12,000
Reduce Carp's capital per unit of income sharing to equal capital per unit of income sharing for Dino [Carp receives cash of $6,000 ($3,000 x 2 – $6,000)]			(3,000)	
Capital per unit of income sharing	$ 8,000	$11,000	$12,000	$12,000
Reduce capital for Carp and Dino to equal capital for Bepp (Carp and Dino receive cash of $2,000 and $1,000, respectively)			(1,000)	(1,000)
Capital per unit of income sharing	$ 8,000	$11,000	$11,000	$11,000
Reduce capital for Bepp, Carp, and Dino to equal capital for Aba (Bepp, Carp, and Dino receive cash of $9,000, $6,000, and $3,000 respectively)		(3,000)	(3,000)	(3,000)
Capital per unit of income sharing after payments of $9,000 to Bepp, $14,000 to Carp, and $4,000 to Dino	$ 8,000	$ 8,000	$ 8,000	$ 8,000

3. a.

Allen & Barr LLP
Journal Entries

2005			
Mar. 31	(1) Organization Costs (applicable to Alba, Inc.)	1,000	
	Barr, Capital		1,000
	To record costs incurred by Barr in organizing Alba, Inc.		
31	(2) Goodwill	9,000	
	Patents	15,000	
	Allen, Capital ($15,000 + $4,500)		19,500
	Barr, Capital		4,500
	To record goodwill (divided equally) and patent invested by		
	Allen to be transferred to Alba, Inc.		
31	(3) Trade Accounts Payable	15,500	
	Allen, Capital ($38,300 + $19,500)	57,800	
	Barr, Capital ($36,200 + $1,000 + $4,500)	41,700	
	Cash		19,500
	Trade Accounts Payable		20,000
	Inventories		50,000
	Short-Term Prepayments		500
	Organization Costs		1,000
	Goodwill		9,000
	Patents		15,000
	To record transfer of net assets to Alba, Inc.		

b.

Alba, Inc.
Journal Entry

2005			
Mar. 31	Cash	19,500	
	Trade Accounts Receivable	20,000	
	Inventories	50,000	
	Short-Term Prepayments	500	
	Organization Costs	1,000	
	Goodwill	9,000	
	Patents	15,000	
	Trade Accounts Payable		15,500
	Common Stock, $1 par		10,000
	Paid-in Capital in Excess of Parr		89,500
	To record acquisition of net assets from Allen & Barr LLP.		

CASE

Your answer to partners Alan Rath and Kyle Stern must be that their question involves a legal interpretation, which you are not licensed or qualified to render. State laws governing the formation and operation of corporations vary; Rath and Stern should request the attorney they have been consulting to answer the question. A CPA who, despite his or her knowledge of the law, essays to practice law may, in addition to jeopardizing his or her CPA license, be accused of performing an act discreditable to the accounting profession.

CHAPTER 4
ACCOUNTING FOR BRANCHES;
COMBINED FINANCIAL STATEMENTS

HIGHLIGHTS OF THE CHAPTER

1. A **branch** is a unit of a business enterprise located some distance from the **home office.** A branch generally caries a stock of merchandise obtained from the home office, makes sales, approves customers' credit, and makes collections on trade accounts receivable.

2. The merchandise of a branch may be obtained exclusively from the home office, or a portion may be purchased from outside suppliers. The cash receipts of the branch may be deposited in a bank account of the home office; branch expenses then are paid from an **imprest cash fund** provided by the home office. The imprest cash fund is replenished periodically by the home office. Alternatively, a branch may maintain its own bank account.

3. Certain units or **segments** of a business enterprise may be operated as **divisions.** A division may consist of either a series of branches or one or more corporations. When a segment is operated as a corporation, it is known as a **subsidiary** of the **parent company.**

4. Costs of organizing a new branch and operating losses during the initial period of operations should be recognized as expenses, not as deferred charges, per AICPA **SOP 98-5.**

5. The accounting records for branches may be **centralized** in the home office or may be **decentralized** so that each branch maintains a complete set of accounting records. If the accounting records are centralized in the home office, each branch prepares daily reports and documents that are used as sources for journal entries in the accounting records of the home office. If a branch maintains its own accounting records, some transactions or events relating to the branch may be recorded by the home office. Periodic financial statements are provided by the branch to the home office so that combined statements may be prepared.

6. The accounting records of a branch include a Home Office ledger account that is credited for assets and services provided by the home office, and for branch net income. The Home Office account is debited for any assets and services provided by the branch to the home office or to other branches, and for branch net losses. The Home Office account thus is an ownership equity-type account representing the net investment of the home office in the branch.

7. A home office maintains a **reciprocal ledger account,** Investment in Branch, which is debited for the assets and other services provided to a branch, and for net income of the branch; it is credited for the assets and services received from the branch, and for branch net losses.

8. A home office generally charges its branches for expenses (such as insurance, interest, property taxes, advertising, and depreciation) incurred for the benefit of the branch. Such expenses must be allocated to branch operations to measure the profitability of each branch.

9. Merchandise shipped by a home office to branches may be billed at home office cost, at home office cost plus a markup, or at branch retail selling price. A shipment of merchandise to a branch is not a sale. Billing at home office cost attributes the entire gross profit on merchandise sold by a branch to the branch. When merchandise is billed at a price above home office cost (or at branch retail selling price), the valuation assigned to branch inventory at the end of the accounting period must be reduced to cost when combined financial statements are prepared.

10. If merchandise is billed to a branch at a price above home office cost and the **perpetual inventory system** is used, the home office debits Investment in Branch for the billed price of the merchandise, credits Inventories for the **cost** of the merchandise, and credits Allowance for Overvaluation of Inventories: Branch for the excess of the billed price over cost. The branch

debits Inventories and credits Home Office at billed prices of merchandise; sales by the branch are debited to Cost of Goods Sold and credited to Inventories at billed prices.

11. A separate income statement and balance sheet for each branch may be prepared for use by enterprise management. The income statement has no unusual features if merchandise is billed to a branch at home office cost. However, if merchandise is billed at a price above cost, the branch trial balance must be adjusted by the home office so that cost of the merchandise sold by the branch is stated at cost to the home office.

12. A **combined balance sheet** for home office and branch shows the financial position of the business enterprise as a single entity. In the working paper for combined financial statements, the assets and liabilities of the branch are substituted for the Investment in Branch ledger account included in the adjusted trial balance of the home office. This is accomplished by elimination of the balances of the Home Office and Investment in Branch reciprocal ledger accounts.

13. If a home office and branch use the **periodic inventory system,** the home office debits Investment in Branch for the billed price of the merchandise shipped, credits Shipments to Branch for the home office cost of the merchandise shipped, and credits any excess of billed price over cost to Allowance for Overvaluation of Inventories: Branch. The branch debits Shipments from Home Office and credits Home Office at billed price. At the end of the accounting period, the home office reduces (debits) Allowance for Overvaluation of Inventories: Branch for the amount of overvaluation applicable to the branch's cost of goods sold and credits the amount of the reduction to the Realized Gross Profit: Branch Sales ledger account.

14. At the end of an accounting period, the balance of the Investment in Branch ledger account may not agree with the balance of the Home Office account. In such cases the reciprocal ledger accounts must be reconciled and brought up to date before combined financial statements are prepared.

15. If the home office operates more than one branch, certain transactions, such as merchandise shipments, may take place between branches. Such interbranch transactions usually are cleared through the Home Office ledger account. For example, if Arlo Branch ships merchandise with a cost of $400 to Boone Branch and the **periodic inventory system** is used, the following journal entries (explanations omitted) are required:

Accounting records of Arlo Branch:

Home Office	400	
Shipments from Home Office		400

Accounting records of Boone Branch:

Shipments from Home Office	400	
Home Office		400

Accounting records of home office:

Investment in Boone Branch	400	
Investment in Arlo Branch		400

16. The transfer of merchandise from one branch to another does not justify increasing the carrying amount of inventories by the additional freight costs incurred because of the indirect routing. Excess freight costs incurred as a result of such transfers are recognized as operating expenses of the home office because the home office makes the decision to transfer the merchandise.

QUESTIONS

True or False

For each of the following statements, circle the **T** or the **F** to indicate whether the statement is true or false.

T F 1. In a centralized accounting system for branches, the branch accounting records are maintained by the home office.

T F 2. Both the Home Office ledger account and the Investment in Branch account are displayed in the combined financial statements for the home office and the branch.

T F 3. The combined net income for the home office and branches would be the same when the home office bills merchandise to branches at home office cost as when the home office bills branches at amounts above home office cost.

T F 4. In most cases, a branch is operated more as a cost center than as a profit center.

T F 5. A branch imprest cash fund is displayed under the heading Investments in the combined balance sheet of the home office and the branch.

T F 6. The Investment in Branch ledger account is displayed as a noncurrent asset in the separate balance sheet of the home office, and the Home Office account is displayed as a long-term liability in the separate balance sheet of the branch.

T F 7. The fiscal year for the home office must coincide with the fiscal year for the branch to facilitate the preparation of combined financial statements.

T F 8. A net loss reported by a branch is recorded by the home office by a debit to the Investment in Branch ledger account.

T F 9. If branch trade accounts receivable are carried in the home office accounting records, doubtful accounts expense of the branch is recorded by the home office by a debit to Branch Loss and a credit to Investment in Branch.

T F 10. If merchandise is billed to a branch at a price above home office cost, the net income reported to the home office by the branch is overstated.

T F 11. Separate financial statements for an enterprise's home office and branches generally are prepared for use by creditors and government agencies.

T F 12. In a working paper for combined financial statements of a home office and branches, the balance of the Shipments to Branch ledger account is eliminated against the balance of the Home Office account.

T F 13. In a separate balance sheet for a home office, the balance of the Allowance for Overvaluation of Inventories: Branch ledger account is deducted from the balance of the Investment in Branch ledger account.

T F 14. The beginning inventories of a branch are reduced to home office cost in the working paper for combined financial statements by a debit to Allowance for Overvaluation of Inventories: Branch and a credit to beginning inventories when the periodic inventory system is used.

T F 15. The perpetual inventory system is impractical for a home office with many branches.

T F 16. If a remittance of cash by a branch has not been recorded by the home office, the balance of the branch's Home Office ledger account exceeds the balance of the home office's Investment in Branch account.

T F 17. Freight costs on merchandise shipments from Cody Branch to Dana Branch in excess of normal freight costs from the home office to Dana Branch should be recognized as operating expenses of Dana Branch.

T F 18. If a new branch is expected to be profitable starting with the second year of operations, a loss incurred by the new branch in the first year should be deferred and recognized as expense over a period of three to five years.

Completion Statements

Fill in the necessary words or amounts to complete the following statements.

1. A _____ is a unit of a business enterprise that sells merchandise at a location some distance from the _____ _____. A branch generally is operated as a _____ of the home office; however, a _____ may be organized as a subsidiary corporation.

2. The Home Office ledger account and the Investment in Branch ledger account are _____ ledger accounts whose balances must be _____ when _____ financial statements for the home office and branch are prepared.

3. If a home office bills merchandise to branches at a price above home office cost, the markup on the unsold merchandise is not _____ and is eliminated for combined financial statements for the home office and its branches.

4. If the Norco Branch remits cash to the home office of Lepore Company and a decentralized accounting system is used, the Norco Branch debits the _____ _____ ledger account and credits Cash; the home office debits Cash and credits the _____ _____ _____ account.

5. Some operating expenses incurred by the home office relate to branch operations and are _____ to the branch by a debit to the _____ _____ _____ ledger account and a credit to the _____ _____ account in the accounting records of the home office.

6. If shipments of merchandise by a home office to branches are billed at 33 1/3% above home office cost, _____% of the amount of the ending inventories of the branch is reported in the Allowance _____ _____ _____ _____: _____ ledger account in the accounting records of the home office.

Multiple Choice

Choose the best answer for each of the following questions and enter the identifying letter in the space provided.

_____ 1. In accounting for branch transactions, it is improper for the home office to:
   a. Credit cash received from a branch to the Investment in Branch ledger account.
   b. Maintain Common Stock and Retained Earnings ledger accounts for only the home office.
   c. Debit shipments of merchandise to the branch from the home office to the Investment in Branch ledger account.
   d. Credit shipments of merchandise to the branch to the Sales ledger account.

_____ 2. The Home Office ledger account in the accounting records of the Tahoe Branch had a credit balance of $12,000 at the end of April, and the Investment in Branch account in the accounting records of the home office had a debit balance of $15,000. The most likely reason for the discrepancy in the two ledger account balances is:
   a. Merchandise shipped by the home office to the branch had not been recorded by the branch.
   b. The home office had not recorded the branch net income for April.
   c. The branch had just collected home office trade accounts receivable in the amount of $3,000.
   d. The branch had not yet recorded the home office net income for April.

_____ 3. Jayhawk Company has numerous branches in the state of Kansas. The home office purchases merchandise and makes shipments to branches from a central warehouse at the request of branch managers. Which of the following would be an improper accounting practice?
   a. The Investment in Branch ledger account is debited in the accounting records of the home office when merchandise is shipped to a branch, and the Shipments to Branch account is credited (assume use of the periodic inventory system).
   b. The home office debits Trade Accounts Receivable and credits Sales when merchandise is shipped to a branch.
   c. Cash received from a branch is credited to the Investment in Branch ledger account by the home office.
   d. Only the home office maintains a Common Stock ledger account and a Retained Earnings account.

_____ 4. Neither the Palmer Branch nor the home office of Rupert Company had completed any intracompany transactions during the last half of May, yet the credit balance of the branch's Home Office ledger account on May 31 was larger than the debit balance of the home office's Investment in Palmer Branch account. The most likely reason for this discrepancy is:
   a. The home office reported a net loss for the month of May.
   b. The branch reported a net loss for the month of May.
   c. The branch returned merchandise to the home office.
   d. The branch reported a net income for the month of May.

_____ 5. Which of the following ledger accounts is displayed in the combined financial statements for a home office and branch?
   a. Shipments to Branch
   b. Home Office
   c. Dividends Declared
   d. Allowance for Overvaluation of Inventories: Branch

_____ 6. The home office of Irby Company bills merchandise to branches at 25% above home office cost. Information taken from the accounting records of Kipp Branch is as follows:

Beginning inventories (at billed prices)	$17,000
Shipments from home office (at billed prices)	42,500
Ending inventories (at billed prices)	20,000
Net loss for accounting period	1,500

The net income or net loss of Kipp Branch, based on home office cost of branch merchandise, is:
a. $7,900 net income
b. $9,400 net loss
c. $6,400 net income
d. $7,000 net income
e. Some other amount

SHORT EXERCISES

1. Below is a partial list of ledger accounts of the Vista Branch of Santee Company, followed by a series of transactions. By placing the appropriate account number in the space provided, indicate the accounts that are debited and credited in **the accounting records of the branch** to record each transaction. The branch uses the perpetual inventory system.

1	Cash	6	Sales	
2	Trade Accounts Receivable	7	Cost of Goods Sold	
3	Inventories	8	Operating Expenses	
4	Trade Accounts Payable	9	Income Summary	
5	Home Office	10	All other ledger accounts	

Transactions	Vista Branch ledger accounts debited	Vista Branch ledger accounts credited
a. Received cash from home office.		
b. Recognized operating expenses (paid in cash) for the accounting period.		
c. Sales were made on account for the accounting period; recognized cost of goods sold for the period.		
d. Collections on trade accounts receivable were received.		
e. Payments by branch to suppliers were made.		
f. Branch remitted cash to home office.		
g. Revenue and expense ledger accounts were closed at the end of the accounting period. (Prepare a journal entry and assume that total revenue exceeds total expenses.)		
h. Closed Income Summary ledger account and notified home office that a net income was earned in the latest accounting period.		

2. The home office of Quilly Company bills Leone Branch at 25% above home office cost for all merchandise shipped to the branch. During January, 2005, the home office shipped merchandise

to the branch at a billed price of $24,000. The branch inventories on January 1 and January 31, 2005, were as follows:

	Jan. 1	Jan. 31
Merchandise received from home office (at billed prices)	$27,600	$32,000
Merchandise purchased from outsiders	12,400	12,000
Total branch inventories	$40,000	$44,000

The home office uses the periodic inventory system.

In the space below, prepare all journal entries (including adjustments) in the accounting records of the home office for January, 2005 to record the foregoing information.

Quilly Company Home Office
Journal Entries

2005			

3. The Investment in Subble Branch ledger account of the home office of Darcy Company and the Home Office account of the branch for the month of January, 2005, are below and on page 44.

Investment in Subble Branch

Balance, Jan. 1	61,000	Cash received from branch	4,500
Shipment of merchandise	6,200	Collection of branch note receivable	2,000
Expenses allocated to branch	1,150		

Home Office

Cash remitted to home office	4,500	Balance, Jan. 1	61,000
Merchandise returned to home office	195	Shipment of merchandise	6,200
		Collection of home office trade account receivable	180

a. Complete the reconciliation of the reciprocal accounts in the space below.

	Investment in Subble Branch ledger account (in home office accounting records)	Home Office ledger account (in branch accounting records)
Balances prior to adjustment	$	$
Add:		
Less:		
Adjusted balances	$	$

b. In the spaces below, prepare a single journal entry for both the home office and the branch to bring each set of accounting records up to date (assume that both use the perpetual inventory system).

Darcy Company Home Office
Journal Entry

2005			
Jan. 31			

Subble Branch
Journal Entry

2005			
Jan. 31			

CASE

In your audit of the financial statements of Wallis Company, which has a single branch in Iowa, for the fiscal year ended January 31, 2005, you review the following home office ledger account:

Allowance for Overvaluation of Inventories: Iowa Branch

Date	Explanation	Debit	Credit	Balance
2005				
Jan. 2	Shipment of merchandise costing $10,000 at a 20% markup on billed price, to stock the branch for its opening.		2,000	2,000 cr
16	Shipment of merchandise costing $40,000 at a 20% markup on billed price, to replenish the branch inventories.		8,000	10,000 cr
31	Reduction of balance by unrealized markup in the branch's ending inventories of $3,000 at billed prices.	600		9,400 cr

a. Describe the errors in the journal entries posted to the foregoing ledger account.

b. Describe, but do not prepare, the journal entry required to correct the foregoing ledger account on January 31, 2005.

SOLUTIONS TO QUESTIONS, SHORT EXERCISES, AND CASE: CHAPTER 4

QUESTIONS

True or False

1. T 2. F 3. T 4. F 5. F 6. F 7. T 8. F 9. F 10. F 11. F 12. F 13. T 14. T 15. F 16. F
17. F 18. F

Completion Statements

1. Branch, home office, profit center, division. 2. Reciprocal, eliminated, combined. 3. Realized.
4. Home Office, Investment in Branch. 5. Allocated, Investment in Branch, Operating Expenses.
6. 25%, for Overvaluation of Inventories: Branch.

Multiple Choice

1. d 2. a 3. b 4. d 5. c 6. c [($39,500 x 0.20) – $1,500 = $6,400]

SHORT EXERCISES

1.

Transactions	Vista Branch ledger accounts debited	Vista Branch ledger accounts credited
a. Received cash from home office.	1	5
b. Recognized operating expenses (paid in cash) for the accounting period.	8	1
c. Sales were made on account for the accounting period; recognized cost of goods sold for the period.	2, 7	6, 3
d. Collections on trade accounts receivable were made.	1	2
e. Payments by branch to suppliers were made.	4	1
f. Branch remitted cash to home office.	5	1
g. Revenue and expense ledger accounts were closed at the end of the accounting period. (Prepare a journal entry and assume that total revenue exceeds total expenses.)	6	7, 8, 9
h. Closed Income Summary ledger account and notified home office that a net income was earned in the latest accounting period.	9	5

2.

Quilly Company Home Office
Journal Entries

2005	Investment in Leone Branch				24,000	
	Shipments to Leone Branch					19,200
	Allowance for Overvaluation of Inventories: Leone Branch					4,800
	To record shipments to branch at 25% above home office cost.					
	Allowance for Overvaluation of Inventories: Leone Branch				3,920	
	Realized Gross Profit: Leone Branch Sales					3,920
	To reduce allowance amount by which ending inventories exceed					
	home office cost.					
		Billed price	**Cost**	**Markup***		
	Beginning inventories	$27,600	$22,080	$ 5,520		
	Add: Shipments from home office	24,000	19,200	4,800		
	Available for sale	$51,600	$41,280	$10,320		
	Less: Ending inventories	(32,000)	(25,600)	(6,400)		
	Cost of goods sold	$19,600	$15,680	$ 3,920		

*A markup of 25% on cost is equal to a markup of 20% on billed price.

3. a.

	Investment in Subble Branch ledger account (in home office accounting records)	**Home Office ledger account (in branch accounting records)**
Balances prior to adjustment	$61,850	$62,685
Add: Collection of home office trade account receivable by branch	180	
Expenses allocated to branch by home office		1,150
Less: Merchandise returned to home office by branch	(195)	
Collection of branch note receivable by home office		(2,000)
Adjusted balances	$61,835	$61,835

b.

Darcy Company Home Office
Journal Entry

2005			
Jan. 31	Inventories	195	
	Trade Accounts Receivable		180
	Investment in Subble Branch		15
	To adjust Investment in Subble Branch ledger account.		

Subble Branch
Journal Entry

2005			
Jan. 31	Operating Expenses	1,150	
	Home Office	850	
	Notes Receivable		2,000
	To adjust Home Office ledger account.		

CASE

a. The two credits to the Allowance for Overvaluation of Inventories: Iowa Branch are of incorrect amount. A 20% markup on billed price is a 25% markup on home office cost; therefore, the January 2, 2005, credit should be $2,500 ($10,000 x 0.25 = $2,500), and the January 16 credit should be $10,000 ($40,000 x 0.25 = $10,000). The January 31 journal entry should be a debit of $11,900, or 20% of branch cost of goods sold of $59,500 ($10,000 + $2,500 + $40,000 + $10,000 – $3,000 = $59,500).

b. The ending balance of the Allowance for Overvaluation of Inventories: Iowa Branch should be $600 ($3,000 x 0.20 = $600). Therefore, the January 31, 2005, journal entry to correct the balance of that account is a debit to Investment in Iowa Branch, $2,500 (the aggregate understatement of the billed prices of the two merchandise shipments to the branch: $500 + $2,000 = $2,500); a debit to Allowance for Overvaluation of Inventories: Iowa Branch, $8,800 ($9,400 – $600 = $8,800); and a credit to Realized Gross Profit: Iowa Branch Sales, $11,300 ($11,900 – $600 = $11,300).

HIGHLIGHTS OF THE CHAPTER

1. A **business combination** occurs when an entity acquires net assets that constitute a business or acquires equity interests of one or more other entities and obtains control over that entity or entities.

2. A **combined enterprise** is an entity that results from a business combination of **constituent companies,** the **combinor** and the **combinee.** The owners of the combinor end up with control of ownership interests in the combined enterprise.

3. In a **friendly takeover** business combination, terms of the combination are worked out by the boards of directors of the constituent companies. A target company in a **hostile takeover** typically resorts to one or more defensive tactics that have colorful designations such as **white knight** and **shark repellent.**

4. In recent years, business combinations have been a popular method for a corporation to diversify its product lines and to enlarge its share of the market for its products. Growth through business combinations often is referred to as **external** growth.

5. The four most common methods for carrying out a business combination are **statutory merger, statutory consolidation, acquisition of common stock,** and **acquisition of assets.**

6. In a **statutory merger,** one corporation issues its common stock for the common stock owned by stockholders of one or more other corporations, which then cease to exist as separate legal entities. The surviving corporation thus obtains the assets and assumes the liabilities of the liquidated corporations.

7. A **statutory consolidation** is similar to a statutory merger, except that a new corporation is formed to issue its common stock for the common stock owned by stockholders of two or more existing corporations, which then go out of existence.

8. In the other two methods for carrying out a business combination, the combinor issues its common stock, cash, debt, or a combination thereof, to acquire the common stock or the net assets of the combinee. These two methods do not involve the liquidation of the combinee.

9. The amount of cash or debt securities, or the number of shares of common stock, to be issued in a business combination usually is established by capitalization of the expected average earnings of the combinee at a desired rate of return and/or determination of the current fair values of the combinee's assets and liabilities.

10. If common stock is issued by the combinor for the outstanding shares of common stock of the combinee, the price is expressed as the ratio of the number of shares of the combinor's common stock to be exchanged for each share of the combinee's common stock. For example, if 100,000 shares of Port Corporation common stock are to be issued in a business combination for the 40,000 outstanding shares of Strode Company common stock, the **exchange ratio** is 2½ to 1.

11. Under current generally accepted accounting principles, there is one permissible method of accounting for business combinations: **purchase.**

12. The **combinor** in a business combination is the constituent company that distributes cash or other assets or incurs liabilities to acquire the common stock or assets of the other constituent company or companies. In a business combination involving an exchange of common stock, the **combinor** generally is the constituent company whose former stockholders retain or receive the larger portion of the voting rights of the combined enterprise.

13. In a business combination, the cost of the combinee includes the total of the consideration paid by the combinor, the **direct** out-of-pocket costs of the business combination, and any **contingent consideration** that is **determinable on the date of the combination.** Other contingent consideration is recognized when the contingency is resolved.

14. The cost of a combinee in a business combination first is allocated to the identifiable assets acquired and liabilities assumed, based on their current fair values on the date of the combination. Any remaining cost not allocated is recognized as **goodwill.** If the total of the current fair values assigned to acquired assets and assumed liabilities **exceeds** the cost of the combinee, the **bargain-purchase excess** is applied pro rata to reduce the values initially assigned to specified assets.

15. The balance sheet issued on the date of a business combination includes the assets and liabilities of all constituent companies involved in the combination; the **retained earnings** is that of the combinor only. The income statement issued by the combinor for the accounting period in which a business combination is completed includes the operating results of the combinee **after the date of the combination only.**

16. The complexity of business combinations and their effects on the financial position and operating results of the reporting entity necessitate extensive disclosure of business combinations in a note to the financial statements.

17. Purchase accounting for business combinations has been criticized by accountants. The principal criticism of purchase accounting centers on its recognition of goodwill (a) on a **residual** basis and (b) for the **combinee only.**

QUESTIONS

True or False

For each of the following statements, circle the **T** or the **F** to indicate whether the statement is true or false.

T F 1. Business combinations provide a method for achieving rapid growth in assets and sales.

T F 2. In a **statutory merger,** a new corporation is formed to issue its common stock for the common stock of two or more existing corporations, which then are liquidated.

T F 3. A **combinee** is a corporation that acquires all or part of the common stock of another corporation.

T F 4. The **exchange ratio** expresses the relationship of the number of shares of the combinor's common stock exchanged for outstanding common stock of the combinee.

T F 5. **Purchase accounting** must be used for all business combinations.

T F 6. Goodwill in a business combination is valued at an amount representing the capitalized value of the average excess earnings of the combinee.

T F 7. Legal fees incurred for the SEC registration statement covering shares of common stock issued in a business combination are included in cost of the combinee.

T F 8. Goodwill recognized in a business combination is entered in the accounting records of the combinee.

T F 9. Out-of-pocket costs of a business combination are recognized as expenses.

Completion Statements

Fill in the necessary words or amounts to complete the following statements.

1. The four most common methods for carrying out a business combination are _____
    _____ , _____ _____ , _____
    _____ _____ _____ , and _____ _____
    _____ .

2. A corporation that issues common stock, cash, debt, or a combination thereof, to acquire all or a
    majority of the common stock of another corporation generally is called a _____ .

3. Additional cash, other assets, or securities that may be issuable in the future in connection with a
    business combination are called _____ _____ .

4. A _____ _____ _____ is an excess of current fair values of net
    assets acquired in a business combination over their cost to the combinor.

5. On April 1, 2005, Peluca Corporation paid $500,000 for all the outstanding common stock of
    Socorro Company in a statutory merger business combination. The carrying amounts of the
    assets and liabilities of Socorro on April 1, 2005, follow:

Cash	$ 10,000
Inventories	150,000
Plant assets (net of accumulated depreciation of $148,000)	250,000
Liabilities	100,000

    On April 1, 2005, the inventories of Socorro had a current fair value of $200,000, and the plant
    assets had a current fair value of $400,000. As a result of the merger with Socorro, Peluca
    recognizes goodwill of $_____ and plant assets of $_____ in its account records.

Multiple Choice

Choose the best answer for each of the following questions and enter the identifying letter in the space
provided.

____ 1. Business combinations often have been challenged under Section 7 of the Clayton Act by:
  a. The U.S. Department of Justice, Antitrust Division
  b. The U.S. Federal Trade Commission
  c. Attorneys general of the several states
  d. Both **a** and **b**

____ 2. The amount of cash or debt securities, or the number of shares of common stock, to be issued
    in a business combination generally is decided by:
  a. Determination of current fair value of the combinee's tangible and intangible assets
      (including goodwill) less liabilities
  b. Capitalization of expected average earnings of the combinee at a desired rate of return
  c. Either **a** or **b** or both **a** and **b**
  d. Neither **a** nor **b**

_____ 3. Out-of-pocket costs of a business combination were as follows:

CPA audit fees for SEC registration statement	$10,000
Legal fees:	
For the business combination	4,000
For SEC registration statement	7,000
Finder's fee	20,000
Printer's charges for printing securities and	
SEC registration statement	2,500
SEC registration fee	500
Total out-of-pocket costs of business	
combination	$44,000

The amount to be debited to the Paid-in Capital in Excess of Par ledger account in the business combination is:
a. $0
b. $20,000
c. $24,000
d. $44,000
e. Some other amount

_____ 4. Seaton Corporation and Marque Company combined in a statutory merger, with Seaton as the combinor. Seaton issued 10,000 shares of its $5 par common stock ($20 current fair value a share) for all 1,000 outstanding shares of Marque's $2 par common stock. Out-of-pocket costs of the business combination may be disregarded. On the date of the combination, the stockholders' equity of Marque was as follows:

Common stock, $2 par	$ 2,000
Additional paid-in capital	60,000
Retained earnings (deficit)	(10,000)
Total stockholders' equity	$52,000

The total amount to be credited to Seaton's Common Stock and Paid-in Capital in Excess of Par ledger accounts is:
a. $50,000
b. $52,000
c. $62,000
d. Some other amount

_____ 5. On March 31, 2005, Meade Company merged into Steele Corporation. Out-of-pocket costs of the business combination totaled $30,000. The separate income statements of the two companies for the fiscal year ended March 31, 2005, prior to any journal entries necessary to record the business combination on that date, showed the following net income: Steele, $500,000; Meade, $100,000. Steele's postmerger income statement for the year ended March 31, 2005, shows net income in the amount of:
a. $470,000
b. $500,000
c. $570,000
d. Some other amount

_____ 6. Stevens Corporation issued cumulative preferred stock with a current fair value of $500,000 for all outstanding common stock of Mullin Company in a statutory merger business combination. Out-of-pocket costs of the combination included $40,000 directly attributable to the merger and $30,000 attributable to the registration of the preferred stock with the SEC The carrying amount of Mullin's identifiable net assets on the date of the combination was $460,000. As a result of the combination, Stevens records an increase in total assets of:

    a. $460,000
    b. $470,000
    c. $540,000
    d. $570,000
    e. Some other amount

_____ 7. The bargain-purchase excess in a business combination is:

    a. Recognized as revenue of the combined enterprise
    b. Added to stockholders' equity of the combined enterprise
    c. Offset against (positive) goodwill of the combined enterprise
    d. Accounted for in some other manner

_____ 8. The cost of the combinee in a business combination involving issuance of bonds payable by the combinor does not include:

    a. Bond issue costs
    b. Contingent consideration determinable on the consummation date of the combination
    c. Present value of the bonds payable issued in the combination
    d. Finder's fee
    e. Any of the foregoing

SHORT EXERCISES

1. On July 1, 2005, More Company merged into Sheaf Corporation in a business combination in which Sheaf issued 50,000 shares of its $10 par common stock (current fair value $15 a share) for all of More's outstanding common stock. On that date, Sheaf's Paid-in Capital in Excess of Par ledger account had a credit balance of $2 million. Data on More's financial position on July 1, 2005, follow:

	Carrying amounts	Current fair values
Total assets	$1,500,000	$1,600,000
Total liabilities	$ 900,000	900,000
Common stock, $1 par	100,000	
Retained earnings	500,000	
Total liabilities & stockholders' equity	$1,500,000	

Out-of-pocket costs of the business combination, paid by Sheaf on July 1, 2005, were as follows:

Finder's, accounting, and legal fees relating to the business combination	$ 90,000
Costs associated with SEC registration statement	30,000
Total out-of-pocket costs of business combination	$120,000

Prepare journal entries for Sheaf Corporation in the space below to record the business combination with More Company.

Sheaf Corporation
Journal Entries

2005			
July 1			
1			
1			

2.   Merz Company merged into Storz Corporation in a business combination completed June 30, 2005. Out-of-pocket costs paid by Storz on June 30, 2005, in connection with the combination were as follows:

Finder's, accounting, and legal fees relating to the business combination	$30,000
Cost associated with notes issued to complete the business combination	20,000
Total out-of-pocket costs of business combination	$50,000

The separate balance sheets of the two companies immediately prior to the business combination were as shown below.

STORZ CORPORATION and MERZ COMPANY
Separate Balance Sheets
(prior to business combination)
June 30, 2005

	Storz Corporation	Merz Company
Current assets	$ 870,000	$ 600,000
Plant assets (net)	3,700,000	2,260,000
Patents (net)	120,000	40,000
Total assets	$4,690,000	$2,900,000
Liabilities	$ 530,000	$ 420,000
Common stock, $20 par	2,400,000	
Common stock, $10 par		750,000
Additional paid-in-capital	840,000	640,000
Retained earnings	1,170,000	1,090,000
Treasury stock, at cost, 10,000 shares	(250,000)	
Total liabilities & stockholders' equity	$4,690,000	$2,900,000

Additional Information:

(1) The current fair values of the identifiable assets and liabilities of Storz and Merz on June 30, 2005, were as follows:

	Storz Corporation	Merz Company
Current assets	$ 990,000	$ 680,000
Plant assets (net)	4,400,000	2,800,000
Patents (net)	144,000	72,000
Liabilities	(530,000)	(420,000)
Net assets	$5,004,000	$3,132,000

(2) There were no intercompany transactions prior to the business combination.

(3) Before the business combination, Storz had 300,000 shares of common stock authorized, 120,000 shares issued, and 110,000 shares outstanding. Merz had 75,000 shares of common stock authorized, issued, and outstanding.

In the space that follows, prepare journal entries for Storz Corporation to record the merger business combination with Merz Company, given that Storz Corporation paid $1 million cash and issued 10% promissory notes at face amount of $3 million for all outstanding common stock of Merz Company. The present value of the promissory notes was $3 million.

©The McGraw-Hill Companies, Inc., 2006

Storz Corporation
Journal Entries

2005			
June 30			
30			
30			

3. On October 31, 2005, Sump Corporation merged with Mark Company in a business combination. Sump exchanged three of its shares of common stock for each share of Mark's outstanding common stock. The current fair value of Sump's common stock on October 31, 2005, was $3.00 a share. October 31 was the fiscal year-end for both companies. There were no intercompany transactions prior to October 31. Out-of-pocket costs of the business combination may be disregarded. The separate balance sheets of Sump and Mark immediately before the merger were as shown below.

SUMP CORPORATION and MARK COMPANY
Separate Balance Sheets
(prior to business combination)
October 31, 2005

	Sump Corporation	Mark Company	
	Carrying amounts	Carrying amounts	Current fair values
Current assets	$120,000	$ 80,000	$110,000
Plant assets (net)	450,000	360,000	420,000
Intangible assets (net)	90,000	20,000	30,000
Total assets	$660,000	$460,000	$560,000
Current liabilities	$105,000	$50,000	$ 50,000
Notes payable	120,000		
Bonds payable		300,000	280,000
Common stock, $1 par	225,000		
Common stock, $5 par		150,000	
Retained earnings (deficit)	210,000	(40,000)	
Total liabilities & stockholders' equity	$660,000	$460,000	

Modern Advanced Accounting, 10/e

Complete the balance sheet below for Sump Corporation immediately after the merger with Mark Company (use the space provided below for computations).

SUMP CORPORATION
Balance Sheet (following business combination)
October 31, 2005

Assets		Liabilities & Stockholders' Equity	
Current assets	$	Current liabilities	$
Plant assets (net)		Notes payable	
Intangible assets (net)		Bonds payable (net)	
Goodwill	_____	Common stock, $1 par	
		Additional paid-in-capital	
		Retained earnings	_____
		Total liabilities & stockholders'	
Total assets	$ _____	equity	$ _____

Computations:

CASE

In a classroom discussion of accounting standards for business combinations, student James expresses puzzlement about the provisions of **FASB Statement No. 141,** "Business Combinations," dealing with determination of the combinor in a business combination involving the exchange of common stock for common stock (see page 49, paragraph **12).** James states that it is his opinion that the issuer of previously unissued common stock should always be the combinor, regardless of which constituent company's former stockholder group either retains or receives the largest portion of voting rights in the combined enterprise.

How would you defend the Financial Accounting Standards Board's standards for identifying the combinor in a stock-for-stock business combination, in response to James? Explain.

SOLUTIONS TO QUESTIONS, SHORT EXERCISES, AND CASE: CHAPTER 5

QUESTIONS

True or False

1. T 2. F 3. F 4. T 5. T 6. F 7. F 8. F 9. F

Completion Statements

1. Statutory merger, statutory consolidation, acquisition of common stock, acquisition of assets.
2. Combinor. 3. Contingent consideration. 4. Bargain-purchase excess. 5. $0, $390,000 [$400,000 − ($510,000 − $500,000) = $390,000].

Multiple Choice

1. d 2. c 3. b ($10,000 + $7,000 + $2,500 + $500 = $20,000) 4. d (10,000 x $20 = $200,000)
5. b 6. b ($500,000 + $40,000 − $70,000 = $470,000) 7. d (Applied to reduce amounts assigned to specified assets) 8. a

SHORT EXERCISES

1.

Sheaf Corporation
Journal Entries

2005			
July 1	Investment in More Company Common Stock		
	(50,000 x $15)	750,000	
	Common Stock (50,000 x $10)		500,000
	Paid-in Capital in Excess of Par		250,000
	To record merger with More Company.		
1	Investment in More Company Common Stock	90,000	
	Paid-in Capital in Excess of Par	30,000	
	Cash		120,000
	To record payment of out-of-pocket costs incurred in		
	merger with More Company.		
1	Assets	1,600,000	
	Goodwill	140,000	
	Liabilities		900,000
	Investment in More Company Common Stock		840,000
	To allocate cost of More Company investment to		
	identifiable assets and liabilities, with the remainder to		
	goodwill.		

2.

Storz Corporation
Journal Entries

2005			
June 30	Investment in Merz Company Common Stock ($1,000,000 + $3,000,000)	4,000,000	
	Cash		1,000,000
	Notes Payable		3,000,000
	To record merger with Merz Company.		
30	Investment in Merz Company Common Stock	30,000	
	Note Issue Costs	20,000	
	Cash		50,000
	To record payment of out-of-pocket costs incurred in merger with Merz Company.		
30	Current Assets	680,000	
	Plant Assets (net)	2,800,000	
	Patents (net)	72,000	
	Goodwill	898,000	
	Liabilities		420,000
	Investment in Merz Company Common Stock		4,030,000
	To allocate cost of Merz Company investment to identifiable assets and liabilities, with remainder to goodwill.		

3.

SUMP CORPORATION
Balance Sheet (following business combination)
October 31, 2005

Assets		Liabilities & Stockholders' Equity	
Current assets	$ 230,000 (1)	Current liabilities	$ 155,000 (5)
Plant assets (net)	870,000 (2)	Notes payable	120,000
Intangible assets (net)	120,000 (3)	Bonds payable (net)	280,000
Goodwill	40,000 (4)	Common stock, $1 par	315,000 (6)
		Additional paid-in-capital	180,000 (7)
		Retained earnings	210,000
		Total liabilities & stockholders' equity	
Total assets:	$1,260,000	equity	$1,260,000

Computations:

(1) $120,000 + $110,000 = $230,000
(2) $450,000 + $420,000 = $870,000
(3) $90,000 + $30,000 = $120,000
(4) (3 x 30,000 x $3) – ($560,000 – $330,000) = $40,000

(5) $105,000 + $50,000 = $155,000
(6) $225,000 + (3 x 30,000 x $1) = $315,000
(7) $90,000 x ($3 – $1) = $180,000

Study Guide

CASE

To justify the Financial Accounting Standards Board's standards for determination of the combinor in a stock-for-stock business combination, one must consider the relevant definition of **combinor** (see page 49, paragraph **12**) as a constituent company entering into a combination whose owners as a group end up with control of the ownership interest in the combined enterprise. The obvious combinor in a business combination affected by the issuance of cash or debt securities is the issuer of those financial instruments, because no unissued common stock has been given to the combinee (in an acquisition of assets) or to the combinee's former stockholders (in a statutory merger, statutory consolidation, or acquisition of common stock). However, the issuer corporation in a stock-for-stock business combination may previously have had few stockholders with minimal stockholdings, as is true for many issuers that are "shell corporations" with only cash and short-term investments, and no operations. To illustrate, assume that Shell Corporation has cash and cash equivalents, $100,000; short-term investments, $400,000; no liabilities; and stockholders' equity, $500,000, represented by 10,000 shares of $1 par common stock (of 100,000 authorized shares) owned by a single stockholder. If Shell Corporation were to issue 40,000 shares of the $1 par common stock to acquire all the outstanding common stock of Active Company having a current fair value of $2,000,000, the former stockholders of Active would control Shell because they own 80% (40,000 ÷ 50,000 = 0.80) of the now outstanding common stock of Shell. Thus, Active would be the combinor.

CHAPTER 6
CONSOLIDATED FINANCIAL STATEMENTS:
ON DATE OF BUSINESS COMBINATION

HIGHLIGHTS OF THE CHAPTER

1. If an investor corporation acquires a controlling interest in the outstanding common stock of an investee corporation that is not liquidated, the investee becomes a **subsidiary** of the investor **parent company.**

2. **Consolidated financial statements** are issued to report the financial position and operating results of a parent company and its subsidiaries as a single **economic entity,** despite the fact that the affiliated companies are separate **legal entities.**

3. In the preparation of consolidated financial statements, assets, liabilities, revenue, and expenses of the parent company and its subsidiaries are totaled; intercompany transactions and balances are eliminated; and the final consolidated amounts are reported in the consolidated balance sheet, income statement, statement of stockholders' equity, and statement of cash flows.

4. In the past, a wide range of **consolidation practices** existed among major corporations in the United States. Many companies excluded from consolidation foreign subsidiaries and domestic finance-related subsidiaries such as insurance companies and banks. However, the Financial Accounting Standards Board has issued a **Statement** requiring the consolidation of all subsidiaries that are **controlled.**

5. The traditional concept of a parent company's controlling financial interest in a subsidiary has been ownership of more than 50% of the subsidiary's voting common stock. However, a parent company **may not actually control** a subsidiary that is in court-supervised liquidation or reorganization, or a subsidiary in a highly restrictive foreign country.

6. In 1999, the FASB proposed to redefine **control** as a parent company's nonshared decision-making ability that enables it to increase the benefits it derives and limit the losses it suffers from the subsidiary's activities. Subsequently, the FASB "shelved" the proposal, leaving the problem of **variable interest entities** unresolved.

7. In a business combination resulting in a parent company–**wholly owned** subsidiary relationship, the subsidiary prepares no journal entries associated with the combination. The parent company's journal entry to record such a business combination includes a debit to the Investment in Subsidiary Common Stock ledger account for the amount of cash or the current fair value of securities issued to effect the combination. The Investment in Subsidiary Common Stock ledger account also is debited with the **direct** out-of-pocket costs of the business combination.

8. Accountants generally use a **working paper for consolidated balance sheet** and **working paper eliminations** to facilitate the preparation of a consolidated balance sheet on the date of a business combination. A consolidated income statement, a consolidated statement of stockholders' equity, and a consolidated statement of cash flows are not appropriate for the accounting period ended on the date of a business combination, because the combining companies were separate **economic** as well as **legal** entities prior to the combination.

9. Working paper eliminations are **working paper entries only;** they are not entered in the accounting records of either the parent company or the subsidiaries. Working paper eliminations on the date of a business combination include differences between current fair values and carrying amounts of the subsidiary's identifiable assets and liabilities because a subsidiary prepares no journal entries for a business combination.

10. The consolidated paid-in capital amounts in a consolidated balance sheet are those of the parent company only. Subsidiaries' paid-in capital amounts **always** are eliminated in consolidation. In addition, consolidated retained earnings on the date of a business combination includes the retained earnings of the **parent company only.**

11. The consolidated balance sheet for a parent company and a **partially owned** subsidiary on the date of a business combination includes the **minority interest** of the subsidiary's stockholders other than the parent company in the net assets of the subsidiary.

12. The **economic unit concept** and the **parent company concept** of consolidated financial statements have different approaches to the display of minority interest in the consolidated financial statements. In the **economic unit concept,** the minority interest in the subsidiary's net assets is displayed in the **stockholders' equity section** of the consolidated balance sheet, and the minority interest in the subsidiary's net income is displayed as a **subdivision of total consolidated income** in the consolidated income statement.

13. In the **parent company concept,** the minority interest in net assets of the subsidiary is displayed as a **liability** in the consolidated balance sheet, and the minority interest in the subsidiary's net income is displayed as an **expense** in the consolidated income statement.

14. In the opinion of the author, the **economic unit concept** of displaying minority interest in consolidated financial statements emphasizes the legal aspects of the separate corporate entities making up the consolidated entity. Because a proposed **Statement** of the FASB mandates its use, the **economic unit concept** has been adopted by the author in the textbook chapters dealing with consolidated financial statements.

15. Three methods have been advanced with respect to the valuation of the minority interest in net assets of subsidiary (and goodwill) in the consolidated balance sheet of a parent company and its **partially owned** subsidiary. The three methods are summarized as follows:

    a. All identifiable assets and liabilities of a partially owned subsidiary are valued on a single basis—current fair value—and only the goodwill of the subsidiary acquired by the parent company is displayed in the consolidated balance sheet. This method is consistent with accounting for business combinations and is widely used.

    b. Current fair values are assigned to a partially owned subsidiary's net assets (including goodwill) only to the extent of the parent company's ownership interest in the net assets. The minority interest is based upon the carrying amounts of the subsidiary's net assets. This method is not consistent with accounting for business combinations.

    c. Same as in **a,** except that minority interest in the consolidated balance sheet includes the minority's share of the implicit current fair value of the subsidiary's **total** goodwill.

16. To illustrate the three methods described in paragraph **15,** assume that Parent Corporation acquired 80% of the common stock of Sub Company for $800,000, and that data for Sub Company on the date of the business combination were as follows:

Carrying amount of net assets	$ 600,000
Current fair value of identifiable net assets	900,000
Current fair value of total net assets, including goodwill ($800,000 ÷ 0.80)	1,000,000

The minority interest and goodwill in the consolidated balance sheet for Parent Corporation and subsidiary on the date of the business combination are computed under each method described in paragraph **15** as follows:

	Minority interest in net assets of subsidiary	Goodwill
a. Minority interest ($900,000 x 0.20)	$180,000	
Goodwill [$800,000 − ($900,000 x 0.80)]		$80,000
b. Minority interest ($600,000 x 0.20)	120,000	
Goodwill [$800,000 − ($900,000 x 0.80)]		$80,000
c. Minority interest ($1,000,000 x 0.20)	200,000	
Goodwill ($1,000,000 − $900,000)		$100,000

17. The minority interest in the subsidiary's net assets and the goodwill as computed in paragraph **16** **are not recognized in the accounting records of either the parent company or the subsidiary.** They are included in the consolidated balance sheet **by means of a working paper elimination.** The following working paper elimination (in journal entry format) for Parent Corporation and subsidiary on the date of the business combination illustrates this. (In the illustration, which incorporates the method described in part **a** of paragraph **15**, amounts not in boldface are assumed.)

Common Stock—Sub	350,000	
Additional Paid-in Capital—Sub	100,000	
Retained Earnings—Sub	150,000	
Various Identifiable Assets—Sub	**300,000**	
Goodwill—Parent	**80,000**	
Investment in Sub Common Stock—Parent		**800,000**
Minority Interest in Net Assets of Subsidiary		**180,000**

To eliminate intercompany investment and equity accounts of subsidiary on date of business combination; to allocate excess of cost over carrying amount of identifiable assets acquired, with remainder to goodwill; and to establish minority interest in net assets of subsidiary on date of combination.

18. If a business combination that results in a parent company–subsidiary relationship involves a bargain-purchase excess, the excess of current fair values of the subsidiary's identifiable net assets over the cost of the parent company's investment is applied pro rata to reduce the amounts initially assigned to specified assets. The proration is accomplished in a working paper elimination.

19. A description of the consolidation policy reflected in consolidated financial statements is included in the "Summary of Significant Accounting Policies" required by **APB Opinion No. 22,** "Disclosure of Accounting Policies."

20. Consolidated financial statements are useful primarily to stockholders and prospective investors in the common stock of the parent company. Creditors of all consolidated corporations and minority stockholders of subsidiaries find only limited use for consolidated financial statements because such statements do not show the financial position, operating results, or cash flows of individual corporations comprising the consolidated group. In addition, consolidated financial statements of a highly diversified corporate group are impossible to categorize into a single operating segment or product classification.

21.   The SEC has authorized **push-down** accounting, for valuations based on parent company investment cost, in the separate financial statements for certain subsidiaries of companies subject to the SEC's authority.

True or False

For each of the following statements, circle the **T** or the **F** to indicate whether the statement is true or false.

T F 1. The parent company concept of consolidated financial statements considers such statements to be an extension of parent company statements, and the minority interest in net assets of subsidiary is displayed as a liability in the consolidated balance sheet.

T F 2. The economic unit concept of consolidated financial statements considers such statements to be those of an economic entity with two classes of stockholders: the dominant interest and the minority interest.

T F 3. Consolidated financial statements are issued to report the financial position and operating results of a parent company and its subsidiaries as a single **legal entity.**

T F 4. Consolidated financial statements for a parent company and its subsidiaries are prepared in essentially the same fashion as combined financial statements for the home office and branches of a business enterprise.

T F 5. The traditional meaning of **controlling financial interest** has been ownership by an investor corporation of 50% or more of the voting common stock of an investee corporation.

T F 6. The parent company's share of the net income or loss of an unconsolidated subsidiary generally is presented on a single line in the consolidated income statement.

T F 7. In a business combination resulting in a parent company–subsidiary relationship, the subsidiary adjusts its asset and liability ledger accounts to reflect their current fair values on the date of combination.

T F 8. Working paper eliminations are entered in accounting records of the parent company.

T F 9. The retained earnings amount of a subsidiary is included in consolidated retained earnings on the date of a business combination.

T F 10. Under methods of computation that are consistent with the parent company concept, the minority interest's share of the subsidiary's goodwill implicit in the parent company's acquisition cost of the subsidiary's common stock **is not included** in the consolidated balance sheet.

T F 11. The disclosure of the consolidation policy followed by a reporting entity generally includes the working paper eliminations for intercompany account balances.

T F 12. Minority stockholders of a subsidiary find consolidated financial statements useful in making investment decisions.

Completion Statements

Fill in the necessary words or amounts to complete the following statements.

1. The principal types of subsidiaries that were excluded from consolidation in past United States accounting practices are _____ subsidiaries and _____-_____ subsidiaries.

2. Generally accepted accounting principles require _____ of one enterprise by another as the basis for consolidated financial statements.

3. The only consolidated financial statement issued on the date of a business combination resulting in a parent company–subsidiary relationship is a consolidated _____ _____.

4. The Eliminations column in a working paper for consolidated financial statements has _____ and _____ rather than debits and credits.

5. Consolidated paid-in capital amounts that are presented in a consolidated balance sheet are those of the _____ _____ only.

6. If Pike Corporation paid $1,392,090 for 75% of the outstanding common stock of Sayles Company, which had identifiable net assets with a current fair value of $1,782,860 on the date of the business combination, the amount of goodwill that generally would be displayed in the consolidated balance sheet on the date of the combination is $_____.

7. Refer to question **6**. The amount of minority interest in net assets of subsidiary that would be displayed in the consolidated balance sheet on the date of the business combination is $_____.

8. _____ financial statements are of limited usefulness to the _____ of the parent company and to _____ stockholders of the subsidiary.

Multiple Choice

Choose the best answer for each of the following questions and enter the identifying letter in the space provided.

_____ 1. What would be the effect on the consolidated financial statements if an unconsolidated subsidiary is accounted for by the cost method of accounting, but consolidated financial statements are prepared for other subsidiaries?
   a. All the unconsolidated subsidiary's ledger account balances would be included individually in the consolidated financial statements.
   b. Consolidated net income would not include any amounts for the unconsolidated subsidiary.
   c. Consolidated net income would be the same as if the subsidiary had been included in the consolidation.
   d. Dividend revenue from the unconsolidated subsidiary would be included in consolidated net income.

____ 2. Consolidated financial statements are appropriate for Pro Corporation, Soy Company, and San Company if:

a. Pro owns all the outstanding common stock of Soy and San; Soy is being liquidated in bankruptcy proceedings

b. Pro owns 55% of the outstanding common stock of Soy and 50% of the outstanding common stock of San.

c. Pro owns 40% of the outstanding common stock of Soy and 85% of the outstanding common stock of San; unrelated Gel Corporation owns 40% of the outstanding common stock of Soy.

d. Pro owns 35% of the outstanding common stock of Soy and 80% of the outstanding common stock of San; San owns 45% of the outstanding common stock of Soy.

____ 3. Plite Corporation owns 92% of the outstanding common stock of Synge company; the other 8% is owned by Probert Corporation. In the consolidated financial statements of Plite Corporation and subsidiary, Probert is considered:

a. An investee
b. A minority interest
c. An affiliate
d. An investor
e. None of the foregoing

____ 4. Consolidated financial statements are appropriate for Pard Corporation, Sax Company , and Sed Company if:

a. Pard owns 80% of the outstanding common stock of Sax and 40% of Sed; Sax owns 30% of Sed.

b. Pard owns 100% of the outstanding common stock of Sax and 90% of Sed; Pard acquired the common stock of Sed one month before the balance sheet date and sold it seven weeks later.

c. Pard owns 100% of the outstanding common stock of Sax and Sed; Sed is in bankruptcy reorganization proceedings.

d. Pard owns 80% of the outstanding common stock of Sax and 40% of Sed; unrelated Vail Company owns 55% of Sed.

Questions **5** and **6** are based on the following information.

Seguro Company's balance sheet on December 31, 2005, was as follows:

Assets	
Cash	$ 80,000
Trade accounts receivable (net)	160,000
Inventories	400,000
Plant assets (net)	720,000
Total assets	$1,360,000
Liabilities & Stockholders' Equity	
Current liabilities	$ 240,000
Long-term debt	400,000
Common stock, $1 par	80,000
Additional paid-in capital	160,000
Retained earnings	480,000
Total liabilities & stockholders' equity	$1,360,000

On December 31, 2005, Penjamo Corporation acquired all the outstanding common stock of Seguro for $1,200,000. On that date, the current fair value of Seguro's inventories was $360,000 and the current fair value of Seguro's plant assets was $800,000. The current fair values of all other identifiable assets and liabilities of Seguro were equal to their carrying amounts.

____ 5. As a result of the acquisition of Seguro by Penjamo, the December 31, 2005, consolidated balance sheet of Penjamo and subsidiary displays goodwill in the amount of:
   a. $400,000
   b. $440,000
   c. $480,000
   d. $520,000
   e. Some other amount

____ 6. Assuming that the unconsolidated balance sheet of Penjamo Corporation on December 31, 2005, included retained earnings of $1,600,000, what amount of retained earnings is displayed in the December 31, 2005, consolidated balance sheet of Penjamo Corporation and subsidiary?
   a. $1,600,000
   b. $2,080,000
   c. $2,240,000
   d. $2,520,000
   e. Some other amount

____ 7. The author of *Modern Advanced Accounting* supports the method of measuring goodwill and minority interest that:
   a. Measures all subsidiary net assets (including goodwill) at current fair value in the consolidated balance sheet
   b. Allocates a portion of the implied total value of the subsidiary's goodwill to minority interest in net assets of subsidiary
   c. Reports at current fair value in the consolidated balance sheet only the portion of subsidiary identifiable net assets acquired by the parent company
   d. Does none of the foregoing

____ 8. Which of the following statements is true?
   a. Consolidated financial statements are useful to creditors of a subsidiary.
   b. Comparison of consolidated financial statements of diversified enterprises may be misleading.
   c. The net assets of a subsidiary that is in liquidation in bankruptcy should be included in a consolidated balance sheet.
   d. Consolidated financial statements are not appropriate for inclusion in the annual reports of publicly owned corporations.

____ 9. The lower portion of a consolidated income statement prepared under the **economic unit concept** of consolidated financial statements may resemble the income statement of :
   a. A partnership
   b. A single proprietorship
   c. A corporation
   d. A parent company

_____ 10. The **parent company concept** of consolidated financial statements considers the minority interest in net assets of a subsidiary to be:
   a. A liability
   b. A part of consolidated stockholders' equity
   c. An item between liabilities and stockholders' equity
   d. Some other classification

SHORT EXERCISES

1.   On September 1, 2005, Polk Corporation acquired 75% of the outstanding common stock of Sword Company for $1,369,050. On that date, the current fair values of Sword's identifiable tangible and intangible net assets totaled $1,714,600.

   a. In the space below, compute Sword's **total** goodwill implicit in the price paid by Polk for th common stock of Sword.

   b. In the space below, compute the amount of goodwill to be displayed in the consolidated balance sheet for Polk and subsidiary under the method of computation supported by the author of *Modern Advanced Accounting*.

   c. In the space below, compute the minority interest in net assets of Sword under the method of computation supported by the author of *Modern Advanced Accounting*.

   d. In the space below, compute the minority interest in net assets of Sword if the total implicit goodwill of Sword is displayed in the consolidated balance sheet.

2. On April 30, 2005, Pemberton Corporation acquired 18,000 of the 20,000 outstanding shares of Solomon Company's $2 par common stock for $180,000 cash; a 10% promissory note payable April 30, 2008, with a face amount and present value of $100,000; and 10,000 shares of Pemberton's unissued $10 par common stock having an April 30, 2005, current fair value of $15 a share. Out-of-pocket costs of the business combination paid by Pemberton on April 30, 2005, totaling $60,000, were allocable 55% to the accounting, legal, and finder's fees related to the combination and 45% to the SEC registration statement for the 10,000 shares of Pemberton common stock.

Balances of Solomon's stockholders' equity ledger accounts on April 30, 2005, were as follows: Common Stock, $40,000; Paid-in Capital in Excess of Par $150,000; Retained Earnings, $120,000. All assets and liabilities of Solomon were carried at amounts equal to current fair value, except plant assets, which were understated by $200,000.

In the space below, prepare the April 30, 2005, journal entries for Pemberton Corporation to record the business combination with Solomon Company (disregard income taxes).

Pemberton Corporation
Journal Entries

2005			
Apr. 30			
30			

3.　Using the information in exercise **2,** prepare the working paper elimination (in journal entry format) for Pemberton Corporation and subsidiary as of April 30, 2005, in the space provided below (disregard income taxes).

Pemberton Corporation and Subsidiary
Working Paper Elimination
April 30, 2005

(a)			

4.　On December 31, 2005, Polly Corporation paid $250,000 to Sandra Sally for all 50,000 shares of Sally Company outstanding common stock. Legal fees paid by Polly on December 31, 2005, in connection with the business combination amounted to $10,000. On the date of the combination, Sally's stockholders' equity amounts were common stock ($1 par), $50,000; additional paid-in capital, $80,000; retained earnings, $70,000. The current fair values of Sally's inventories and plant assets (net) exceeded their carrying amounts by $30,000 and $70,000, respectively. Sally had no noncurrent assets other than plant assets.

In the space below, prepare a working paper elimination (in journal entry format) for Polly Corporation and subsidiary on December 31, 2005 (disregard income taxes).

Polly Corporation and Subsidiary
Working Paper Elimination
December 31, 2005

(a)			

Case

As controller of Posten Corporation, a large, non–publicly owned corporation that has just completed a business combination with Salker Company, a manufacturing enterprise with widely recognized products, you have explained to Posten's majority stockholder and chief executive officer, Charles Posten, the accounting standards for business combinations, including goodwill and bargain-purchase excess. You point out that, based on your preliminary computations, a significant amount of goodwill will have to be recognized in the consolidated balance sheet of Posten and Salker on the date of the business combination. You also inform Charles Posten that, although Salker is in a different operating segment than is Posten Corporation, the disclosures of basic and diluted earnings per share required for publicly owned enterprises do not apply to nonpublic enterprises such as Posten Corporation and Salker Company. Responding to your statement that amortization of goodwill will be deductible over a 15-year period for income tax purposes, Charles Posten asks whether the goodwill might be allocated to the valuation of shorter-lived noncurrent assets as is done for bargain-purchase excess; in other words, might a different standard for goodwill recognition apply to nonpublic companies, as is true for earnings per share?

How should you respond to Charles Posten's question? Explain, including actions that might be taken under generally accepted accounting principles to reduce the portion of cost of Salker Company's common stock that must be allocated to goodwill.

SOLUTIONS TO QUESTIONS, SHORT EXERCISES, AND CASE: CHAPTER 6

QUESTIONS

True or False

1. T 2. T 3. F 4. T 5. F 6. F 7. F 8. F 9. F 10. T 11. F 12. F

Completion Statements

1. Foreign, finance-related. 2. Control. 3. Balance sheet. 4. Increases, decreases. 5. Parent company.
6. $54,945 [$1,392,090 – ($1,782,860 x 0.75) = $54,945]. 7. $445,715 ($1,782,860 x 0.25 = $445,715).
8. Consolidated, creditors, minority.

Multiple Choice

1. d 2. d 3. b 4. a 5. b [$1,200,000 – ($720,000 – $40,000 + $80,000) = $440,000] 6. a 7. d 8. b
9. a 10. a

SHORT EXERCISES

1.
a. Implied current fair value of Sword's
total net assets ($1,369,050 ÷ 0.75) $1,825,400
Less: Total current fair values of
Sword's identifiable tangible and
intangible net assets   1,714,600
Sword's total goodwill implicit in the
cost of Sword's common stock $ 110,800

b. Cost of Polk's investment in Sword $1,369,050
Less: Polk's share of total current fair
values of Sword's net assets
($1,714,600 x 0.75)   1,285,950
Amount of goodwill in consolidated
balance sheet $ 83,100

c. Minority interest in net assets of Sword
under the method of computation
supported by the author ($1,714,600 x
0.25) $ 428,650

d. Minority interest in net assets of Sword
if the total implicit goodwill of Sword
is displayed in the consolidated
balance sheet ($1,825,400 x 0.25) $ 456,350

2.

Pemberton Corporation
Journal Entries

2005				
Apr. 30	Investment in Solomon Company Common Stock		430,000	
	Cash			180,000
	Notes Payable			100,000
	Common Stock			100,000
	Paid-in Capital in Excess of Par			50,000
	To record acquisition of 18,000 shares of Solomon Company's			
	outstanding common stock in a business combination.			
	(Income taxes are disregarded.)			
30	Investment in Solomon Company Common Stock		33,000	
	Paid-in Capital in Excess of Par		27,000	
	Cash			60,000
	To record payment of out-of-pocket costs of business			
	combination with Solomon Company.			

3.

Pemberton Corporation and Subsidiary
Working Paper Elimination
April 30, 2005

	(a) Common Stock—Solomon	40,000	
	Additional Paid-in Capital—Solomon	150,000	
	Retained Earnings—Solomon	120,000	
	Plant Assets—Solomon	200,000	
	Goodwill—Pemberton	4,000	
	Investment in Solomon Company Common		
	Stock—Pemberton		463,000
	Minority Interest in Net Assets of Subsidiary		51,000
	To eliminate intercompany investment and equity accounts of		
	subsidiary on date of business combination; to increase		
	subsidiary's plant assets to current fair value; to recognize		
	goodwill acquired by parent company; and to establish		
	minority interest in subsidiary on date of combination		
	($510,000 x 0.10 = $51,000). (Income tax effects are		
	disregarded).		

4.

Polly Corporation and Subsidiary
Working Paper Elimination
December 31, 2005

	(a) Common Stock—Sally	50,000	
	Additional Paid-in Capital—Sally	80,000	
	Retained Earnings—Sally	70,000	
	Inventories—Sally	30,000	
	Plant Assets (net)—Sally [$70,000 – ($300,000 – $260,000)]	30,000	
	Investment in Sally Company Common Stock—Polly ($250,000 + $10,000)		260,000
	To eliminate intercompany investment and equity accounts of		
	subsidiary on date of business combination; and to allocate		
	$40,000 excess of current fair values of subsidiary's		
	identifiable net assets over Polly's cost to subsidiary's plant		
	assets. (Income tax effects are disregarded.)		

CASE

You should inform Charles Posten of the difference between **accounting standards,** such as accounting for business combinations, and **disclosure standards,** such as for operating segments. You should point out that the **accounting standards** incorporated in generally accepted accounting principles are the same for nonpublic enterprises as for publicly owned enterprises, whereas **disclosure standards** for such items as earnings per share differ between the two types of enterprises. You might offer to reexamine the identifiable assets of Salker Company, including any not recognized in Salker's balance sheet, for amortizable identifiable intangible assets such as customer lists, trade names, secret formulas, and noncompete agreements by Salker's former stockholders, which might be assigned part of the total cost of Posten Corporation's investment in Salker's common stock (if not already done), with an accompanying reduction in goodwill to be recognized in the business combination.

CHAPTER 7
CONSOLIDATED FINANCIAL STATEMENTS: SUBSEQUENT TO DATE OF BUSINESS COMBINATION

HIGHLIGHTS OF THE CHAPTER

1. A parent company may select either the **equity method** or the **cost method** of accounting for the operating results of consolidated subsidiaries.

2. In the **equity method** of accounting for a subsidiary's operating results, the parent company enters in its accounting records its share of the subsidiary's net income or net loss, as well as its share of dividends declared by the subsidiary.

3. Proponents of the equity method of accounting claim that the method is consistent with the accrual basis of accounting, and that it stresses the **economic substance** of the parent company–subsidiary relationship.

4. In the **cost method** of accounting for a subsidiary's operating results, the parent company accounts for the subsidiary's operations only to the extent that dividends are declared to the parent by the subsidiary.

5. Supporters of the cost method of accounting claim that the method appropriately recognizes the **legal form** of the parent company–subsidiary relationship.

6. A parent company that uses the equity method of accounting for a subsidiary's operations prepares the following journal entries (explanations omitted) to account for its share of a subsidiary's dividend declarations and net income, respectively (disregarding income tax effects).

Intercompany Dividends Receivable	XXX	
Investment in Subsidiary Common Stock		XXX
Investment in Subsidiary Common Stock	XXX	
Intercompany Investment Income		XXX

7. In addition to the equity method journal entries for a subsidiary described in paragraph **6,** a parent company that accounts for a subsidiary by the equity method must prepare a journal entry to record its share of the depreciation and amortization of differences between current fair values and carrying amounts of the subsidiary's net assets on the date of the business combination.

8. To illustrate the accounting described in paragraph **7,** assume that on March 1, 2005, Prague Corporation paid $1,600,000 for 80% of the outstanding common stock of Slovak Company. On that date, the current fair values of Slovak's identifiable net assets totaled $1,900,000—the same as their carrying amounts. Thus, goodwill of $80,000 was recognized in the Prague-Slovak business combination [$1,600,000 − ($1,900,000 x 0.80) = $80,000]. In addition to journal entries recording its share of Slovak's net income or loss, Prague would prepare the following journal entry on February 28, 2006, the end of the fiscal year (assuming that goodwill was partially impaired on that date).

Loss on Impairment of Goodwill	2,000	
Investment in Slovak Company		
Common Stock		2,000

To recognize 2½% impairment loss on goodwill
attributable to Slovak Company for year ended February
28, 2006, as follows (disregarding income taxes):

Goodwill, Mar. 1, 2005	$80,000
Impairment loss for year ended	
Feb. 28, 2006: ($80,000 x 0.025)	$ 2,000

9. If a parent company accounts for a subsidiary's operations by the equity method of accounting, the parent company's closing entries include a credit to the Retained Earnings of Subsidiary ledger account for the parent's share of the subsidiary's adjusted net income not distributed as dividends during the accounting period. For example, if the adjusted net income of a 95%-owned subsidiary for a fiscal year was $100,000 and the subsidiary declared dividends in the amount of $40,000, the parent company's closing entries at the end of the fiscal year would include a credit of $57,000 to the Retained Earnings of Subsidiary ledger account [($100,000 – $40,000) x 0.95 = $57,000].

10. In the **cost method** of accounting for a subsidiary's operating results, the parent company prepares no journal entries to record its share of the subsidiary's net income or losses. Dividends declared by a subsidiary from net income subsequent to the business combination are recorded by the parent company under the cost method of accounting with a debit to Intercompany Dividends Receivable and a credit to Intercompany Dividend Revenue in the amount of the parent company's share of the subsidiary's dividends.

11. Use of the cost method of accounting for a subsidiary's operating results requires more working paper eliminations than the equity method. However, **the consolidated amounts are identical, regardless of whether the equity method or the cost method of accounting is used to account for a subsidiary's operating results.**

12. The equity method of accounting for a subsidiary's operations is preferable to the cost method for a number of reasons, chief of which is the equity method's emphasis on **economic substance**, rather than **legal form**, of the parent company-subsidiary relationship.

QUESTIONS

True or False

For each of the following statements, circle the **T** or the **F** to indicate whether the statement is true or false.

T   F   1. Supporters of the cost method of accounting for a subsidiary's operations claim it is consistent with the accrual basis of accounting.

T   F   2. Dividends receivable by the parent company from a subsidiary accounted for by the equity method are credited to the Intercompany Investment Income ledger account in the parent company's accounting records.

T   F   3. Consolidated financial statement amounts will be the same regardless of whether a parent company uses the equity method or the cost method of accounting to record the results of a subsidiary's operations.

T F 4. If the parent company uses the equity method of accounting for a wholly owned subsidiary's operations, consolidated retained earnings in the consolidated balance sheet is the same amount as the balance of the parent company's Retained Earnings ledger account.

T F 5. In effect, the consolidation process reclassifies the parent company's equity method Intercompany Investment Income ledger account balance to the revenue and expense components of that account's balance.

T F 6. If a parent company uses the equity method of accounting for a subsidiary's operations, the parent company closes its share of the subsidiary's net income not distributed as dividends to the Retained Earnings of Subsidiary ledger account.

T F 7. The only time a parent company prepares an equity method journal entry debiting Intercompany Investment Income and crediting Investment in Subsidiary Common Stock is when the subsidiary's operations result in a net loss.

T F 8. Journal entries to reflect depreciation and amortization of the differences between current fair values and carrying amounts of a subsidiary's identifiable net assets on the date of the business combination are entered in the accounting records of the subsidiary.

T F 9. If a parent company uses the cost method of accounting for a subsidiary's operations, the parent company's Intercompany Dividend Revenue ledger account is placed on the same line as the reciprocal subsidiary ledger account in the working paper for consolidated financial statements.

T F 10. The cost method of accounting for a subsidiary's operations emphasizes the legal form of the parent company–subsidiary relationship.

Completion Statements

Fill in the necessary words or amounts to complete the following statements.

1. In the _____ method of accounting for a subsidiary's operations, the parent company accounts for dividends from the subsidiary as _____ _____.

2. Journal entries for the depreciation and amortization of the differences between current fair values and carrying amounts of a subsidiary's net assets on the date of a business combination are recorded in the _____ _____ accounting records.

3. In the working paper for consolidated financial statements for a subsidiary accounted for by the cost method of accounting, the working paper elimination for the parent company's investment and the subsidiary's equity ledger accounts includes the balances on the date of the _____ _____.

4. Except when intercompany profits (gains) or losses exist in assets to be consolidated, the parent company's net income and combined retained earnings ledger accounts balances are identical to the related consolidated amount under the _____ method of accounting for a subsidiary's operations.

Multiple Choice

Choose the best answer for each of the following questions and enter the identifying letter in the space provided.

_____ 1.   For the fiscal year ended December 31, 2005, Pike Corporation's 85%-owned subsidiary, Shasta Company, declared dividends totaling $20,000 and had a net income of $50,000. Year 2005 depreciation and amortization of the date-of-business-combination differences between the current fair values and carrying amounts of Shasta's identifiable net assets totaled $15,000. The net amount of 2005 intercompany revenue recorded by Pike for its ownership interest in Shasta under the cost method of accounting is:
a. $20,000
b. $29,750
c. $42,500
d.   Some other amount

_____ 2.   Which of the following journal entry formats is appropriate under the equity method of accounting to record the parent company's share of a subsidiary's dividend declaration?

a. Intercompany Dividends Receivable	XXX	
Investment in Subsidiary Common Stock		XXX
b. Cash	XXX	
Intercompany Dividend Revenue		XXX
c. Intercompany Dividends Receivable	XXX	
Intercompany Dividend Revenue		XXX
d. Investment in Subsidiary Common Stock	XXX	
Intercompany Dividend Revenue		XXX

_____ 3.   In the equity method of accounting for a subsidiary's operations, the parent company's share of the subsidiary's adjusted net income not distributed as dividends is credited in a closing entry to the following ledger account:
a.   Intercompany Investment Income
b.   Retained Earnings of Subsidiary
c.   Retained Earnings
d.   Investment in Subsidiary Common Stock

_____ 4.   Which of the following is a characteristic of the cost method of accounting for a subsidiary's operations?
a.   Parent company net income equals consolidated net income.
b.   More working paper eliminations are required than for the equity method of accounting.
c.   Consolidated amounts differ from the comparable amounts under the equity method of accounting.
d.   None of the foregoing

_____ 5.   Which of the following is an advantage of the equity method as compared with the cost method of accounting for a subsidiary's operations?
a.   The equity method produces more realistic consolidated amounts than the cost method does.
b.   A Retained Earnings of Subsidiary ledger account is not required for the equity method.
c.   The equity method facilitates issuance of unconsolidated financial statements for the parent company, if required by the SEC or for another purpose.
d.   None of the foregoing

6.   How is the portion of consolidated earnings to be assigned to minority interest in net income of subsidiary computed?
a.   The net income of the parent company is subtracted from the subsidiary's net income to compute the minority interest.
b.   The subsidiary's entire net income is allocated to the minority interest.
c.   The amount of the subsidiary's net income recognized for consolidation purposes is multiplied by the minority's percentage ownership.
d.   The amount of consolidated net income determined in the working paper for consolidated financial statements is multiplied by the minority interest percentage on the balance sheet date.

7.   In the equity method of accounting for an investment in a subsidiary, dividends from the subsidiary are accounted for by the parent company as:
a.   Revenue, unless declared from retained earnings of the subsidiary earned prior to the business combination
b.   Revenue, if the dividends were declared from retained earnings
c.   A reduction in the carrying amount of the Investment in Subsidiary Common Stock ledger account
d.   A deferred credit

8.   Powell Corporation owns 80% of the outstanding common stock of Sylvester Company, for which it uses the equity method of accounting. Compare the consolidated net income of Powell and Sylvester (X) with Powell's net income (Y) if it consolidated Sylvester.
a. $X > Y$
b. $X = Y$
c. $X < Y$
d.   The comparison cannot be determined.

9.   A parent company that uses the equity method of accounting for its investment in a 70%-owned subsidiary that had a net income of $20,000 and declared $5,000 in dividends prepared only the following journal entries (explanations omitted):

Investment in Subsidiary Common Stock	14,000	
Intercompany Investment Income		14,000
Intercompany Dividends Receivable	3,500	
Intercompany Dividend Revenue		3,500
Cash	3,500	
Intercompany Dividend Receivable		3,500

What effect do these journal entries have on the parent company's unconsolidated balance sheet?
a.   The balance sheet is fairly stated.
b.   The Investment in Subsidiary Common Stock ledger account is overstated and the Retained Earnings ledger account is understated.
c.   The Investment in Subsidiary Common Stock ledger account is understated and the Retained Earnings ledger account is understated.
d.   The Investment in Subsidiary Common Stock ledger account is overstated and the Retained Earnings ledger account is overstated.

_____ 10. Squire Company, the 90%-owned subsidiary of Paladin Corporation, had a net income of $60,000 and declared and paid dividends of $20,000 for the fiscal year ended March 31, 2006. Depreciation and amortization of differences between current fair values and carrying amounts of Squire's identifiable net assets for the year ended March 31, 2006, totaled $10,000. The amount of the working paper elimination of Paladin Corporation and subsidiary for minority interest in net income of subsidiary for the year ended March 31, 2006, is:

    a. $2,000
    b. $4,000
    c. $5,000
    d. $6,000
    e. Some other amount

SHORT EXERCISES

1.   Indicate by placing a check mark in the appropriate column whether each of the items in the table below applies to, or is a characteristic of, the equity method, the cost method, or both methods of accounting for a subsidiary's operations.

Item	Applicable to	
	Equity method	Cost method
a. Use of Retained Earnings of Subsidiary ledger account		
b. Use of Intercompany Dividend Revenue ledger account		
c. Appropriate for any subsidiary		
d. Parent company journal entry for depreciation and amortization of date-of-business-combination differences between current fair values and carrying amounts of subsidiary's net assets		
e. Use of Intercompany Dividends Receivable ledger account		
f. Parent company retained earnings balance not equal to consolidated retained earnings (and there are no intercompany profits or losses on the balance sheet date)		
g. Necessitates more working paper eliminations		
h. Emphasizes economic substance of parent company–subsidiary relationship		

2.   On July 1, 2005, Pioneer Corporation acquired all the outstanding common stock of Sagamore Company for a total cost of $550,000, including direct out-of-pocket costs of the business combination. The $150,000 difference between the total cost and the carrying amounts of Sagamore's identifiable net assets was allocable as follows:

Inventories (all sold during fiscal year ended June 30, 2006)	$ 40,000
Building (10-year remaining economic life)	60,000
Goodwill	50,000
Total difference	$150,000

Sagamore declared a $35,000 dividend on June 28, 2006, payable July 8, 2006, and had a net income of $60,000 for the fiscal year ended June 30, 2006. The goodwill was unimpaired as of June 30, 2006.

a. In the space below, prepare journal entries for Pioneer Corporation to record Sagamore Company's operations for the year ended June 30, 2006, under the equity method of accounting.

b. In the space below, prepare a journal entry for Pioneer Corporation to record Sagamore Company's operations for the year ended June 30, 2006, under the cost method of accounting.

Pioneer Corporation
Journal Entries

a.	2006			
	June 28			
	30			
	30			
b.	2006			
	June 28			

3.   The Investment in Sagehen Company Common Stock and Intercompany Investment Income ledger accounts of Pheasant Corporation for its 80%-owned subsidiary, Sagehen Company, for the fiscal year ended August 31, 2006, were as follows:

Investment in Sagehen Company Common Stock

Date	Explanation	Debit	Credit	Balance
2005				
Aug. 31	Balance forward			847,965 dr
2006				
Aug. 15	Dividend declared by subsidiary ($50,000 x 0.80)		40,000	807,965 dr
31	Net income of subsidiary ($120,000 x 0.80)	96,000		903,965 dr
31	Depreciation and amortization of differences between current fair values and carrying amounts of subsidiary's identifiable net assets ($30,000 x 0.80)		24,000	879,965 dr

Intercompany Investment Income

Date	Explanation	Debit	Credit	Balance
2006				
Aug. 31	Net income of subsidiary ($120,000 x 0.80)		96,000	96,000 cr
31	Depreciation and amortization of differences between current fair values and carrying amounts of subsidiary's identifiable net assets ($30,000 x 0.80)	24,000		72,000 cr

For the fiscal year ended August 31, 2006, Pheasant Corporation had net sales of $10,000,000 and total costs and expenses of $8,500,000. Pheasant did not declare or pay dividends for the year ended August 31, 2006.

In the space below, prepare an aggregate closing entry on August 31, 2006, for Pheasant Corporation.

Pheasant Corporation
Closing Entry

2006			
Aug. 31			

Modern Advanced Accounting, 10/e

4. The working paper elimination for Pegasus Corporation and subsidiary on May 31, 2005, the date of the business combination, was as follows (in journal entry format, explanation omitted):

Pegasus Corporation and Subsidiary
Working Paper Elimination
May 31, 2005

(a) Common Stock—Steele	20,000	
Additional Paid-in Capital—Steele	60,000	
Retained Earnings—Steele	70,000	
Inventories—Steele	30,000	
Plant Assets (net)—Steele	120,000	
Goodwill—Pegasus [$290,000 – ($300,000 x 0.70)]	80,000	
Investment in Steele Company Common Stock—Pegasus		290,000
Minority Interest in Net Assets of Subsidiary ($300,000 x 0.30)		90,000

Steele accounts for inventories by the first-in, first-out method. On May 31, 2005, the composite economic life of Steele's plant assets was 10 years. Pegasus's goodwill was unimpaired at May 31, 2006. Steele includes depreciation expense in cost of goods sold.

For the fiscal year ended May 31, 2006, Steele had a net income of $60,000. On May 31, 2006, Steele declared dividends of $8,000, payable in June, 2006.

a. In the space below, prepare journal entries for Pegasus Corporation to record the operations of Steele Company for the year ended May 31, 2006, under the equity method of accounting. Omit explanations and disregard income taxes.

Pegasus Corporation
Journal Entries

2006			
May 31			

b. In the space on page 84, prepare working paper eliminations (in journal entry format) on May 31, 2006, for Pegasus Corporation and subsidiary. Omit explanations and disregard income taxes.

Pegasus Corporation and Subsidiary
Working Paper Eliminations
May 31, 2006

	(a)		
	(b)		

CASE

You are audit manager of Strong & Company, CPAs, a San Antonio firm. Karen Black, the controller of client PreSolve Corporation, asks you for advice on converting retroactively, to the equity method from the cost method, the accounting for PreSolve's investment in Selvidge Company, a 75%-owned subsidiary acquired four years ago. Black's action is in response to a recent SEC ruling that requires PreSolve to file unconsolidated, as well as consolidated, financial statements in its **Form 10-K** Annual Report to the SEC.

Explain to Karen Black what data must be gathered, and the components of a single journal entry required, to convert retroactively PreSolve Corporation's accounting for its investment in Selvidge Company to the equity method from the cost method.

SOLUTIONS TO QUESTIONS, SHORT EXERCISES, AND CASE: CHAPTER 7

QUESTIONS

True or False

1. F 2. F 3. T 4. F 5. T 6. T 7. F 8. F 9. F 10. T

Completion Statements

1. Cost, intercompany revenue. 2. Parent company's. 3. Business combination. 4. Equity.

Multiple Choice

1. d ($20,000 x 0.85 = $17,000) 2. a 3. b 4. b 5. c 6. c 7. c 8. d (There is no mention of intercompany profits or losses.) 9. d 10. c [($60,000 – $10,000) x 0.10 = $5,000]

SHORT EXERCISES

1.

Item	Applicable to	
	Equity method	Cost method
a. Use of Retained Earnings of Subsidiary ledger account	√	
b. Use of Intercompany Dividend Revenue ledger account		√
c. Appropriate for any subsidiary	√	√
d. Parent company journal entry for depreciation and amortization of date-of-business-combination differences between current fair values and carrying amounts of subsidiary's net assets	√	
e. Use of Intercompany Dividends Receivable ledger account	√	√
f. Parent company retained earnings balance not equal to consolidated retained earnings (and there are no intercompany profits or losses on the balance sheet date)		√
g. Necessitates more working paper eliminations		√
h. Emphasizes economic substance of parent company–subsidiary relationship	√	

2.

Pioneer Corporation
Journal Entries

<table>
<tr><td>a.</td><td>2006</td><td></td><td></td><td></td></tr>
<tr><td></td><td>June 28</td><td>Intercompany Dividends Receivable</td><td>35,000</td><td></td></tr>
<tr><td></td><td></td><td>Investment in Sagamore Company Common Stock</td><td></td><td>35,000</td></tr>
<tr><td></td><td></td><td>To record dividend declared by Sagamore Company, payable July 8, 2006.</td><td></td><td></td></tr>
<tr><td></td><td>30</td><td>Investment in Sagamore Company Common Stock</td><td>60,000</td><td></td></tr>
<tr><td></td><td></td><td>Intercompany Investment Income</td><td></td><td>60,000</td></tr>
<tr><td></td><td></td><td>To record 100% of net income of Sagamore Company for the year ended June 30, 2006.</td><td></td><td></td></tr>
<tr><td></td><td>30</td><td>Intercompany Investment Income</td><td>46,000</td><td></td></tr>
<tr><td></td><td></td><td>Investment in Sagamore Company Common Stock</td><td></td><td>46,000</td></tr>
<tr><td></td><td></td><td>To amortize differences between Sagamore Company's assets current fair values and carrying amounts on July 1, 2005:</td><td></td><td></td></tr>
<tr><td></td><td></td><td>Inventories—to cost of goods sold $40,000
Building—depreciation ($60,000 ÷ 10)   6,000
Total difference applicable to Year 2006 $46,000</td><td></td><td></td></tr>
<tr><td>b.</td><td>June 28</td><td>Intercompany Dividends Receivable</td><td>35,000</td><td></td></tr>
<tr><td></td><td></td><td>Intercompany Dividend Revenue</td><td></td><td>35,000</td></tr>
<tr><td></td><td></td><td>To record dividend declared by Sagamore Company, payable July 8, 2006.</td><td></td><td></td></tr>
</table>

3.

Pheasant Corporation
Closing Entry

<table>
<tr><td>2006</td><td></td><td></td><td></td></tr>
<tr><td>Aug. 31</td><td>Net Sales</td><td>10,000,000</td><td></td></tr>
<tr><td></td><td>Intercompany Investment Income</td><td>72,000</td><td></td></tr>
<tr><td></td><td>Costs and Expenses</td><td></td><td>8,500,000</td></tr>
<tr><td></td><td>Retained Earnings of Subsidiary ($96,000 − $24,000 − $40,000)</td><td></td><td>32,000</td></tr>
<tr><td></td><td>Retained Earnings</td><td></td><td>1,540,000</td></tr>
<tr><td></td><td colspan="3">To close revenue and expense ledger accounts; to transfer net income legally available for dividends to retained earnings; and to segregate 80% share of adjusted net income of subsidiary not distributed as dividend by subsidiary.</td></tr>
</table>

Pegasus Corporation
Journal Entries

2006			
May 31	Investment in Steele Company Common Stock ($60,000 x 0.70)	42,000	
	Intercompany Investment Income		42,000
31	Intercompany Dividends Receivable ($8,000 x 0.70)	5,600	
	Investment in Steele Company Common Stock		5,600
31	Intercompany Investment Income [($30,000 + $12,000) x 0.70]	29,400	
	Investment in Steele Company Common Stock		29,400

b.

Pegasus Corporation and Subsidiary
Working Paper Eliminations
May 31, 2006

	(a) Common Stock—Steele	20,000	
	Additional Paid-in Capital—Steele	60,000	
	Retained Earnings—Steele	70,000	
	Plant Assets (net) —Steele ($120,000 – $12,000)	108,000	
	Goodwill—Pegasus	80,000	
	Cost of Goods Sold—Steele ($30,000 + $12,000)	42,000	
	Intercompany Investment Income—Pegasus ($42,000 – $29,400)	12,600	
	Investment in Steele Company Common Stock—Pegasus ($290,000 + $42,000 – $5,600 – $29,400)		297,000
	Dividends declared—Steele		8,000
	Minority Interest in Net Assets of Subsidiary [$90,000 – ($8,000 x 0.30)]		87,600
	(b) Minority Interest in Net Income of Subsidiary [($60,000 – $42,000) x 0.30]	5,400	
	Minority Interest in Net Assets of Subsidiary		5,400

CASE

To convert PreSolve Corporation's investment in Selvidge Company retroactively to the equity method from the cost method of accounting, Karen Black must accumulate the following data:

(1) 75% of Selvidge's aggregate net income, less net loss, for the first three years since the business combination.

(2) 75% of the depreciation and amortization of differences between the current fair values and carrying amounts of Selvidge's identifiable net assets (on the business combination date) for the first three years since the combination. (This may be accumulated to some extent from the working paper eliminations under the cost method for the first three years' consolidated financial statements.)

(3)   Impairment, if any, of goodwill that was recognized in the business combination, for the first three years since the combination. (This, too, may be accumulated to some extent from prior-year cost-method working paper eliminations.)

(4)   Dividend revenue recognized by PreSolve under the cost method of accounting for the first three years since the business combination.

Having gathered these data, Black may prepare a single journal entry to convert the accounting for PreSolve's investment in Selvidge to the equity method **as of the beginning of the fourth year,** as follows:

Debit Investment in Selvidge Company Common Stock for the net of (1) – (2) – (3) – (4)

Debit Retained Earnings for the amount of (3)

Credit Retained Earnings of Subsidiary for the net of (1) – (2) – (4)

This journal entry may then be accompanied by the conventional equity method journal entries for Selvidge's operations for the fourth year, except that, assuming Selvidge's dividends declared and paid to PreSolve during that year had been credited to Intercompany Dividend Revenue, that account would be debited and Investment in Selvidge Company Common Stock would be credited for the amount of the dividends.

HIGHLIGHTS OF THE CHAPTER

1. A parent company and its subsidiaries may enter into a number of business transactions with each other subsequent to the date of the business combination. Both the parent company and the subsidiary should account for these related party intercompany transactions in a manner that facilitates the consolidation process.

2. Among the transactions (other than dividends) between a parent company and its subsidiaries are loans on promissory notes or open account, operating leases of property, and rendering of services. None of these transactions involves an element of intercompany profit or loss, because the balances of the ledger accounts used to record these intercompany transactions are offset in the preparation of consolidated financial statements.

3. A parent company often carries out all of an affiliated group's borrowings from financial institutions. The parent company then makes loans to its subsidiaries for their working capital or other needs at an interest rate exceeding the parent's borrowing rate. These loans and related interest revenue or expense and interest receivable or payable should be recorded in **intercompany** ledger accounts by each of the affiliated companies.

4. If the parent company **discounts** at a bank a promissory note receivable from a subsidiary, the subsidiary transfers the note payable and related accrued interest from the **intercompany** ledger accounts to accounts for liabilities payable to **outsiders.**

5. Intercompany rent revenue and expense and intercompany management fee revenue and expense also are accounted for in clearly designated **intercompany** ledger accounts in the accounting records of both the parent company and the subsidiary. Accounts for intercompany assets and liabilities and revenue and expenses from loans, rent, and management fees are placed on the same line in the working paper for consolidated financial statements so that they are eliminated without a working paper elimination.

6. To illustrate the technique described in paragraph **5,** assume that management fees for services rendered by Plato Corporation to Socrates Company during the fiscal year ended July 31, 2006, totaled $146,800, of which $15,200 remained unpaid on July 31, 2006. These amounts would be presented as shown below in the working paper for consolidated financial statements of Plato Corporation and subsidiary for the year ended July 31, 2006.

	Plato Corporation	Socrates Company	Eliminations increase (decrease)	Consolidated
Income Statement				
Revenue:				
Intercompany revenue (expenses)	$146,800	$(146,800)		
Balance Sheet				
Assets:				
Intercompany receivables (payables)	$ 15,200	$ (15,200)		

7. Because there is no element of intercompany profit or loss in the interest, rent, or management fee transactions, there are no income tax effects associated with the elimination of the intercompany revenue and expenses.

8.   Transactions between a parent company and its subsidiaries that may involve an element of profit (gain) or loss include intercompany sales of merchandise, plant assets, or intangible assets, and intercompany leases of property under sales-type/capital leases. Such intercompany profits and losses are **unrealized** until the related assets or their products are sold to outsiders. In addition, a **realized intercompany gain or loss** may result from a parent or subsidiary company's acquisition of its affiliate's bonds **in the open market.**

9.   Elimination of **unrealized** intercompany profits (gains) or losses, and inclusion of **realized** gains and losses, for consolidated financial statements are essential to prevent a parent company's management from manipulating consolidated net income.

10.   Intercompany sales of merchandise may be made at a price equal to the selling affiliate's cost. If so, the selling affiliate offsets intercompany cost of goods sold against intercompany sales in its separate income statement; no working paper elimination is required for consolidated financial statements. Any resultant intercompany receivables and payables are offset in the usual fashion in the working paper for consolidated financial statements.

11.   Intercompany sales of merchandise typically are made at a gross profit, which may be equal to, larger than, or less than the gross profit margin on sales to outsiders. The intercompany profit is **realized** through the purchasing affiliate's sales of the merchandise to outsiders. Consequently, the **unrealized** intercompany profit in the purchasing affiliate's inventories on the date of a consolidated balance sheet must be eliminated through an appropriate working paper elimination.

12.   The intercompany profit in **beginning** inventories is considered to be realized on a first-in, first-out basis through the purchasing affiliate's sales of the merchandise to outsiders during the ensuing year. Because the selling affiliate in essence closed its Intercompany Sales and Intercompany Cost of Goods Sold ledger accounts of the prior accounting period to its Retained Earnings account, the selling affiliate's beginning retained earnings balance is overstated, from a consolidated viewpoint, by the amount of the unrealized intercompany profit in the purchasing affiliate's beginning inventories.

13.   To illustrate the issues of intercompany sales of merchandise set forth in paragraphs **11** and **12**, assume that Peters Corporation's sales of merchandise to its 80%-owned subsidiary, Styles Company, during the fiscal year ended December 31, 2006, were summarized as follows:

	Selling price	Cost	Gross profit (25%)
Beginning inventories	$ 60,000	$ 45,000	$ 15,000
Sales	360,000	270,000	90,000
Totals	$420,000	$315,000	$105,000
Less: Ending Inventories	80,000	60,000	20,000
Cost of goods sold	$340,000	$255,000	$ 85,000

The December 31, 2006, working paper elimination (in journal entry format) for Peters Corporation and subsidiary, disregarding income tax effects, is as follows:

Retained Earnings—Peters	15,000	
Intercompany Sales—Peters	360,000	
Intercompany Cost of Goods Sold—Peters		270,000
Cost of Goods Sold—Styles		85,000
Inventories—Styles		20,000

To eliminate intercompany sales, cost of goods sold, and unrealized profit in inventories. (Income tax effects are disregarded.)

14. If intercompany sales are made by a partially owned subsidiary to its parent company or to another subsidiary, the resultant intercompany profits or losses must be taken into consideration in the computation of minority interest in the selling subsidiary's beginning retained earnings and its net income or net loss for the accounting period.

15. Intercompany sales of plant assets or intangible assets are rare transactions. The intercompany gain or loss on such sales is realized in transactions with outsiders after the passage of many accounting periods, in contrast to the typical realization of intercompany profit in inventories during the accounting period immediately following the period of the intercompany sales transactions.

16. If Stebbins Company, a 90%-owned subsidiary of Pippin Corporation, sold land with a cost of $100,000 to its parent company for $175,000, the $75,000 intercompany gain is accounted for as follows, in a working paper elimination (in journal entry format) at the end of the accounting period in which the intercompany sale took place:

Intercompany Gain on Sale of Land—Stebbins	75,000	
Land—Pippin		75,000

To eliminate unrealized intercompany gain on sale of land. (Income tax effects are disregarded.)

17. For accounting periods subsequent to the period of Stebbins Company's sale of land to Pippin Corporation, as long as Pippin continued to own the land, the working paper elimination (in journal entry format) is as follows (disregarding income tax effects):

Retained Earnings—Stebbins ($75,000 x 0.90)	67,500	
Minority Interest in Net Assets of Subsidiary ($75,000 x 0.10)	7,500	
Land—Pippin		75,000

To eliminate unrealized intercompany gain in land. (Income tax effects are disregarded.)

18. The eliminated intercompany gain illustrated in paragraphs **16** and **17** is taken into account in the computation of (a) the minority interest in Stebbins Company's net income in the year of sale and (b) the minority interest in Stebbin's beginning retained earnings for subsequent periods during which Pippin Corporation continued to own the land.

19. The working paper elimination, on the date of sale, for an intercompany gain on the sale of a **depreciable** plant asset or an intangible asset is identical to the comparable date-of-sale elimination for land as illustrated in paragraph **16**. For example, if on April 30, 2006, the end of a fiscal year, Pasteur Corporation sold to its partially owned subsidiary, Salk Company, for $50,000 a machine with a carrying amount of $40,000, the April 30, 2006, working paper elimination (in journal entry format) for Pasteur Corporation and subsidiary is as follows (disregarding income tax effects):

Intercompany Gain on Sale of Machinery—Pasteur	10,000	
Machinery—Salk		10,000

To eliminate unrealized intercompany gain on sale of machinery. (Income tax effects are disregarded.)

20. In subsequent years, the intercompany profit element in Salk Company's depreciation expense also must be eliminated for consolidated financial statements. If Salk assigned to the machine acquired from Pasteur Corporation an economic life of five years, the straight-line method of depreciation, and no residual value, the working paper elimination (in journal entry format) for Pasteur Corporation and subsidiary on April 30, 2007, is as follows (disregarding income tax effects):

Retained Earnings—Pasteur	10,000	
Accumulated Depreciation—Salk ($10,000 ÷ 5)	2,000	
Machinery—Salk		10,000
Depreciation Expense—Salk		2,000

To eliminate unrealized intercompany gain in machinery and related depreciation. (Income tax effects are disregarded.)

21. The $2,000 credit to Salk Company's depreciation expense in the working paper elimination in paragraph **20** represents a **realization** of a portion of Pasteur's intercompany gain on the sale of the machinery. Thus, the $2,000 is treated as an increase in Pasteur Corporation's net income, and it does not enter into the computation of the minority interest in net income of Salk.

22. At the end of each of the four remaining years of the economic life of Salk Company's machine, the **credit** amounts of the working paper elimination for intercompany gain are the same as the amounts shown in paragraph **20.** However, the **unrealized** portion of the intercompany gain decreases in each succeeding year, as indicated by the following summary of the **debit** amounts of the working paper eliminations (in journal entry format) for April 30, 2008 and 2009:

	Year Ended April 30,	
	2008	2009
Retained Earnings—Pasteur	$8,000	$6,000
Accumulated Depreciation—Salk	4,000	6,000

23. An intercompany lease of property under a sales-type/capital lease requires working paper eliminations with features that resemble eliminations for both intercompany sales of merchandise and intercompany sales of plant assets. For example, if on June 30, 2005, the end of a fiscal year, Planck Corporation leased a machine carried in its inventories at $6,000 to its 80%-owned subsidiary, Sunder Company, on a three-year sales-type lease requiring Sunder to pay $3,000 to Planck on June 30, 2005, 2006, and 2007, the present value of the minimum lease payments at Planck's 10% interest rate implicit in the lease (known to Sunder and less than Sunder's incremental borrowing rate) is $8,207 ($3,000 x 2.735537 = $8,207). Assuming that Sunder uses straight-line depreciation, a five-year economic life, and no residual value for the machine, working paper eliminations (in journal entry format, explanations omitted, and income taxes disregarded) on June 30, 2005 and 2006, are as follows:

24. **June 30, 2005**

Intercompany Liability under Capital Lease—Sunder ($8,207 – $3,000)	5,207	
Unearned Intercompany Interest Revenue—Planck ($9,000 – $8,207)	793	
Intercompany Sales—Planck	8,207	
Intercompany Cost of Goods Sold—Planck		6,000
Intercompany Lease Receivables—Planck ($9,000 – $3,000)		6,000
Leased Equipment —Capital Lease—Sunder ($8,207 – $6,000)		2,207

25. **June 30, 2006**

Intercompany Liability under Capital Lease—Sunder ($5,207 – $2,479)	2,728	
Unearned Intercompany Interest Revenue—Planck ($793 – $521)	272	
Retained Earnings—Planck ($8,207 – $6,000)	2,207	
Intercompany Lease Receivables—Planck ($6,000 – $3,000)		3,000
Leased Equipment—Capital Lease—Sunder ($2,207 – $441)		1,766
Depreciation Expense —Sunder ($2,207 ÷ 5)		441

26. In the June 30, 2006, working paper for consolidated financial statements of Planck Corporation and subsidiary, Planck's intercompany interest revenue, $521 ($5,207 x 0.10 = $521) is offset against Sunder's intercompany interest expense of $521 on the same line of the income statement section.

27. Working paper eliminations for intercompany gains or losses on intercompany sales of intangible assets resemble the eliminations for depreciable plant assets illustrated in paragraphs **19** and **20**, except that there typically is no separate ledger account for accumulated amortization.

28. No intercompany gain or loss results from the **direct** acquisition of one affiliate's bonds by another affiliate because the cost of the investment to the acquirer **exactly offsets** the issuance proceeds of the debt. However, intercompany gains or losses may be **realized** when one affiliate acquires **in the open market** the outstanding bonds of another affiliate.

29. To illustrate the realized gain or loss when one affiliate acquires another affiliate's outstanding bonds in the open market, assume that on March 31, 2005, the end of a fiscal year, Peale Corporation acquired in the open market for $442,919 (a 15% yield), $500,000 face amount of the $750,000 total outstanding 10%, five-year bonds payable of Stole Company, Peale's wholly owned subsidiary. The bonds had been issued by Stole on March 31, 2003, for $695,928 (a 12% yield), with interest payable annually each March 31. On March 31, 2005, the balance of Stole's Discount on 10% Bonds Payable ledger account was $36,028.

30. Based on the facts in paragraph **29,** the appropriate working paper elimination (in journal entry format) for Peale Corporation and subsidiary on March 31, 2005, is as follows (disregarding income tax effects):

Intercompany 10% Bonds Payable—Stole	500,000	
Discount on Intercompany 10% Bonds Payable—Stole [$36,028 x ($500,000 ÷ $750,000)]		24,019
Investment in Stole Company Bonds—Peale		442,919
Gain on Extinguishment of Bonds—Stole [($500,000 – $24,019) – $442,919]		33,062

To eliminate subsidiary's bonds acquired by parent, and to recognize gain on the extinguishment of the bonds. (Income tax effects are disregarded).

31. In the working paper elimination illustrated in paragraph **30,** the gain resulting from the parent company's acquisition of the subsidiary's bonds is attributed to the subsidiary. The parent company is considered to have acted as agent for the subsidiary in the acquisition of the bonds.

32. In the three years subsequent to Peale Corporation's acquisition of Stole Company's bonds, the $33,062 **realized** gain on the acquisition will be **recorded** through the differences in the discount amortization (by the interest method) of the two affiliates. This is illustrated by the following working paper elimination (in journal entry format) for Peale Corporation and subsidiary on March 31, 2006:

Intercompany Interest Revenue—Peale ($442,919 x 0.15)	66,438	
Intercompany Bonds Payable—Stole	500,000	
Discount on Intercompany Bonds Payable—Stole [$24,019 – ($57,118 - $50,000)]		16,901
Investment in Stole Company Bonds—Peale [$442,919 + ($66,438 – $50,000)]		459,357
Intercompany Interest Expense—Stole [($500,000 – $24,019) x 0.12]		57,118
Retained Earnings—Stole		33,062

To eliminate subsidiary's bonds owned by parent, and related interest revenue and expense; and to increase subsidiary's **beginning** retained earnings by amount of unamortized gain on the extinguishment of the bonds. (Income tax effects are disregarded).

33.   The $9,320 difference between Peale's intercompany interest revenue ($66,438) and Stole Company's intercompany interest expense ($57,118) represents a portion of the $33,062 realized gain that was recorded during the fiscal year ended March 31, 2005. However, because the entire $33,062 gain was **recognized** in the consolidated income statement of Peale Corporation and subsidiary for the year ended March 31, 2005, the working paper elimination in paragraph **32** effectively eliminates the $9,320 difference.

34.   Working paper eliminations for intercompany profits (gains) and losses must be analyzed carefully for the computation of minority interest in net income of a partially owned subsidiary.

QUESTIONS

True or False

For each of the following statements, circle the **T** or the **F** to indicate whether the statement is true or false.

T   F   1.   A parent or subsidiary company's acquisition of its affiliate's outstanding bonds in the open market may result in a realized intercompany gain or loss.

T   F   2.   If intercompany sales of merchandise are made at cost, the working paper elimination is the same regardless of whether all of the merchandise was sold by the purchasing affiliate or some of the merchandise remained in the purchaser's inventories on the date of the consolidated financial statements.

T   F   3.   The consolidated inventories of a parent company and its subsidiaries are overstated by the cost of merchandise received from an affiliate that remains unsold in the purchasing affiliate's inventories on the date of the consolidated balance sheet.

T   F   4.   A subsidiary that purchases merchandise from its parent company debits Intercompany Inventories and credits Trade Accounts Payable under the perpetual inventory system.

T   F   5.   If a partially owned subsidiary sells merchandise to its parent company, any intercompany profit in the parent company's ending inventories must be taken into account in the computation of minority interest in the subsidiary's net income for the accounting period of the sale.

T F 6. The $10,000 intercompany profit in the beginning inventories of a 90%-owned subsidiary that purchased merchandise from its parent company is handled as follows in the end-of-period working paper elimination: Decrease Retained Earnings—Subsidiary by $9,000; decrease Minority Interest in Net Assets of Subsidiary by $1,000; and decrease Inventories—Subsidiary by $10,000.

T F 7. The intercompany gain in a parent company's sale of land to its subsidiary generally is realized for consolidated financial statement purposes in the accounting period following that in which the sale took place.

T F 8. From the point of view of the consolidated entity, the intercompany gain element of annual depreciation expense of a subsidiary represents a realization of a portion of the parent company's original intercompany gain on its sale of depreciable plant assets to the subsidiary.

T F 9. The gain on a parent company's open-market acquisition of its subsidiary's outstanding bonds is entered in the accounting records of the parent company.

T F 10. The gain on a subsidiary's open-market acquisition of its parent company's outstanding bonds is recognized in the consolidated income statement for the accounting period of the acquisition.

T F 11. Intercompany interest revenue and expense resulting from an intercompany sales-type/capital lease are eliminated by a working paper elimination.

T F 12. The typical difference between a working paper elimination for an intercompany sale of an intangible asset and a comparable elimination for an intercompany sale of a depreciable plant asset is the absence of an Accumulated Amortization ledger account for the intangible asset.

T F 13. Separate ledger accounts should be established by both the parent company and the subsidiary to account for intercompany transactions.

T F 14. In the preparation of a working paper for consolidated financial statements for a business combination, the intercompany revenue and expenses are placed on the same line so that they are eliminated without formal working paper eliminations.

T F 15. All intercompany notes receivable—including those discounted at a bank by the holder—are eliminated in the working paper for consolidated financial statements.

T F 16. If a parent company discounts a note receivable from a subsidiary at a bank, the subsidiary debits Intercompany Interest Expense and credits Intercompany Interest Payable for the interest accrued on the note to the date of discounting.

T F 17. There is no income tax effect accounted for when intercompany rent revenue and expense are eliminated in a working paper for consolidated financial statements.

T F 18. Accountants use working paper eliminations to reconcile differences between the balances of reciprocal intercompany ledger accounts.

©The McGraw-Hill Companies, Inc., 2006

Completion Statements

Fill in the necessary words or amounts to complete the following statements.

1. Intercompany sales of merchandise, plant assets, or intangible assets generally involve an element of _____ profit (gain) or loss. A parent or subsidiary company's acquisition of its affiliate's outstanding bonds in the open market may result in a _____ gain or loss.

2. Failure to eliminate intercompany profits (gains) and losses for consolidated financial statements would result in the statements' reflecting the results of _____ transactions within the consolidated group.

3. _____ intercompany sales are those from a parent company to subsidiaries. _____ intercompany sales are those from subsidiaries to the parent company. _____ intercompany sales are between subsidiaries of the same parent company.

4. The gross profit in intercompany sales of merchandise is realized through the _____ affiliate's sales of the merchandise to _____.

5. The intercompany profit in a subsidiary's beginning inventories resulting from the parent company's sales of merchandise to the subsidiary is considered in consolidation to be an overstatement of the _____ _____ ledger account of the _____ _____.

6. The FASB-recommended accounting for intercompany profit resulting from upstream or lateral intercompany sales is consistent with the _____ _____ concept of consolidated financial statements.

7. An intercompany gain on the sale of a depreciable plant asset is considered to be realized through the _____ of the asset.

8. The realized gain or loss resulting from a subsidiary's open-market acquisition of its parent company's outstanding bonds is attributed to the _____ _____.

9. Intercompany rent revenue and expense are recorded for the type of lease contract between parent company and subsidiary known as a (or an) _____ lease.

Multiple Choice

Choose the best answer for each of the following questions and enter the identifying letter in the space provided.

Questions **1** through **3** are based on the following information.

During the fiscal year ended May 31, 2006, Swope Company, the 80%-owned subsidiary of Pone Corporation, sold merchandise to its parent company at billed prices totaling $360,000, representing a 20% markup on Swope's cost. On May 31, 2006, Pone's inventories included merchandise totaling $54,000 purchased from Swope—a $12,000 increase over the comparable June 1, 2005, amount.

_____ 1. The **total** amount to be eliminated for consolidated costs of goods sold of Pone Corporation and subsidiary for the fiscal year ended May 31, 2006, is:
   a. $58,000
   b. $60,000
   c. $300,000
   d. Some other amount

_____ 2. In the working paper elimination (in journal entry format) for Pone Corporation and subsidiary on May 31, 2006, Minority Interest in Net Assets of Subsidiary is debited in the amount of:
   a. $0
   b. $1,400
   c. $7,000
   d. Some other amount

_____ 3. In the working paper elimination (in journal entry format) for Pone Corporation and subsidiary on May 31, 2006, Inventories—Pone is credited in the amount of:
   a. $7,000
   b. $9,000
   c. $54,000
   d. Some other amount

Questions **4** and **5** are based on the following information: On November 1, 2006, the beginning of a fiscal year, Parsifal Corporation sold to its 85%-owned subsidiary, Sazerac Company, for $75,000 a machine with a cost and a carrying amount to Parsifal of $100,000 and $60,000, respectively, on that date. Sazerac adopted the straight-line method of depreciation and established a six-year economic life and no residual value for the machine.

_____ 4. In the November 1, 2006, journal entry to record the acquisition of the machine, Sazerac Company credits Accumulated Depreciation of Machinery in the amount of:
   a. $0
   b. $30,000
   c. $40,000
   d. Some other amount

_____ 5. In the working paper elimination (in journal entry format) for Parsifal Corporation and subsidiary on October 31, 2007, the end of the fiscal year, Depreciation Expense—Sazerac is credited in the amount of:
   a. $0
   b. $2,500
   c. $12,500
   d. Some other amount

Questions **6** through **8** are based on the following information: On July 31, 2006, the end of a fiscal year, Senegal Company, the 99%-owned subsidiary of Portugal Corporation, acquired in the open market for $93,660 (a 10% yield) plus accrued interest, $100,000 face amount of Portugal's outstanding 8% bonds payable due August 1, 2010. Portugal had issued $500,000 face amount of the bonds on August 1, 2005, for $480,552 (a 9% yield). Interest on the bonds is payable annually each August 1.

©The McGraw-Hill Companies, Inc., 2006

_____ 6. In Senegal Company's July 31, 2006, journal entry to record the acquisition of the bonds, Cash is credited in the amount of:
   a. $93,660
   b. $100,000
   c. $101,660
   d. Some other amount

_____ 7. In the working paper elimination (in journal entry format) for Portugal Corporation and subsidiary on July 31, 2006, Discount on Intercompany Bonds Payable—Portugal is credited in the amount of:
   a. $3,240
   b. $3,892
   c. $16,198
   d. $19,462
   e. Some other amount

_____ 8. In the working paper elimination (in journal entry format) for Portugal Corporation and subsidiary on July 31, 2006, the gain on Senegal's acquisition of Portugal's bonds is credited to:
   a. Gain on Extinguishment of Bonds—Portugal
   b. Retained Earnings—Senegal
   c. Retained Earnings—Senegal and Minority Interest in Net Assets of Subsidiary
   d. Retained Earnings—Portugal

_____ 9. If a parent company discounts at a bank a note receivable from a subsidiary, the subsidiary prepares a journal entry that includes:
   a. A debit to Intercompany Interest Expense and a credit to Interest Payable
   b. A debit to Interest Expense and a credit to Intercompany Interest Payable
   c. A debit to Interest Expense and a credit to Interest Payable
   d. A debit to Intercompany Interest Expense and a credit to Intercompany Interest Payable

_____ 10. The elimination of intercompany interest revenue and expense on intercompany loans usually is accomplished by:
   a. A working paper elimination
   b. Placing the intercompany items in adjacent columns on the same line of the working paper for consolidated financial statements
   c. A journal entry in the accounting records of the parent company
   d. None of the foregoing methods

SHORT EXERCISES

1. In the spaces on page 99, prepare working paper eliminations (in journal entry format) for each of the following independent situations, on the date indicated in the working paper. Disregard income tax considerations.

   a. Price Corporation acquired 80% of the outstanding common stock of Stewart Company on April 1, 2006. During the fiscal year ended March 31, 2007, Price sold merchandise to Stewart for $50,000, at a gross profit of $9,500. One-half of the merchandise had been sold by Stewart Company as of March 31, 2007.

Price Corporation and Subsidiary
Working Paper Elimination
March 31, 2007

b. Included in the Machinery ledger account of Smith Company, 90%-owned subsidiary of Press Corporation, on September 30, 2007, the end of a fiscal year, was a machine with a cost of $20,000 and accumulated straight-line depreciation of $4,000. When Smith had acquired the machine from Press on October 1, 2005, the machine had a carrying amount to Press of $17,500 and no residual value to Smith.

Press Corporation and Subsidiary
Working Paper Elimination
September 30, 2007

c. On September 1, 2006, the beginning of a fiscal year, Staple Company, the 80%-owned subsidiary of Pindar Corporation, acquired in the open market for $97,321 (a 12% yield), $100,000 face amount of the outstanding 9%, five-year bonds of Pindar due August 31, 2007 (interest payable annually each August 31). Pindar had issued $500,000 face amount of the bonds at a yield of 10%. The carrying amount of the intercompany bonds in Pindar's accounting records on September 1, 2006, was $99,091.

Pindar Corporation and Subsidiary
Working Paper Elimination
September 1, 2006

2. Included among the December 31, 2006, end-of-fiscal-year working paper eliminations (in journal entry format) for Photon Corporation and its 90%-owned subsidiary, Stengel Company, was the following:

Intercompany Gain on Sale of Machinery—Stengel	15,000	
Machinery—Photon		15,000

To eliminate unrealized intercompany gain on sale of machinery this date, disregarding income taxes. Machinery is to be depreciated by straight-line method over economic life of four years, with no residual value.

In the spaces below, prepare working paper eliminations (in journal entry format) for Photon Corporation and subsidiary on December 31, 2007, and December 31, 2008. Disregard income taxes.

Photon Corporation and Subsidiary
Working Paper Elimination
December 31, 2007

Photon Corporation and Subsidiary
Working Paper Elimination
December 31, 2008

3. On April 30, 2006, Sommer Company, the 75%-owned subsidiary of Padgett Corporation, issued $1,000,000 face amount of 7%, four-year bonds due April 30, 2010, for $966,879, an 8% yield. Interest on the bonds is payable annually each April 30. On May 1, 2007, Padgett acquired in the open market $400,000 face amount of Sommer's outstanding 7% bonds for $379,749, a 9% yield. Both companies have an April 30 fiscal year.

   a. In the spaces on page 101 prepare journal entries for both Padgett Corporation and Sommer Company to record all transactions and events relating to the bonds through April 30, 2008, except for transfer of bonds to an intercompany ledger account. Both enterprises use the interest method of accumulation or amortization of bond discount or premium.

Padgett Corporation
Journal Entries

May 1, 2007			
Apr. 30, 2008			

Sommer Company
Journal Entries

Apr. 30, 2006			
Apr. 30, 2007			
Apr. 30, 2008			

b. In the space below, prepare a working paper elimination (in journal entry format) for Padgett Corporation and subsidiary on April 30, 2008, the end of the fiscal year. Disregard income taxes.

Padgett Corporation and Subsidiary
Working Paper Elimination
April 30, 2008

4. The journal entries of Presser Corporation and Stasser Company, its wholly owned subsidiary, on December 31, 2006, a fiscal year end, to record a sales-type/capital lease with an implicit interest rate of 10%, were as follows:

Presser Corporation

Intercompany Lease Receivables ($2,000 x 5)	10,000	
Intercompany Cost of Goods Sold	7,000	
Intercompany Sales		8,340
Unearned Intercompany Interest Revenue ($10,000 – $8,340)		1,660
Inventories		7,000

To record sales-type lease with Stasser Company at inception and cost of leased equipment.

Cash	2,000	
Intercompany Lease Receivables		2,000

To record receipt of first payment on intercompany lease.

Stasser Company

Leased Equipment—Capital Lease	8,340	
Intercompany Liability under Capital Lease (net)		8,340

To record intercompany capital lease at inception.

Intercompany Liability under Capital Lease (net)	2,000	
Cash		2,000

To record lease payment for first year of intercompany lease.

In the spaces below, prepare working paper eliminations (in journal entry format) for Presser Corporation and subsidiary on December 31, 2006, and December 31, 2007, assuming that Stasser used straight-line depreciation, a 10-year economic life, and no residual value for the leased equipment. Omit explanations and disregard income taxes.

Presser Corporation and Subsidiary
Working Paper Elimination
December 31, 2006

Presser Corporation and Subsidiary
Working Paper Elimination
December 31, 2007

5. On June 30, 2006, Pontiac Corporation loaned $50,000 to a subsidiary, Southwest Company, on a 90-day, 9% promissory note. On July 15, 2006, Pontiac discounted the Southwest note at Eastern Bank at a 12% discount rate.

In the space below, prepare journal entries for Pontiac Corporation to record the receipt and the discounting of the Southwest note. Round computations to the nearest dollar.

Pontiac Corporation
Journal Entries

2006			
June 30			
July 15			

Case

You are the controller of Plumm Corporation, the publicly owned parent company of 85%-owned Swann Company and 92%-owned Sully Company. In your consultation with Lawrence Stoke, recently hired as chief accountant after three years of public accounting experience, you learn that Stoke is well versed in all aspects of working paper eliminations for consolidated financial statements except for the computation of minority interest in net income of subsidiaries. Stokes asks you to provide written instructions on that computation for him, covering especially the realized and unrealized intercompany profits (gains) or losses on the following:

- Swann's and Sully's sales of merchandise to Plumm this year
- Plumm's sale to Sully two years ago at a gain of a machine with an economic life of five years on the sale date
- Plumm's open-market acquisition this year of outstanding bonds of Swann at a substantial discount
- Plumm's sale this year of a patent to Sully

Provide Lawrence Stoke with the written instructions that he requested.

SOLUTIONS TO QUESTIONS, SHORT EXERCISES, AND CASE: CHAPTER 8

QUESTIONS

True or False

1. T 2. T 3. F 4. F 5. T 6. F 7. F 8. T 9. F 10. T 11. F 12. T 13. T 14. T 15. F 16. F 17. T 18. F

Completion Statements

1. Unrealized, realized. 2. Related-party. 3. Downstream, Upstream, Lateral. 4. Purchasing, outsiders.
5. Retained Earnings, parent company. 6. Economic unit. 7. Depreciation. 8. Parent company.
9. Operating.

Multiple Choice

1. d [($360,000 x 5/6) + ($348,000 x 1/6) = $358,000] 2. b [($42,000 x 1/6) x 0.20 = $1,.400] 3. b
($54,000 x 1/6 = $9,000) 4. a 5. b ($15,000 ÷ 6 = $2,500) 6. c ($93,660 + $8,000 = $101,660) 7. a
{[($500,000 – $480,552) – ($43,250 – $40,000)] x 0.20 = $3,240} 8. a 9. a 10.b

SHORT EXERCISES

1. a.

Price Corporation and Subsidiary
Working Paper Elimination
March 31, 2007

	Intercompany Sales—Price	50,000	
	Intercompany Cost of Goods Sold—Price ($50,000 – $9,500)		40,500
	Cost of Goods Sold—Stewart ($9,500 x 1/2)		4,750
	Inventories—Stewart ($9,500 x 1/2)		4,750
	To eliminate intercompany sales, costs of goods sold, and unrealized profit in inventories. (Income tax effects are disregarded.)		

b.

Press Corporation and Subsidiary
Working Paper Elimination
September 30, 2007

	Retained Earnings—Press ($2,500 – $250)	2,250	
	Accumulated Depreciation—Smith [($2,500 ÷ 10) x 2]	500	
	Machinery—Smith ($20,000 – $17,500)		2,500
	Depreciation Expense—Smith ($2,500 ÷ 10)		250
	To eliminate unrealized intercompany gain in machinery and related depreciation. (Income tax effects are disregarded.)		

c.

Pindar Corporation and Subsidiary
Working Paper Elimination
September 1, 2006

Intercompany Bonds Payable—Pindar	100,000	
Discount on Intercompany Bonds Payable—Pindar ($100,000 − $99,091)		909
Investment in Pindar Corporation Bonds—Staple		97,321
Gain on Extinguishment of Bonds—Pindar ($99,091 − $97,321)		1,770
To eliminate parent's bonds acquired by subsidiary, and to recognize gain on the extinguishment of the bonds. (Income tax effects are disregarded.)		

2.

Photon Corporation and Subsidiary
Working Paper Elimination
December 31, 2007

Retained Earnings—Stengel ($15,000 x 0.90)	13,500	
Minority Interest in Net Assets of Subsidiary ($15,000 x 0.10)	1,500	
Accumulated Depreciation—Photon	3,750	
Machinery—Photon		15,000
Depreciation Expense—Photon ($15,000 ÷ 4)		3,750
To eliminate unrealized intercompany gain in machinery and related depreciation. (Income tax effects are disregarded.)		

Photon Corporation and Subsidiary
Working Paper Elimination
December 31, 2008

Retained Earnings—Stengel [($15,000 − $3,750) x 0.90]	10,125	
Minority Interest in Net Assets of Subsidiary [($15,000 − $3,750) x 0.10)]	1,125	
Accumulated Depreciation—Photon ($3,750 x 2)	7,500	
Machinery—Photon		15,000
Depreciation Expense—Photon ($15,000 ÷ 4)		3,750
To eliminate unrealized intercompany gain in machinery and related depreciation. (Income tax effects are disregarded.)		

3. a.

Padgett Corporation
Journal Entries

May 1, 2007	Investment in Sommer Company Bonds	379,749	
	Cash		379,749
	To record acquisition of $400,000 face amount of Sommer		
	Company's 7% bonds.		
Apr. 30, 2008	Cash ($400,000 x 0.07)	28,000	
	Investment in Sommer Company Bonds	6,177	
	Intercompany Interest Revenue		34,177
	To record receipt of annual interest on Sommer Company's 7%		
	bonds. Effective interest is computed as follows: $379,749 x		
	0.09 = $34,177.		

Sommer Company
Journal Entries

Apr. 30, 2006	Cash	966,879	
	Discount on Bonds Payable ($1,000,000 – $966,879)	33,121	
	Bonds Payable		1,000,000
	To record issuance of 7% bonds payable due Apr. 30, 2006, at		
	a discount.		
Apr. 30, 2007	Interest Expense	77,350	
	Cash ($1,000,000 x 0.07)		70,000
	Discount on Bonds Payable		7,350
	To record payment of annual interest on 7% bonds. Effective		
	interest is computed as follows: $966,879 x 0.08 = $77,350.		
Apr. 30, 2008	Intercompany Interest Expense ($389,692 x 0.08)	31,175	
	Interest Expense ($584,537 x 0.08)	46,763	
	Cash ($1,000,000 x 0.07)		70,000
	Discount on Intercompany Bonds Payable ($31,175 –		
	$28,000)		3,175
	Discount on Bonds Payable ($46,763 – $42,000)		4,763
	To record payment of annual interest on 7% bonds payable.		

©The McGraw-Hill Companies, Inc., 2006

b.

Padgett Corporation and Subsidiary
Working Paper Elimination
April 30, 2008

	Intercompany Interest Revenue—Padgett	34,177	
	Intercompany Bonds Payable—Sommer	400,000	
	Discount on Intercompany Bonds Payable—Sommer ($10,308 − $3,175)		7,133
	Investment in Sommer Company Bonds—Padgett ($379,479 + $6,177)		385,926
	Intercompany Interest Expense—Sommer		31,175
	Gain on Extinguishment of Bonds—Sommer ($389,692 − $379,749)		9,943
	To eliminate subsidiary's bonds acquired by parent, and related interest revenue and expense; and to recognize gain on extinguishment of the bonds. (Income tax effects are disregarded.)		

4.

Presser Corporation and Subsidiary
Working Paper Elimination
December 31, 2006

	Intercompany Liability under Capital Lease—Stasser ($8,340 − $2,000)	6,340	
	Unearned Intercompany Interest Revenue—Presser	1,660	
	Intercompany Sales—Presser	8,340	
	Intercompany Cost of Goods Sold—Presser		7,000
	Intercompany Lease Receivables—Presser ($10,000 − $2,000)		8,000
	Leased Equipment—Capital Lease—Strasser ($8,340 − $7,000)		1,340

Presser Corporation and Subsidiary
Working Paper Elimination
December 31, 2007

	Intercompany Liability under Capital Lease—Stasser [$6,340 − ($2,000 − $634)]	4,974	
	Unearned Intercompany Interest Revenue—Presser ($1,660 − $634)	1,026	
	Retained Earnings—Presser ($8,340 − $7,000)	1,340	
	Intercompany Lease Receivables—Presser ($8,000 − $2,000)		6,000
	Leased Equipment—Capital Lease—Stasser ($1,340 − $134)		1,206
	Depreciation Expense—Stasser ($1,340 ÷ 10)		134

5.

Pontiac Corporation
Journal Entries

2006			
June 30	Intercompany Notes Receivable	50,000	
	Cash		50,000
	To record loan to Southwest Company on 90-day, 9% promissory		
	note.		
July 15	Cash	49,847	
	Interest Expense ($1,278 – $937)	341	
	Intercompany Notes Receivable		50,000
	Intercompany Interest Revenue ($50,000 x 0.90 x 15/360)		188
	To record discounting of 90-day, 9% note receivable from		
	Southwest Company dated June 30, 2006, at a discount rate of		
	12%. Cash proceeds computed as follows: $51,125 maturity		
	value of note, less $1,278 discount ($51,125 x 0.12 x 75/360 =		
	$1,278), equals $49,847.		

CASE

Plumm Corporation and Subsidiaries
Instructions for Computation of Minority Interest in
Net Income of Subsidiaries

1. To compute the minority interest in net income of Swann Company, make the following adjustments to Swann's reported net income for the year:

   (a) Deduct the unrealized intercompany profit in Plumm's ending inventory resulting from Swann's sales of merchandise to Plumm.

   (b) Add the realized gain resulting from Plumm's open-market acquisition of Swann's outstanding bonds.

   Then, multiply the result of the above computation by 15% to measure the minority interest in net income of Swann.

2. To compute the minority interest in net income of Sully Company, make the following adjustment to Sully's reported net income for the year: Deduct the unrealized intercompany profit in Plumm's ending inventory resulting from Sully's sales of merchandise to Plumm. Then, multiply the result by 8% to measure the minority interest in net income of Sully.

   Note that Plumm's sales of a machine and a patent to Sully have no effect on the minority interest in net income of Sully.

CHAPTER 9
CONSOLIDATED FINANCIAL STATEMENTS: INCOME TAXES, CASH FLOWS, AND INSTALLMENT ACQUISITIONS

HIGHLIGHTS OF THE CHAPTER

1. Income tax accounting requirements for business combinations often differ from generally accepted accounting principles. Consequently, the current fair values assigned to identifiable net assets of a combinee in a business combination often include deferred income tax liabilities or assets attributable to differences between financial accounting and income tax accounting for the combination.

2. Generally, **income tax allocation** accounting is appropriate in the parent company's accounting records for undistributed earnings of subsidiaries. Income taxes attributed to domestic subsidiaries' undistributed earnings are computed under the assumption that the undistributed earnings had been distributed as dividends and the parent company had availed itself of all possible tax planning alternatives, credits, and deductions. The resultant parent company journal entry generally is in the following form:

Income Taxes Expense	XXX	
Income Taxes Payable		XXX
Deferred Income Tax Liability		XXX

   To provide for income taxes on intercompany investment income from subsidiary.

3. The amount credited to Income Taxes Payable in the journal entry illustrated in paragraph **2** is for income taxes attributable to dividends received by the parent company from the subsidiary during the accounting period. The credit to the Deferred Income Tax Liability ledger account is for the amount of income taxes attributable to undistributed earnings of the subsidiary.

4. Under current federal income tax laws, an affiliated group of corporations may file a **consolidated income tax return,** with intercompany profits (gains) and losses eliminated from consolidated taxable income. If the parent and subsidiary companies do not qualify for, or do not choose to file, consolidated income tax returns, income taxes accrued or paid on intercompany profits (gains) must be deferred (assuming the criteria for recognizing deferred tax assets without a valuation allowance are met).

5. To illustrate the deferral of income taxes attributable to intercompany profits, assume that intercompany profits of $15,000 and $20,000, respectively, were attributable to the beginning and ending inventories of Sprackle Company resulting from merchandise purchases from its parent company, Prangle Corporation. If the income tax rate is 40%, the following working paper eliminations (in journal entry format) are appropriate for Prangle Corporation and subsidiary at the end of the year:

Deferred Income Tax Asset—Prangle	8,000	
Income Taxes Expense—Prangle		8,000

   To defer income taxes provided on separate income tax returns of parent applicable to unrealized intercompany profits in subsidiary's inventories at end of year ($20,000 x 0.40 = $8,000).

Income Taxes Expense—Prangle	6,000	
Retained Earnings—Prangle		6,000

   To provide for income taxes attributable to realized intercompany profits in subsidiary's inventories at beginning of year ($15,000 x 0.40 = $6,000)

6. The deferral of income taxes attributable to an intercompany gain on sale of land is accomplished with a working paper elimination (in journal entry format) at the end of the accounting period of the sale, such as the following:

Deferred Income Tax Asset—Parent   XXX
   Income Taxes Expense —Parent   XXX
To defer income taxes provided on separate income tax returns of parent company applicable to unrealized intercompany gain in subsidiary's land at end of period.

7. In years subsequent to the intercompany sale of land, as long as the acquiring affiliate owns the land, a working paper elimination similar to the one illustrated in paragraph **6** is appropriate except that the credit is to the retained earnings of the selling affiliate.

8. The deferral of income taxes attributed to an intercompany gain on sale of a depreciable plant asset at the end of an accounting period is accomplished by a working paper elimination identical in format to the one illustrated in paragraph **6**. In working paper eliminations of subsequent years of the economic life of the depreciable plant asset, a portion of the deferred income taxes attributable to the intercompany gain element of the acquiring affiliate's depreciation expense is allocated to the income taxes expense of the selling affiliate.

9. A working paper elimination should be used to provide for income taxes attributable to the realized gain or loss on one affiliate's open-market acquisition of another affiliate's outstanding bonds at the end of an accounting period. The working paper elimination (in journal entry format) would be as follows:

Income Taxes Expense—Subsidiary   XXX
   Deferred Income Tax Liability—Subsidiary   XXX
To provide for income taxes attributable to subsidiary's realized gain on parent company's acquisition of the subsidiary bonds.

10. In accounting periods subsequent to the acquisition of the bonds, the **actual income tax effects** of the difference between intercompany interest revenue and expense would represent the reversal of the deferred income tax liability illustrated in paragraph **9**.

11. In the preparation of a consolidated statement of cash flows, special problems arise with respect to the minority interest in net income of subsidiary, cash dividends applicable to minority stockholders, and changes in the parent company's ownership of common stock of the subsidiary.

12. A parent company may obtain control of a subsidiary company in a **series of common stock acquisitions,** rather than in a single transaction constituting a business combination. If so, the parent company logically should determine the current fair value of the subsidiary's identifiable net assets on the date the parent attains a controlling interest in the subsidiary. Prior to attaining a controlling interest, the investor company begins applying the equity method of accounting at the time when the investment is sufficient to enable the investor to exercise significant operating and financial influence over the investee.

13. Application of the equity method of accounting in conjunction with the installment acquisition of a subsidiary's outstanding common stock may lead to the piecemeal recognition of goodwill. For example, assume that Pogue Corporation acquired outstanding common stock of Stigue Company as follows:

July 1, 2003	30%
July 1, 2004	15%
July 1, 2005	35%

Under generally accepted accounting principles, Pogue begins applying the equity method for its investment in Stigue's common stock during the year beginning July 1, 2003. Any goodwill is computed separately on that date, on July 1, 2004, and on July 1, 2005. A business combination is considered to have taken place on July 1, 2005, when a controlling interest of 80% was achieved.

QUESTIONS

True or False

For each of the following statements, circle the **T** or the **F** to indicate whether the statement is true or false.

T F 1. Estimated future tax effects of differences between the tax bases and amounts otherwise appropriate to assign to assets and liabilities are one of the variables in estimates of current fair values for a combinee in a business combination.

T F 2. The amount of undistributed earnings of a domestic subsidiary included in parent company net income under the equity method of accounting is accounted for as a temporary difference between taxable income and financial income of the parent company.

T F 3. Income taxes attributable to unrealized intercompany profits (gains) are deferred in consolidated financial statements if the affiliated group files a consolidated income tax return.

T F 4. A working paper elimination (in journal entry format) for income taxes attributable to realized intercompany profits in a subsidiary's beginning inventories includes a credit to Deferred Income Tax Asset—Parent.

T F 5. If income tax accounting for a business combination differs from financial accounting, the combinor debits or credits a deferred income tax asset or liability.

T F 6. A working paper elimination (in journal entry format) for income taxes attributable to a subsidiary's realized gain on the parent company's acquisition of the subsidiary's bonds includes a debit to Income Taxes Expense—Parent.

T F 7. In a consolidated statement of cash flows, the minority interest in net income of subsidiary is displayed in net cash provided by operating activities.

T F 8. A parent company's acquisition of common stock from minority stockholders of a subsidiary is displayed in a consolidated statement of cash flows as a cash flow from financing activities.

T F 9. If a parent obtains control of a subsidiary in a series of outstanding common stock acquisitions, current fair values of the subsidiary's identifiable net assets logically should be ascertained on the date when the parent company attains the controlling interest in the subsidiary.

T F 10. An investor enterprise may use the cost method of accounting for installment investments in an eventual subsidiary once the investor owns more than 20% of the investee's outstanding common stock but prior to the time the investor attains a controlling interest in the subsidiary.

T F 11. Retroactive application of the equity method of accounting is required when an investor enterprise attains significant influence (usually 20% common stock ownership) over the investee enterprise.

T F 12. Separate computations of goodwill may be made on more than one date when a parent company obtains control of a subsidiary in a series of outstanding common stock acquisitions.

Completion Statements

Fill in the necessary words or amounts to complete the following statements.

1. If Potash Corporation acquired 15% of the outstanding common stock of Silicone Company on October 1, 2005, another 20% on April 1, 2006, and the remaining 65% on October 1, 2006, Potash should logically determine the current fair values of Silicone's identifiable assets on _____.

2. If a parent company and its subsidiaries do not file consolidated income tax returns, _____ _____ _____ is required for a subsidiary's _____ _____.

3. Only dividends paid to _____ _____ and _____ stockholders are reported as cash flows from financing activities in a consolidated statement of cash flows.

4. If a business combination meets the requirements for a "tax-free corporate reorganization" under the income tax law, a _____ _____ may result between provisions for depreciation and amortization in the combinee's financial statements and income tax returns.

5. Deferred income taxes attributable to an unrealized intercompany gain in a depreciable plant asset reverse as _____ _____ _____ _____ for the asset.

6. An acquisition by the parent company of additional shares of common stock _____ _____ a subsidiary does not change the amount of consolidated cash.

Multiple Choice

Choose the best answer for each of the following questions and enter the identifying letter in the space provided.

_____ 1. On May 1, 2005, Pilsner Corporation acquired for $50,000 cash 5% of the outstanding common stock of Seaward Company. On that date both the carrying amounts and the current fair values of Seaward's identifiable net assets were $1 million. During the fiscal year ended April 30, 2006, Seaward had a net income of $60,000 and declared dividends of $20,000. On May 1, 2006, Pilsner acquired the remainder of Seaward's outstanding common stock for cash. Pilsner's May 1, 2006, journal entries include a credit to the Retained Earnings ledger account in the amount of:
   a. $0
   b. $2,000
   c. $40,000
   d. Some other amount

_____ 2. Proust Corporation sells merchandise to its wholly-owned subsidiary, Samuel Company. Intercompany profit in Samuel's January 1, 2006, inventories was $50,000, and in Samuel's December 31, 2006, inventories was $40,000. If Proust is subject to an income tax rate of 40%, the December 31, 2006, working paper eliminations (in journal entry format) for Proust Corporation and subsidiary should change Proust's income taxes expense by:
   a. An increase of $4,000
   b. A decrease of $4,000
   c. An increase of $20,000
   d. A decrease of $16,000
   e. Some other amount

_____ 3. Sexton Company, a wholly-owned domestic subsidiary of Poltroon Corporation, had a net income of $60,000 and declared dividends of $20,000 for 2006. In Poltroon's equity method journal entries for Sexton's 2006 operating results, Sexton's $40,000 increase in retained earnings is treated as:
   a. A permanent difference between Poltroon's financial income and taxable income
   b. An increase in Poltroon's Retained Earnings ledger account balance
   c. A temporary difference between Poltroon's financial income and taxable income
   d. None of the foregoing

_____ 4. In an installment acquisition of a controlling interest in an eventual subsidiary, the investor–parent company applies the equity method of accounting for the investment in the investee–subsidiary when the parent acquires:
   a. The first investment in the investee's common stock
   b. At least 20% of the investee's common stock
   c. More than 50% of the investee's common stock
   d. At lease 50% of the investee's common stock

_____ 5. The realized intercompany profit in the beginning inventories of Piedmont Corporation, parent company of Sturdwick Company, was $60,000, and the unrealized intercompany profit in Piedmont's ending inventories was $80,000. Piedmont and Sturdwick file separate income tax returns, and both affiliates are subject to income taxes at a rate of 40%. If the criteria for recording deferred tax assets without a valuation allowance are met, the working paper elimination of Piedmont Corporation and subsidiary should:
   a. Debit Income Taxes Expense—Sturdwick for $24,000
   b. Debit Deferred Income Tax Asset—Sturdwick for $24,000
   c. Credit Deferred Income Tax Liability—Piedmont for $32,000
   d. Do none of the foregoing

_____ 6. In a consolidated statement of cash flows, a parent company's gain or loss on disposal of part of an investment in a subsidiary is displayed as:
   a. A cash flow from financing activities
   b. An adjustment to consolidated net income of the parent company and subsidiary
   c. A decrease in minority interest in net assets of subsidiary
   d. An increase in minority interest in net assets of subsidiary

_____ 7. In the journal entry for a business combination, the combinor recognizes a deferred income tax liability if:

a. A portion of the current fair value of the combinee's net assets is not deductible for income taxes.

b. The combinee had temporary differences between financial income and taxable income prior to the business combination.

c. The affiliated group expects to file consolidated income tax returns.

d. The business combination was not a "tax-free corporate reorganization."

SHORT EXERCISES

1. The accountant for Progress Corporation prepared the following working paper eliminations (in journal entry format) on March 31, 2006:

Progress Corporation and Subsidiary
Working Paper Eliminations
March 31, 2006

Retained Earnings—Sanford	3,225	
Minority Interest in Net Assets of Subsidiary	525	
Intercompany Sales—Sanford	100,000	
Intercompany Cost of Goods Sold—Sanford		75,000
Cost of Goods Sold—Progress		23,750
Inventories—Progress		5,000

To eliminate intercompany sales, cost of goods sold, and unrealized intercompany profit in inventories.

Retained Earnings—Progress	9,000	
Accumulated Depreciation—Sanford	4,500	
Machinery—Sanford		12,000
Depreciation Expense—Sanford		1,500

To eliminate unrealized intercompany gain in machinery and related depreciation. Gain element in depreciation is computed as follows: $12,000 ÷ 8 = $1,500 (based on eight-year economic life of machinery).

Prepare additional working paper eliminations in the space on page 116 that are required to recognize the income tax effects associated with the foregoing eliminations. Use an income tax rate of 40%, and assume that the criteria for recognizing deferred tax assets without a valuation allowance are met.

Progress Corporation and Subsidiary
Working Paper Eliminations
March 31, 2006

2. The following data are from the consolidated financial statements of Pagani Corporation and its subsidiary, Sharpe Company, for the fiscal year ended December 31, 2006:

Increase in net current assets except cash	$ 49,000
Consolidated net income	624,000
Depreciation and amortization expense	82,000
Gain on disposal of part of investment in Sharpe Company common stock	144,000
Minority interest in net income of subsidiary	46,000
Proceeds on disposal of part of investment in Sharpe Company common stock	423,000
Investment income from Irving Company (an influenced investee that declared no cash dividends during the year)	86,000

In the space below, compute the net cash provided by operating activities for the consolidated statement of cash flows (indirect method) of Pagani Corporation and subsidiary for the year ended December 31, 2006.

3. On January 2, 2005, when the current fair value and carrying amount of Simpole Company's identifiable net assets was $640,000, Panker Corporation acquired 10% of Simpole's outstanding common stock for $80,000. Simpole declared dividends of $50,000 on December 31, 2005, and had a net income of $140,000 for the fiscal year ended December 31, 2005. On January 2, 2006, when the current fair value of Simpole's identifiable net assets was the same as carrying amount, Panker acquired 60% of Simpole's outstanding common stock for $500,000 cash. Both Panker and Simpole recognize goodwill impairment when it occurs.

In the space below, prepare journal entries for Panker Corporation on the dates indicated. Omit explanations and disregard income taxes and out-of-pocket costs of the common stock acquisitions. Assume no impairment of goodwill.

Panker Corporation
Journal Entries

2005			
Jan. 2			
Dec. 31			
2006			
Jan. 2			
2			

4. Consolidated balance sheets for Parker Corporation and subsidiary, Solat Company, on December 31, 2006 and 2005, were as follows:

	December 31,	
	2006	2005
Cash	$ 58,000	$ 40,000
Other current assets	850,000	758,000
Plant assets	1,290,000	1,000,000
Less: Accumulated depreciation	(350,000)	(280,000)
Goodwill	52,000	52,000
Totals	$1,900,000	$1,570,000
Current liabilities	$ 421,000	$ 335,000
Long-term debt	400,000	375,000
Common stock, no par or stated value	600,000	500,000
Minority interest in net assets of subsidiary	69,000	60,000
Retained earnings	410,000	300,000
Totals	$1,900,000	$1,570,000

Parker Corporation owned 70% of the common stock of Solat Company throughout 2006. For 2006, Solat had a net income of $80,000 and Parker had a net income of $220,000, including its share of the net income of Solat. Both companies declared and paid cash dividends in 2006. There were no disposals of plant assets or payments on long-term debt during 2006. Additional common stock was issued in 2006 by Parker in exchange for plant assets, unimpaired goodwill was computed under the parent company concept on the business combination date, and there was no "current fair value excess" on that date.

Complete the consolidated statement of cash flows for 2006 below. (Do not use a working paper disregard supplemental disclosure of cash flow information related to cash paid during the year for interest and income taxes.)

Parker Corporation and Subsidiary
Consolidated Statement of Cash Flows (indirect method)
For Year Ended December 31, 2006

Net cash provided by operating activities **(Exhibit 1)**	$
Cash flows from investing activities:	
Acquisition of plant assets	
Cash flows from financing activities:	
Long-term borrowings	$
Payment of cash dividends, including $_____ to minority stockholders	
Net cash used in financing activities	_____
Net increase in cash	$ 20,0(
Cash, beginning of year	40,0(
Cash, end of year	$ 60,0(

Exhibit 1 Cash flows from operating activities:

Net income	$220,0(
Adjustments to reconcile net income to net cash provided by operating activities:	

Exhibit 2 Noncash investing and financing activities:

CASE

Following is an excerpt from a note to the financial statements of Asarco, Incorporated, a publicly owned enterprise, for the year ended December 31, 1994, as shown in *Accounting Trends & Techniques,* 49th ed., AICPA (Jersey City: 1995), p. 417:

> U.S. deferred tax liabilities have net been provided on approximately $251.9 million in 1994 ($267.0 million in 1993 and $167.0 million in 1992) of undistributed earnings of foreign subsidiaries and nonconsolidated associated companies more than 50% owned, because assets representing those earnings are permanently invested. It is not practicable to determine the amount of income taxes that would be payable upon remittance of assets that represent those earnings. The amount of foreign withholding taxes that would be payable upon remittance of assets that represent those earnings would be approximately $.3 million in 1994 ($2.8 million in 1993 and $3.4 million in 1992).

Does the foregoing excerpt provide adequate informative disclosure regarding the company's accounting for deferred income taxes attributable to undistributed earnings of subsidiaries and investees? Explain.

SOLUTIONS TO QUESTIONS, SHORT EXERCISES, AND CASE: CHAPTER 9

QUESTIONS

True or False

1. F 2. T 3. F 4. F 5. T 6. F 7. T 8. F 9. T 10. F 11. T 12. T

Completion Statements

1. October 1, 2006. 2. Income tax allocation, undistributed earnings. 3. Parent company, minority.
4. Temporary difference. 5. Depreciation expense is recorded. 6. Directly from.

Multiple Choice

1. a 2. a [($50,000 – $40,000) x 0.40 = $4,000] 3. c 4. b 5. a ($60,000 x 0.40 = $24,000) 6. b 7. a

SHORT EXERCISES

1.

Progress Corporation and Subsidiary
Working Paper Eliminations
March 31, 2006

Deferred Income Tax Asset—Sanford	2,000	
Income Taxes Expense—Sanford		2,000
To defer income taxes provided on separate income tax returns of subsidiary applicable to unrealized intercompany profits in parent company's inventories on Mar. 31, 2006 ($5,000 x 0.40 = $2,000)		
Income Taxes Expense—Sanford	1,500	
Retained Earnings—Sanford ($1,500 x 0.86)		1,290
Minority Interest in Net Assets of Subsidiary ($1,500 x 0.14)		210
To provide for income taxes attributable to intercompany profits in parent company's inventories on Mar. 31, 2005 ($3,750 x 0.40 = $1,500)		
Income Taxes Expense—Progress	600	
Deferred Income Tax Asset—Progress	3,000	
Retained Earnings—Progress		3,600
To provide for income tax expense on intercompany gain realized through subsidiary's depreciation ($1,500 x 0.40 = $600); and to defer taxes applicable to remainder of unrealized intercompany gain [($9,000 – $1,500) x 0.40 = $3,000].		

2. Cash flows from operating activities:

Net income	$624,000
Adjustments to reconcile net income to net cash provided by operating activities:	
Depreciation and amortization expense	82,000
Minority interest in net income of subsidiary	46,000
Gain on disposal of investment in Sharpe Company common stock	(144,000)
Investment income from Irving Company	(86,000)
Net increase in net current assets	(49,000)
Net cash provided by operating activities	$473,000

3.

Panker Corporation
Journal Entries

2005			
Jan. 2	Investment in Simpole Company Common Stock	80,000	
	Cash		80,000
Dec. 31	Dividends Receivable ($50,000 x 0.10)	5,000	
	Dividend Revenue		5,000
2006			
Jan. 2	Investment in Simpole Company Common Stock	500,000	
	Cash		500,000
2	Investment in Simpole Company Common Stock	9,000	
	Retained Earnings of Subsidiary [$14,000 – $5,000]		9,000

Study Guide

4.

Parker Corporation and Subsidiary
Consolidated Statement of Cash Flows (indirect method)
For Year Ended December 31, 2006

Net cash provided by operating activities (**Exhibit 1**)		$308,000
Cash flows from investing activities:		
Acquisition of plant assets		(190,000) (1)
Cash flows from financing activities:		
Long-term borrowings	$ 25,000	
Payment of cash dividends, including $15,000 (2) to		
minority stockholders	(125,000) (3)	
Net cash used in financing activities		(100,000)
Net increase in cash		$ 18,000
Cash, beginning of year		40,000
Cash, end of year		$ 58,000

Exhibit 1 Cash flows from operating activities:	
Net income	$220,000
Adjustments to reconcile net income to net cash provided	
by operating activities:	
Depreciation and amortization expense	70,000 (4)
Minority interest in net income of subsidiary	24,000 (5)
Net increase in net current assets	(6,000)(6)
Net cash provided by operating activities	$308,000

Exhibit 2 Noncash investing and financing activities:	
Common stock issued for plant assets	$100,000

(1)	$1,290,000 – $1,000,000 – $100,000 = $190,000
(2)	($80,000 x 0.30) – ($69,000 – $60,000) = $15,000
(3)	$220,000 – ($410,000 – $300,000) + $15,000 = $125,000
(4)	($350,000 – $280,000) = $70,000
(5)	$80,000 x 0.30 = $24,000
(6)	($850,000 – $758,000) – ($421,000 – $335,000) = $6,000

CASE

The note to financial statements of Asarco, Incorporated is unclear as to the provision for income taxes (if any) on undistributed earnings of **domestic** subsidiaries, and the meaning of **nonconsolidated associated companies more than 50% owned.** Perhaps those items are explained elsewhere in the notes to financial statement or the company's annual report to stockholders. Clarity and precision in the language of notes to financial statements are essential to their **usefulness.**

HIGHLIGHTS OF THE CHAPTER

1. If a parent company acquires all or part of the minority interest in a subsidiary, purchase accounting (including recognition of goodwill) is applied to the acquisition.

2. If a parent company disposes of a portion of its common stockholdings in a subsidiary, a gain or loss is recognized in the parent's accounting records and in the consolidated income statement. The gain or loss is measured as the difference between the cash or current fair value of consideration received by the parent and the carrying amount of the subsidiary common stock sold. The gain or loss is not an extraordinary item. For accounting periods subsequent to the date of the parent company's disposal of a portion of its subsidiary common stockholdings, the minority interest in the subsidiary's net income and net assets is larger than prior to the disposal.

3. If a subsidiary issues additional shares of common stock to the public, thus increasing the minority interest in the net income and net assets of the subsidiary, the parent company generally recognizes a gain or loss. A gain results if the price per share for the subsidiary's common stock issued to the public **exceeded** the carrying amount per share of the parent company's investment in the subsidiary. A loss to the parent company results from the converse situation. The parent company's gain or loss generally is displayed as a nonoperating item in both the consolidated income statement and the parent's income statement.

4. A subsidiary's issuance of additional shares of common stock to the parent company also results in a nonoperating gain or loss to the parent company if an existing minority interest in net assets of the subsidiary is changed by the subsidiary's common stock issuance.

5. Some combinees in a business combination have preferred stock as well as common stock outstanding. If the parent company acquires less than 100% of the subsidiary's preferred stock, the preferences associated with the preferred stock must be considered in the measurement of the minority interest in net income and net assets of the subsidiary.

6. Preferred stock of a subsidiary does not enter into the measurement of goodwill acquired in a business combination because the preferred stock substantively may be considered **debt** rather than **equity** of the subsidiary. Thus, the amount paid by the parent company for the subsidiary's **common** stock is the measure of the amount of goodwill acquired in a business combination.

7. The **call price** of a subsidiary's preferred stock is used in the measurement of both the cost of the parent company's investment in the preferred stock and the minority interest of preferred stockholders in the net assets of the subsidiary on the date of the business combination. The call price is both the preferred stockholders' maximum claim on the subsidiary's net assets and the amount that the subsidiary would pay to retire the preferred stock.

8. Dividends received by a parent company on its investment in a subsidiary's preferred stock are recognized as **intercompany revenue** under the cost method of accounting. If a subsidiary passes dividends on cumulative preferred stock owned by the parent company, the parent accrues the passed dividends under the equity method of accounting. Minority preferred stockholders' dividends are included in the measurement of minority interest in net income of the subsidiary.

9. The amount of consolidated retained earnings is not affected by a subsidiary's stock dividends. All accumulated earnings of the consolidated group **not distributed to the parent company's stockholders or capitalized by the parent company** are included in consolidated retained earnings.

10. Treasury stock of a subsidiary on the date of a business combination is treated as **retired** stock in the consolidated financial statements. A working paper elimination is prepared to reflect the "retirement" of the treasury stock by the par or stated value method. Comparable treatment is accorded to treasury stock acquired by the subsidiary from minority stockholders subsequent to the date of a business combination. In addition, goodwill is recognized if the cost of the acquired treasury stock exceeds the carrying amount of the relevant minority interest in net assets.

11. **Indirect shareholdings** exist if a subsidiary and the parent company jointly own a controlling interest in another subsidiary, or a subsidiary is itself the parent company of its own subsidiary. Accountants who prepare working papers for consolidated financial statements for parent–subsidiary relationships involving indirect shareholdings must follow carefully the common stock ownership percentages and apply the equity method of accounting for the indirectly owned subsidiary's operating results accordingly.

12. **Reciprocal shareholdings** involve subsidiary ownership of the parent company's common stock. Reciprocal shareholdings are in substance **treasury stock** to the consolidated entity; thus, working paper eliminations (in journal entry format) such as the following are appropriate for reciprocal shareholdings.

| Treasury Stock—Parent | XXX | |
| Investment in Parent Company Common Stock—Subsidiary | | XXX |

To transfer subsidiary's investment in parent company's common stock to treasury stock category.

| Intercompany Dividend Revenue—Subsidiary | XXX | |
| Dividends Declared—Parent | | XXX |

To eliminate parent company dividends received by subsidiary.

QUESTIONS

True or False

For each of the following statements, circle the **T** or the **F** to indicate whether the statement is true or false.

T F 1. Purchase accounting is used for a parent company's acquisition of all or part of the minority interest in net assets of a subsidiary.

T F 2. Accounting for a parent company's disposal of part of its investment in a subsidiary is similar to the accounting for disposal of any noncurrent asset.

T F 3. Under generally accepted accounting principles, the gain or loss on a parent company's disposal of a part of its investment in a subsidiary is an extraordinary item.

T F 4. If a subsidiary issues additional shares of common stock to the public, there may be a nonoperating gain or loss to the parent company.

T F 5. Unlike the interest of minority common stockholders, the interest of minority preferred stockholders in the net assets of a subsidiary is not residual.

T F 6. Preferred stock of a subsidiary may in substance be considered debt rather than owners' equity.

T F 7. In a consolidated balance sheet, the liquidation value per share of a subsidiary's preferred stock is used to measure the minority preferred stockholders' interest in the subsidiary's net assets.

T F 8. A parent company should use the cost method of accounting for preferred dividends received from a subsidiary.

T F 9. A parent company uses the equity method of accounting for cumulative preferred dividends passed by a subsidiary.

T F 10. The amount of consolidated retained earnings is reduced by the amount of a subsidiary's retained earnings capitalized as a stock dividend.

T F 11. Treasury stock of a subsidiary on the date of a business combination is displayed as treasury stock in the consolidated balance sheet.

T F 12. If a subsidiary acquires for its treasury all or part of the common stock owned by minority stockholders of the subsidiary, the parent company recognizes a gain or loss on the transaction.

T F 13. Shares of parent company common stock owned by a subsidiary are in substance treasury stock of the consolidated entity.

Completion Statements

Fill in the necessary words or amounts to complete the following statements.

1. A parent company uses _____ accounting for the acquisition of all or part of the minority interest in net assets of subsidiary.

2. If a parent company attains control of a subsidiary by a series of acquisitions of the subsidiary's common stock, _____ _____ is used to account for the carrying amount of subsidiary common stock later disposed of by the parent.

3. A parent company credits a _____ _____ ledger account for a gain resulting from a subsidiary's issuance of additional common stock to the public.

4. In a consolidated balance sheet, the _____ _____ of a subsidiary's preferred stock is used to compute the _____ _____ of preferred stockholders in net assets of the subsidiary.

5. Treasury stock of a subsidiary on the date of a business combination is treated as _____ stock in consolidated financial statements.

6. A subsidiary's ownership of parent company common stock is known as a _____ _____.

Multiple Choice

Choose the best answer for each of the following questions and enter the identifying letter in the space provided.

_____ 1. Among the journal entries of Pleasanton Corporation during 2006 was the following (explanation omitted):

Investment in Subsidiary Common Stock	15,613	
Nonoperating Gain		15,613

A probable reason for the journal entry is:
a. Pleasanton disposed of some of its subsidiary common stockholdings at a gain.
b. The subsidiary acquired part of its minority stockholders' common stock for an amount of cash larger than the carrying amount of the minority interest.
c. The subsidiary issued additional common stock to the public at a price per share higher than the carrying amount per share of Pleasanton's investment in the subsidiary.
d. None of the foregoing

_____ 2. On April 1, 2005, Paloma Corporation paid $341,575 cash for 700 shares of Sardinia Company's 1,000 outstanding shares of $2 par, 8% cumulative preferred stock and 850 of Sardinia's 1,000 outstanding shares of $10 par common stock. Out-of-pocket costs of the business combination may be disregarded. Current fair values of Sardinia's identifiable net assets were the same as their carrying amounts on April 1, 2005. On the date of the business combination, Sardinia had additional paid-in capital of $150,000 and retained earnings of $200,250. Sardinia's preferred stock was callable at $2.25 a share plus preferred dividends in arrears, and had a liquidation preference of $2.10 a share. Preferred dividends were not in arrears. The portion of the $341,575 cost of Paloma's investment in Sardinia that is allocated to Sardinia's preferred stock is:
a. $0
b. $1,400
c. $1,470
d. Some other amount

_____ 3. Refer to the facts in question **2.** The amount to be created to Minority Interest in Net Assets of Subsidiary—Common in the April 1, 2005, working paper elimination (in journal entry format) for Paloma Corporation and subsidiary is:
a. $51,236
b. $60,000
c. $60,278
d. Some other amount

_____ 4. Subsequent to the date of a business combination, the subsidiary acquired for its treasury some of the common stock owned by minority stockholders. In the working paper for consolidated financial statements for the parent company and its subsidiary, the cost of the common stock acquired is treated as:
a. An increase in consolidated investments
b. A reduction of consolidated stockholders' equity
c. An increase in consolidated treasury stock
d. None of the foregoing

_____ 5. The 92%-owned subsidiary of Poker Corporation declared a 10% stock dividend on its 10,000 shares of $5 par common stock. Current fair value of the dividend shares was $12 a share. The journal entry for Poker's receipt of the dividend shares from the subsidiary is:

a. Investment in Subsidiary Company Common Stock (920 x $5)   4,600
    Intercompany Investment Income   4,600

b. Retained Earnings of Subsidiary (920 x $12)   11,040
    Retained Earnings   11,040

c. Investment in Subsidiary Company Common Stock (920 x $12)   11,040
    Intercompany Investment Income   11,040

d. None of the foregoing

_____ 6. Which of the following transactions or events does not result in a gain or loss to a parent company?

a. Parent company's disposal of a part of its investment in the subsidiary's common stock
b. Subsidiary's issuance of additional shares of common stock to the public, with minority stockholders waiving their preemptive right
c. Subsidiary's acquisition of shares of its common stock owned by minority stockholders, such shares to be treasury stock
d. Subsidiary's issuance of additional shares of common stock to the parent company, with resultant change in minority interest in net assets of subsidiary

_____ 7. In the journal entry to record the disposal of a 10% interest in its wholly-owned subsidiary to an outsider, a parent company credited the Realized Gain on Disposal of Investment in Subsidiary ledger account. In the consolidated income statement for the accounting period of the disposal, the gain account balance is:

a. Excluded, because it was eliminated as an intercompany gain
b. Displayed as an extraordinary item
c. Included in income before extraordinary item
d. Included in minority interest in net income of subsidiary

_____ 8. Single Company owned 22% of the outstanding common stock of Stokker Company throughout 2006. On January 2, 2007, Plenary Corporation acquired 75% of the outstanding common stock of Single and 40% of the outstanding common stock of Stokker. In the working paper elimination for Plenary Corporation and subsidiaries on January 2, 2007, the amount of Single's Retained Earnings of Investee ledger account applicable to Stokker is:

a. Eliminated
b. Included in consolidated retained earnings
c. Combined with Plenary's Retained Earnings of Subsidiary ledger account established to record the business combination with Single and Stokker
d. Handled in some other manner

SHORT EXERCISES

1   Separate balance sheets for Pat Corporation, Set Company, and Syn Company on December 31, 2005, are shown below:

Pat Corporation, Set Company, and Syn Company
Separate Balance Sheets
December 31, 2005

Assets	Pat Corporation	Set Company	Syn Company
Various assets	$361,000	$195,000	$100,000
Investment in Set Company common stock (80%)	74,000		
Investment in Syn Company common stock (30%)	15,000		
Investment in Syn Company common stock (60%)		30,000	
Total assets	$450,000	$225,000	$100,000
Liabilities & Stockholders' Equity			
Liabilities	$156,000	$ 50,000	$ 70,000
Common stock, no par or stated value	234,000	100,000	50,000
Retained earnings (deficit)	60,000	75,000	(20,000)
Total liabilities & stockholders' equity	$450,000	$225,000	$100,000

Additional Information:

(1)   All investment ledger accounts are maintained under the cost method of accounting.

(2)   Assets of Pat Corporation include $15,000 receivable from Set Company, and assets of Syn Company include $5,000 receivable from Pat.

(3)   Pat Corporation had acquired 60% of Set Company's outstanding common stock for $48,000 on January 2, 2005, when Set had a deficit of $20,000. Pat Corporation had acquired an additional 20% of Set's outstanding stock for $26,000 on April 1, 2005, when Set had retained earnings of $10,000. Current fair values of Set's identifiable net assets were equal to their carrying amounts on both dates.

(4)   Syn Company's common stock had been issued for cash to Pat Corporation, Set Company, and outsiders on April 1, 2005, when Syn was organized.

(5)   Set had a net income of $30,000 for the first quarter of 2005 and a net income of $100,000 for all of 2005. Set declared a cash dividend of $5,000 on December 20, 2005, payable in 2006.

(6)   Goodwill, if any, was unimpaired at December 31, 2005.

a.   In the spaces below and on page 129, prepare adjusting entries for Set Company and Pat Corporation on December 31, 2005, to restate their Investment ledger accounts to the equity method of accounting. Disregard income taxes.

Set Company
Adjusting Entry
December 31, 2005

Pat Corporation
Adjusting Entries
December 31, 2005

b. Complete the consolidated balance sheet for Pat Corporation and subsidiaries in the space below. Show supporting computations for goodwill, minority interest in net assets of subsidiaries, and consolidated retained earnings.

Pat Corporation and Subsidiaries
Consolidated Balance Sheet
December 31, 2005

Assets		Liabilities & Stockholders' Equity	
Various assets	$	Liabilities	$
Goodwill			
Total assets	$_____	Total liabilities & stockholders' equity	$_____

Computation of goodwill:

Computation of minority interest in net assets of subsidiaries:

Computation of consolidated retained earnings:

2.　　On June 1, 2005, the beginning of a fiscal year, Passaic Corporation acquired for $208,000 92% of the 10,000 outstanding shares of Seaview Company's $1 par common stock in a business combination. On the date of the combination, stockholders' equity of Seaview was composed of the following:

Common stock $1	$ 12,000
Additional paid-in capital	96,000
Retained earnings	122,000
Total paid in capital and retained earnings	$230,000
Less: 2,000 shares of treasury stock, at cost	22,000
Total stockholders' equity	$208,000

On October 1, 2005, Seaview acquired in the open market 5,000 shares of Passaic's 1 million outstanding shares of $5 par common stock for $100,000. On May 21, 2006, Passaic declared a cash dividend of $1.20 a share on the common stock, payable June 7, 2006, to stockholders of record May 31, 2006.

Prepare working paper eliminations (in journal entry format) for Passaic Corporation and subsidiary on May 31, 2006, other than for elimination of intercompany investment. Disregard income taxes. Use the space provided below.

Passaic Corporation and Subsidiary
Working Paper Eliminations
May 31, 2006

3. On December 31, 2005, after closing entries, the balances of Packy Corporation's two ledger accounts related to its 90%-owned subsidiary, Stamper Company, which Packy had established with a 90% interest on January 2, 2005, were as follows:

Investment in Stamper Company Common Stock	$162,200 dr
Retained Earnings of Subsidiary	63,000 cr

Stamper's stockholders' equity on December 31, 2005, was as follows:

Common stock, $5 par	$ 50,000
Additional paid-in capital	60,000
Retained earnings	70,000
Total stockholders' equity	$180,000

On January 2, 2006, Packy paid $26,000 for the 1,000 shares of Stamper's common stock owned by minority stockholders of Stamper.

In the space below, prepare a working paper elimination (in journal entry format) for Packy Corporation and subsidiary on January 2, 2006, after Packy's acquisition of the minority interest in Stamper. Disregard income taxes.

Packy Corporation and Subsidiary
Working Paper Elimination
January 2, 2006

CASE

APB Opinion No. 30, "Reporting the Results of Operations . . . ," specified two criteria for **extraordinary items:** unusual in nature and infrequent in occurrence. Nonetheless, now superseded **FASB Statement No. 4,** ". . . Extinguishments of Debt," required extraordinary item classification for material gains or losses on extinguishment of debt, despite the absence of the two specified criteria, because of enterprise management's ability to determine the amount and times of such gains and losses.

Given that management of a parent company is able to determine the timing—if not the amount—of nonoperating gains or losses resulting from a subsidiary's issuance of additional shares of common stock to the public or the parent, with minority stockholders waiving their preemptive right, should extraordinary item treatment be accorded to such gains and losses if material? Explain.

SOLUTIONS TO QUESTIONS, SHORT EXERCISES, AND CASE: CHAPTER 10

QUESTIONS

True or False

1. T   2. T   3. F   4. T   5. T   6. T   7. F   8. T   9. T   10. F   11. F   12. F   13. T

Completion Statements

1. Purchase.   2. Specific identification.   3. Nonoperating gain.   4. Call price, minority interest.
5. Retired.   6. Reciprocal shareholding.

Multiple Choice

1. c   2. d (700 x $2.25 = $1,575)   3. d {[($2,000 + $10,000 + $150,000 + $200,250) – (1,000 x $2.25)] x
0.15 = $54,000}   4. d (reduction of subsidiary's stockholders' equity) 5. d (no entry) 6. c   7. c   8. a

SHORT EXERCISES

1. a.

Set Company
Adjusting Entry
December 31, 2005

	Intercompany Investment Income (Loss) ($20,000 x 0.60)	12,000	
	Investment in Syn Company Common Stock		12,000
	To record 60% of Syn Company's $20,000 net loss for period		
	Apr. 1 – Dec. 31, 2005.		

Pat Corporation
Adjusting Entries
December 31, 2005

	Intercompany Investment Income (Loss) ($20,000 x 0.30)	6,000	
	Investment in Syn Company Common Stock		6,000
	To record 30% of Syn Company's $20,000 net loss for period		
	Apr. 1 – Dec. 31, 2005.		
	Investment in Set Company Common Stock	60,400	
	Intercompany Investment Income (Loss)		60,400
	To adjust investment in Set Company to equity method of		
	accounting as follows (disregarding income taxes):		
	$30,000 (Set net income for Jan. 2–Mar. 31, 2005,		
	no goodwill) x .0.60 $18,000		
	($70,000 – $12,000) (Set net income for		
	Apr. 1–Dec. 31,2005, adjusted for Set's		
	share of Syn's net loss) x 0.80 46,400		
	Dividend from Set on Dec. 20, 2005 ($5,000 x 0.80) (4,000)		
	Net increase in Investment account $60,400		

b.

Pat Corporation and Subsidiaries
Consolidated Balance Sheet
December 31, 2005

Assets		Liabilities & Stockholders' Equity	
Various assets	$636,000	Liabilities	$256,000
Goodwill	4,000	Minority interest in net assets of subsidiaries	35,600
		Common stock, no par or stated value	234,000
		Retained earnings	114,400
		Total liabilities & stockholders'	
Total assets	$640,000	equity	$640,000

Computation of goodwill:

Acquisition of Set common stock, Apr. 1, 2005 ($26,000 – $22,000)	$ 4,000
Impairment loss	-0-
Goodwill, Dec. 31, 2005	$ 4,000

Computation of minority interest in net assets of subsidiaries:

In Set Company [($175,000 – $12,000) x 0.20]	$ 32,600
In Syn Company ($30,000 x 0.10)	3,000
Minority interest in net assets of subsidiaries, Dec. 31, 2005	$ 35,600

Computation of consolidated retained earnings:

Pat retained earnings, Dec. 31, 2005, prior to adjustment	$ 60,000
Total adjustments to Pat's retained earnings through intercompany investment income (loss)	54,400
Consolidated retained earnings, Dec. 31, 2005 (same as Pat's adjusted retained earnings)	$114,400

2.

Passaic Corporation and Subsidiary
Working Paper Eliminations
May 31, 2006

Common Stock—Seaview (2,000 x $1)	2,000	
Additional Paid-in Capital—Seaview (2,000 x $8)	16,000	
Retained Earnings—Seaview (2,000 x $2)	4,000	
Treasury Stock		22,000
To account for subsidiary's treasury stock as though it had been retired.		
Treasury Stock—Passaic	100,000	
Investment in Passaic Corporation Common		
Stock—Seaview		100,000
To transfer subsidiary's investment in parent company's common stock to treasury stock.		
Intercompany Dividend Revenue—Seaview (5,000 x $1.20)	6,000	
Dividends Declared—Passaic		6,000
To eliminate parent company dividends received by subsidiary.		

3.

Packy Corporation and Subsidiary
Working Paper Elimination
January 2, 2006

Common Stock—Stamper	50,000	
Additional Paid-in Capital—Stamper	60,000	
Retained Earnings—Stamper ($70,000 – $63,000)	7,000	
Retained Earnings of Subsidiary—Packy	63,000	
Goodwill—Packy [$26,000 – ($180,000 x 0.10)]	8,000	
Investment in Stamper Company Common Stock—Packy		
($162,000 + $26,000)		188,000
To eliminate intercompany investment and equity accounts of		
subsidiary; to exclude from consolidated retained earnings the		
amount attributable to former minority stockholders of		
subsidiary; and to provide for goodwill attributable to acquisition		
of minority interest in net assets subsidiary. (Income tax effect		
are disregarded.)		

CASE

Given the infrequency and unusual nature of a subsidiary's issuance of additional shares of common stock to the public or to the parent company, extraordinary item treatment for such gains or losses may be appropriate. A gain or loss from a subsidiary's issuance of common stock may be initiated by the subsidiary (at the parent company's behest) in a public offering of the stock, or by the parent company if the subsidiary issues the stock to the parent, rather than by independent entities.

CHAPTER 11
INTERNATIONAL ACCOUNTING STANDARDS; ACCOUNTING FOR FOREIGN CURRENCY TRANSACTIONS

HIGHLIGHTS OF THE CHAPTER

1. Recent political and economic events have focused on the pressing need for more uniformity in international accounting standards. Two organizations in the forefront of attempts to achieve such uniformity are the International Accounting Standards Board (IASB) and the Financial Accounting Standards Board (FASB).

2. Currently, the International Accounting Standard Committee, parent of the 17-member IASB, headquartered in London, has a membership of accounting organizations of over 100 countries. The American Institute of Certified Public Accountants is the U.S. member of the IASC. International Accounting Standards issued by the IASB have no authoritative support unless they are adopted by the standard-setting organizations of IASB members' countries.

3. Through 2000, the IASB had issued about 40 **International Accounting Standards (IAS**s) (now incorporated in **International Financial Reporting Standards**) dealing with a number of topics. In 1993, the IASB revised 11 of its IASs to establish **benchmark** (preferred) accounting treatments with permissible alternatives. Several **IAS**s have dealt with topics in other chapters of the textbook; the standards in those pronouncements differ somewhat from U.S. generally accepted accounting principles.

4. In 2002, the FASB joined with the IASB in a **convergence project**, the goal of which was to compare the two Boards' existing standards and conform the two sets of standards into the highest quality solution.

5. In most countries of the world, the currencies of other countries are bought and sold as **commodities** or **money-market instruments.** The buying and selling of foreign currencies results in variations in **exchange rates** between the currencies of two countries. **Spot rates** apply to current exchanges of money; **forward rates** apply to foreign currency transactions to be completed on a future date.

6. **FASB Statement No. 52,** "Foreign Currency Translation," and **FASB Statement No. 133,** "Accounting for Derivative Instruments and Hedging Activities," established accounting standards for transactions involving foreign currencies. These standards are incorporated in the discussion and illustrations in Chapter 11 of the textbook.

7. **Multinational enterprises** are business enterprises that carry on operations in more than one nation, through a network of branches, divisions, or subsidiaries. Multinational enterprises obtain raw material and capital in countries where such resources are plentiful, manufacture products where wages and other operating costs are lowest, and sell the products in countries that provide the most profitable markets.

8. Merchandise or loan transactions between a U.S. multinational enterprise and a foreign supplier, customer, or lender generally require journal entries for **foreign currency transactions gains** or **losses,** which result from the variations in exchange rates for foreign currencies. For example, if a U.S. enterprise purchased merchandise on May 1, 2005, from a South Korean supplier for 1 million won (₩), on a date when the selling spot rate was ₩1 = $0.0014, and acquired a ₩1 million draft for transmittal to the South Korean supplier on May 31, 2005, when the selling spot rate was ₩1 = $0.0015, there would be a $100 **foreign currency transaction loss.** The $100 loss is the difference between the $1,500 required to acquire the ₩1 million draft on May 31, 2005, and the $1,400 trade account payable to the South Korean supplier recognized on May 1, 2005.

These amounts are recorded by the U.S. enterprise as follows:

2005

May 1	Inventories	1,400	
	Trade Accounts Payable		1,400
	To record purchase from South Korean supplier for ₩1 million, translated at selling spot rate of ₩1 = $0.0014.		

May 31	Trade Accounts Payable	1,400	
	Foreign Currency Transaction Losses	100	
	Cash		1,500
	To record payment for ₩1 million draft to settle liability to South Korea supplier and recognition of foreign currency transaction loss.		

9. The journal entries in paragraph **8** illustrate the **two-transaction perspective** for foreign currency transaction gains and losses. Under this concept, the purchase of merchandise from a foreign supplier is considered to be a separate and distinct transaction from the settlement of the liability to the foreign supplier. An opposing view, known as the **one-transaction perspective**, is that a foreign currency transaction gain or loss should be applied to correct the cost of merchandise purchased from the foreign supplier. The one-transaction perspective was rejected by the Financial Accounting Standards Board.

10. A U.S. multinational enterprise's sale of merchandise to a foreign customer, with payment to be received in the local currency of the customer, requires restatement of the local currency amount of the sale to U.S. dollars at the buying spot rate in effect on the date of sale. For example, if a U.S. enterprise sold merchandise costing $30,000 to a Greek customer for 10 million Greek drachmas (Drs), with the buying spot rate for the drachma $0.004648, the U.S. enterprise would debit Trade Accounts Receivable $46,480 (Drs10,000,000 x $0.004648 = $46,480) and credit Sales for the same amount. If the buying spot rate for the drachma increased by the date that the U.S. enterprise received Drs10 million from the Greek customer, the U.S. enterprise would realize a foreign currency transaction gain; a decrease in the buying spot rate for the drachma would produce a foreign currency transaction loss.

11. The purchase and sale transactions illustrated in paragraphs **8** and **10** demonstrate that **increases** in the selling spot rate between the dates of initiating and paying for a purchase denominated in a foreign currency generate foreign currency transaction **losses; decreases** in the selling spot rate produce foreign currency transaction **gains.** Conversely, **increases** in the buying spot rate between the dates of initiating and receiving payment for a sale denominated in a foreign currency result in foreign currency transaction **gains; decreases** in the buying spot rate create foreign currency transaction **losses.**

12. If financial statements are prepared between the dates of a foreign currency–denominated transaction and the payment of cash to settle the transaction, a U.S. multinational enterprise's payables (or receivables) are adjusted to reflect the end-of-period exchange rate. The resultant **unrealized** foreign currency transaction gain or loss is accounted for in the same manner as the **realized** foreign currency transaction loss illustrated in paragraph **8.** Both realized and unrealized foreign currency transaction gains and losses are included in the measurement of net income for the accounting period in which the transaction gains and losses are recognized. Foreign currency transaction gains and losses are not extraordinary items.

13. A multinational enterprise may **hedge** its exposure to exchange rate fluctuations by acquiring or selling **forward contracts.** For example, a U.S. enterprise that has a liability payable in British pounds would acquire a forward contract for an appropriate number of British pounds to minimize the risk of having to use more dollars in the future to acquire British pounds.

14. In **FASB Statement No. 133,** the FASB established different accounting procedures for forward contracts, which are **derivative instruments.** Two of the five classes of forward contracts identified by the FASB are discussed and illustrated in Chapter 11 of the textbook; a third type is mentioned in Chapter 12 thereof.

15. **IAS 21,** "Accounting for the Effects of Changes in Foreign Exchange Rates," has provisions essentially the same as those of **FASB Statement No. 52,** except for the lack of coverage of forward contracts. **IAS 39,** "Financial Instruments: . . . ," deals with such contracts.

16. Both the FASB and the SEC require numerous quantitative and qualitative disclosures of foreign currency transaction gains and losses and forward contracts, as well as all other derivative instruments.

QUESTIONS

True or False

For each of the following statements, circle the **T** or the **F** to indicate whether the statement is true or false.

T   F   1. The International Accounting Standards Board attempts to solicit general acceptance of international accounting standards that it adopts.

T   F   2. **Spot rates** are applicable to current exchanges of one currency for another.

T   F   3. A U.S. multinational enterprise pays the foreign currency trader's buying spot rate for a desired amount of foreign currency.

T   F   4. If a U.S. multinational enterprise needed HK$250,000 (Hong Kong dollars), and the spot exchange rates were: buying—HK$1 = $0.1725; selling—HK$1 = $0.1728, the U.S. enterprise would pay $43,125 for a draft denominated in HK$250,000.

T   F   5. Foreign currency transaction gains and losses result from commercial bargaining between business enterprises in different countries.

T   F   6. A U.S. multinational enterprise may hedge the risk of fluctuations in exchange rates by acquiring or selling a forward contract for the desired amount of foreign currency.

T   F   7. A foreign currency transaction gain or loss is included in the measurement of income before extraordinary items.

T   F   8. Supporters of the one-transaction perspective approach for accounting for foreign currency transaction gains and losses emphasize the cash payment aspects of a foreign currency transaction.

T   F   9. The IASC has established internationally accepted standards for trading of securities on international exchanges.

T   F   10. The provisions of **IAS 21,** "Accounting for the Effects of Changes in Foreign Exchange Rates" are identical to those of **FASB Statement No. 52,** "Foreign Currency Translation."

Completion Statements

Fill in the necessary words or amounts to complete the following statements.

1. In most countries of the world, a foreign country's currency is treated as though it were a
   _____ - _____ _____ or a
   _____.

2. Exchange rates that apply to foreign currency transactions to be consummated in the future are
   termed _____ _____.

3. If the buying spot rate and selling spot rate for the Malaysian dollar (M$) are M$1 = $0.4300 and
   M$1 = $0.4305, respectively, a U.S. multinational enterprise would receive
   $_____ from a foreign currency dealer in exchange for a M$300,000 draft
   received from a Malaysian customer.

4. Supporters of the two-transaction perspective for accounting for foreign currency transaction
   gains and losses argue that an importer's assumption of the risk of exchange rate fluctuations is a
   _____ decision, not a _____ decision.

5. Investments in forward contracts are _____ _____.

6. If the buying spot rate increases between the time of a sale of merchandise denominated in a
   foreign currency and the receipt of the foreign currency, the seller realizes a foreign currency
   transaction _____.

Multiple Choice

Choose the best answer for each of the following questions and enter the identifying letter in the space
provided.

____ 1. International Accounting Standards are:
   a. Issued by the IASB
   b. Binding on members of the International Monetary Fund
   c. Adopted by the SEC
   d. Adopted by the FASB

____ 2. A U.S. multinational enterprise realizes a foreign currency transaction gain on a purchase
   from a foreign supplier denominated in the foreign currency if, between the dates of purchase
   and payment, the:
   a. Selling spot rate for the foreign currency increases
   b. Buying spot rate for the foreign currency increases
   c. Selling spot rate for the foreign currency decreases
   d. Buying spot rate for the foreign currency decreases

____ 3. **IAS 21,** "Accounting for the Effects of Changes in Foreign Exchange Rates," does not
   address forward contracts:
   a. Not designated as a hedge
   b. Designated as a hedge of a firm commitment
   c. Designated as a hedge of a net investment
   d. Of any type

____ 4. On July 1, 2005, Occidental Corporation purchased merchandise on 30-day open account
   from a New Zealand supplier at an invoice cost of 100,000 New Zealand dollars (NZ$). On
   that date, spot exchange rates were: buying—NZ$1 = $0.777; selling—NZ$1 = $0.7785. On

July 31, 2005, Occidental acquired a draft for NZ$100,000 for $77,600. In the journal entry to record the acquisition of the NZ$100,00 draft, Occidental recognizes a foreign currency:
a. Transaction loss of $100
b. Transaction loss of $250
c. Transaction gain of $250
d. Transaction gain of $23,400

____ 5. Watt Company, a U.S. multinational enterprise, purchased goods from Kluger Company of Germany on March 1, 2005, for 30,000 euros (€) when the selling spot rate was €1 = $1.0895. Watt's fiscal year-end was March 31, 2005, when the selling spot rate was €1 = $1.0845. Watt acquired €30,000 and paid the invoice on April 20, 2005, when the selling spot rate was €1 = $1.0945. What amounts are displayed in Watt's income statements as foreign currency transaction gains or losses for the years ended March 31, 2005, and 2006?

	2005	2006
a.	$0	$0
b.	$0	$150 loss
c.	$150 loss	$0
d.	$150 gain	$300 loss

SHORT EXERCISES

1. On May 17, 2005, Canton Corporation, a U.S. multinational enterprise, purchased merchandise from a Taiwan supplier on 30-day open account for 400,000 Taiwan dollars (NT$). On May 25, 2005, Canton sold all the Taiwanese merchandise to a Colombia customer on 30-day open account for 952,000 Colombian pesos (Col$). Canton prepares interim financial statements monthly. Relevant spot exchange rates are shown below:

Date	Currency	Spot Exchange Rates	
		Buying	**Selling**
May 17, 2005	NT$1	$0.024	$0.029
May 25, 2005	Col$1	0.015	0.016
May 31, 2005	NT$1	0.023	0.028
May 31, 2005	Col$1	0.016	0.017

In the space below, prepare journal entries for Canton Corporation to reflect the foregoing data. Canton uses the perpetual inventory system.

Canton Company
Journal Entries

2005			
May 17			
25			
25			
31			
31			

2. On July 1, 2005, Trans-Pac Corporation acquired a 60-day forward contract for 1 million Japanese yen (¥1,000,000) at the forward rate of ¥1 = $0.0083, which was $0.0003 in excess of the selling spot rate for yen on that date. The contract was not designated as a hedge. On July 31, 2005, when Trans-Pac prepared monthly financial statements, the appropriate forward rate was ¥ = $0.0081. On August 30, 2005, when the forward rate was ¥ = $0.0079, Trans-Pac paid for the contract and received the yen. The interest rate is 6%.

In the space below, prepare journal entries for Trans-Pac Corporation on July 1 and 31 and August 30, 2005.

Trans-Pac Corporation
Journal Entries

2005			
July 1			
31			
Aug. 30			

CASE

FASB Statement No. 52, "Foreign Currency Translation," requires both realized and unrealized foreign currency transaction gains and losses to be included in the measurement of net income of a multinational enterprise for the accounting period in which the transaction gains and losses were recognized.

What is your opinion of this requirement? Explain.

SOLUTIONS TO QUESTIONS, SHORT EXERCISES, AND CASE: CHAPTER 11

QUESTIONS

True or False

1. T 2. T 3. F 4. F 5. F 6. T 7. T 8. T 9. F 10. F

Completion Statements

1. Money-market instrument, commodity. 2. Forward rates. 3. $129,000 (M$300,000 x $0.43 = $129,000). 4. Financial-type, merchandising. 5. Derivative instruments. 6. Gain.

Multiple Choice

1. a 2. c 3. d 4. c ($77,850 – $77,600 = $250} 5. d [€30,000 x ($1.0895 – $1.0845) = $150; €30,000 x ($1.0845 – $1.0945) = $300]

SHORT EXERCISES

1.
Canton Company
Journal Entries

2005			
May 17	Inventories (NT$400,000 x $0.029)	11,600	
	Trade Accounts Payable		11,600
	To record purchase from Taiwanese supplier for NT$4,000,000,		
	translated at selling spot rate of NT$1 = $0.029.		
25	Trade Accounts Receivable (Col$952,000 x $0.015)	14,280	
	Sales		14,280
	To record sale of Taiwanese merchandise to Colombian customer		
	for Col$952,000, translated at buying spot rate of Col$1 =		
	$0.015.		
25	Cost of Goods Sold	11,600	
	Inventories		11,600
	To record cost of Taiwanese merchandise sold to Colombian		
	customer.		
31	Trade Accounts Payable ($11,600 – $11,200)	400	
	Foreign Currency Transaction Gains		400
	To record foreign currency transaction gain applicable to May		
	17 purchase from Taiwanese supplier. Account payable		
	translated at NT$1 = $0.028.		
31	Trade Accounts Receivable ($15,232 – $14,280)	952	
	Foreign Currency Transaction Gains		952
	To record foreign currency transaction gain applicable to May		
	25 sale to Colombian customer. Account receivable translated at		
	Col$1 = $0.016.		

2.

Trans-Pac Corporation
Journal Entries

2005			
July 1	Investment in Forward Contract (¥1,000,000 x $0.0083)	8,300	
	Forward Contract Payable		8,300
	To record forward contract for ¥1,000,000, at forward rate of ¥1		
	= $0.0083.		
31	Foreign Currency Transaction Losses	199	
	Investment in Forward Contract		199
	To recognize fair value of forward contract investment and		
	resultant transaction loss [¥1,000,000 x ($0.0083 – $0.0081) –		
	($200 x 0.06 x 30/360) = $199].		
Aug. 30	Investment in Yen (¥1,000,000 x $0.0079)	7,900	
	Forward Contract Payable	8,300	
	Foreign Currency Transaction Losses	201	
	Cash		8,300
	Investment in Forward Contract ($8,300 – $199)		8,101
	To recognize settlement of forward contract, fair value of		
	investment in yen, and transaction loss as follows:		
	Carrying amount of contract July 31 $8,101		
	Fair value of contract Aug. 30 7,900		
	Transaction loss $ 201		

CASE

On the surface, it appears that the inclusion of unrealized foreign currency transaction gains in the measurement of net income for the accounting period in which the gains were recognized is inconsistent with lower-of-cost-or-market (LCM) accounting for inventories. In LCM accounting, unrealized losses, but no unrealized gains, are included in the measurement of net income in the periods in which they are recognized. However, inventories are longer-lived than are trade accounts receivable and trade accounts payable denominated in a foreign currency. For that reason, inclusion of unrealized foreign currency transaction gains on such receivables and payables in the measurement of net income of the period of their recognition may be a unique version of the "mark-to-market" accounting used for trading and available-for-sale securities investments. (There is considerable support among accountants for current fair value accounting for all nonmonetary assets.) Further, investments in forward contracts, which generate unrealized foreign currency transaction gains in certain circumstances, although having specified maturity dates, are also unlike inventories. In summary, the unique characteristics of trade accounts receivable and payable denominated in a foreign currency and of forward contracts warrant specialized accounting for foreign currency transaction gains and losses, as set forth in **FASB Statement No. 52,** "Foreign Currency Translation," and **FASB Statement No. 133,** "Accounting for Derivative Instruments and Hedging Activities."

CHAPTER 12
TRANSLATION OF FOREIGN CURRENCY
FINANCIAL STATEMENTS

HIGHLIGHTS OF CHAPTER

1. U.S. multinational enterprises must **translate** to the U.S. dollar the financial statements of their foreign divisions, branches, subsidiaries, or other investees that are denominated in foreign **functional currencies.** Translation of foreign investees' financial statements is a problem because of fluctuations in exchange rates between the dollar and other currencies.

2. An entity's **functional currency** is the currency of the primary economic environment in which the entity operates; generally, that is the currency of the environment in which an entity primarily generates and expends cash.

3. The functional currency of an entity with operations that are relatively self-contained and integrated within a country generally is the currency of that country. However, the U.S. dollar may be the functional currency of a foreign branch of a U.S. multinational enterprise if the branch's operations are an extension of the home office's operations. **FASB Statement No. 52,** "Foreign Currency Translation," provided several guidelines for the determination of an entity's functional currency.

4. Three methods of foreign currency translation have been developed—the **current/noncurrent method,** the **monetary/nonmonetary method,** and the **current rate method.** (A fourth method, the **temporal method,** essentially is the same as the monetary/nonmonetary method.) The three methods differ principally in translation techniques for balance sheet amounts.

5. In the **current/noncurrent method** of foreign currency translation, current assets and current liabilities of the foreign investee are translated at the **current** exchange rate in effect on the balance sheet date. All other assets and liability accounts, and the owners' equity accounts, are translated at **historical** rates in effect when the items originally were recognized in the accounting records. In the income statement, depreciation and amortization expense are translated at historical rates applicable to the related assets, and all other expense and revenue items are translated at an **average** exchange rate for the accounting period.

6. Although proponents of the current/noncurrent method claim that it best reflects **liquidity** aspects of a foreign investee's financial position, critics point out that with respect to inventories, the current/noncurrent method represents a departure from historical cost, because it requires the translation of inventories at the **current** rate rather than at historical rates.

7. In the **monetary/nonmonetary method** of foreign currency translation, monetary assets and liabilities are translated at the current exchange rate. (Monetary assets and liabilities are claims or obligations expressed in a fixed monetary amount.) All other assets, liabilities, and owners' equity items are translated at appropriate historical rates. In the income statement, depreciation and amortization expense and cost of goods sold are translated at appropriate historical rates; all other revenue and expense items are translated at average exchange rates for the accounting period.

8. The **current rate method** of foreign currency translation was proposed by critics of the monetary/nonmonetary method, who claimed the latter method incorrectly stressed the **parent company** aspects of a foreign investee's financial position and operating results. In the current rate method, all balance sheet items other than owners' equity are translated at the current exchange rate. Owners' equity items are translated at historical rates. Revenue and expenses are translated at the current exchange rate if practicable; otherwise, an average rate for the accounting period is used.

9. **FASB Statement No. 52,** "Foreign Currency Translation," adopted the current rate method for **translating** a foreign entity's financial statements from the entity's **functional currency** to the **reporting currency** of the parent company (the U.S. dollar for a U.S. multinational enterprise). Account balances must be **remeasured** to the foreign entity's functional currency if the accounting records are not maintained in the functional currency. **Remeasurement** essentially is accomplished by the **monetary/nonmonetary method** described in paragraph **7.** If a foreign entity's functional currency is the U.S. dollar, **remeasurement** eliminates the need for **translation.**

10. In the **remeasurement** of the trial balance of a foreign division or branch, or the financial statements of a foreign subsidiary or other investee, to its U.S. dollar functional currency, the amounts in foreign currency are multiplied by the appropriate exchange rate to obtain the amounts in U.S. dollars. A debit balance (loss) or credit balance (gain) **foreign currency transaction gain or loss** is computed to balance the remeasured trial balance or financial statements. This foreign currency transaction gain or loss enters into the measurement of combined or consolidated net income. Home office or intercompany accounts may be "remeasured" by substitution of the balance in U.S. dollars of the reciprocal account in the multinational company's accounting records.

11. In the **translation** of the trial balance of a foreign division or branch, or the financial statements of a foreign subsidiary or other investee, from a foreign functional currency to U.S. dollars, the amounts in foreign currency are multiplied by the appropriate current exchange rate to obtain the amounts in U.S. dollars. Debit balance or credit balance **foreign currency translation adjustments** are computed to balance the translated trial balance or financial statements. Foreign currency translation adjustments are displayed in the statement of comprehensive income.

12. Other matters covered in **FASB Statement No. 52** include certain foreign currency transaction gains and losses excluded from net income, functional currency in highly inflationary economies, income taxes related to foreign currency translation, and disclosure of foreign currency translation.

13. **FASB Statement No. 52** has been criticized for a number of reasons, especially for its alleged establishment of an indefensible distinction between **foreign currency transaction gains and losses** and **foreign currency translation adjustments.**

QUESTIONS

True or False

For each of the following statements, circle the **T** or the **F** to indicate whether the statement is true or false.

T F 1. The current/noncurrent method of foreign currency translation is consistent with the historical cost valuation principle.

T F 2. In the monetary/nonmonetary method of foreign currency translation, cost of goods sold is translated at an average exchange rate for the accounting period.

T F 3. The current rate method of foreign currency translation emphasizes the local currency aspects of the foreign investee's operations.

T F 4. The Foreign Currency Transaction Gains and Losses ledger account balance is used to balance the translated trial balance or financial statements of a foreign investee of a U.S. multinational enterprise.

T F 5. The current/noncurrent method is used in the translation of foreign currency financial statements to the reporting currency from the functional currency.

T F 6. The functional currency of a foreign entity in a highly inflationary economy is the reporting currency of the U.S. parent, home office, or investor enterprise.

T F 7. Foreign currency translation adjustments are displayed in the stockholders' equity section of a translated balance sheet.

T F 8. **FASB Statement No. 52,** "Foreign Currency Translation," requires the use of the current rate method for both remeasurement and translation of foreign currency financial statements.

Completion Statements

Fill in the necessary words or amounts to complete the following statements.

1. Foreign currency financial statements of a subsidiary of a U.S. multinational enterprise must be _____ from the foreign currency to the U.S. dollar functional currency.

2. In the current/noncurrent method of foreign currency translation, inventories are translated at the _____ rate, and in the monetary/nonmonetary method of translation, inventories are translated at the _____ rate.

3. **FASB Statement No. 52,** "Foreign Currency Translation," requires disclosure of

    _____ _____ _____
    for an accounting period.

4. In remeasurement, inventories are restated at the _____ rate; in translation, inventories are restated at the _____ rate.

5. An excess of credit balance amounts over debit balance amounts in a remeasured trial balance of a foreign entity produces a balancing foreign currency transaction _____.

6. A highly inflationary economy is one having a cumulative inflation of 100% over a _____ year period.

Multiple Choice

Choose the best answer for each of the following questions and enter the identifying letter in the space provided.

_____ 1. If a parent company bills all sales to a foreign subsidiary in U.S. dollars and is to be paid in U.S. dollars, the balance of the Intercompany Purchases ledger account in the subsidiary's income statement is remeasured to U.S. dollars, the functional currency, by the use of the:
   a. Average exchange rate for the accounting period
   b. Exchange rate at the beginning of the period
   c. Exchange rate at the end of the period
   d. Balance of the parent company's Intercompany Sales ledger account for sales to the foreign subsidiary

_____ 2.   Erie Corporation acquired with U.S. dollars all the outstanding common stock of Manitoba Company, a Canadian corporation whose functional currency is the U.S. dollar. On the date of the business combination, a portion of the balance of Erie's Investment in Manitoba Company Common Stock ledger account was allocable to goodwill. One year later, after an exchange rate decrease between the U.S. dollar and the Canadian dollar, the unimpaired goodwill is carried in the consolidated balance sheet of Erie Corporation and subsidiary at:
a.   An increased amount
b.   The same amount
c.   A lesser amount
d.   An increased or a lesser amount, depending on management's policy

_____ 3.   The current/noncurrent and monetary/nonmonetary methods of foreign currency translation differ principally in the translation of:
a.   Sales and cost of goods sold
b.   Depreciation expense and cost of goods sold
c.   Inventories and cost of goods sold
d.   Amortization expense and cost of goods sold

_____ 4.   Which of the following statements about the current rate method of foreign currency translation is correct?
a.   It is generally accepted in the United States.
b.   It emphasizes the reporting currency aspects of a foreign investee's operations.
c.   It requires use of the current exchange rate for translating all financial statement amounts of the foreign investee.
d.   None of the foregoing

_____ 5.   Delnora Company owns a foreign subsidiary with 3,600,000 local currency units (LCU) of plant assets before accumulated depreciation on December 31, 2005. Of this amount, LCU2,400,000 were acquired in 2003, when the exchange rate was LCU1.6 to $1, and LCU1,200,000 were acquired in 2004, when the exchange rate was LCU1.8 to $1. The exchange rate in effect on December 31, 2005, was LCU2 to $1. The weighted average of exchange rates that were in effect during 2005 was LCU1.92 to $1. Assuming that the plant assets are depreciated by the straight-line method over a 10-year economic life with no residual value, how much depreciation expense relating to the foreign subsidiary's plant assets is reported in Delnora's income statement for 2005 if the U.S. dollar is the functional currency of the subsidiary?
a. $180,000
b. $187,500
c. $200,000
d. $216,667
e.   Some other amount

6. Jemco, Inc., used the current rate method for translating foreign currency amounts on December 31, 2005. On that date, Jemco had foreign subsidiaries with 1,500,000 local currency units (LCU) in long-term receivables and LCU2,400,000 in long-term debt. The exchange rate in effect when the specific transactions occurred involving those foreign currency amounts was LCU2 to $1. The exchange rate in effect on December 31, 2005, was LCU1.5 to $1. The translation of the foregoing foreign currency amounts to U.S. dollars on December 31, 2005, results in long-term receivables and long-term debt, respectively of:
   a. $750,000 and $1,200,000
   b. $750,000 and $1,600,000
   c. $1,000,000 and $1,200,000
   d. $1,000,000 and $1,600,000
   e. Some other amounts

7. How are foreign currency translation adjustments resulting from translating foreign currency financial statements to U.S. dollars currently reported?
   a. Displayed as an ordinary item in the income statement for the accounting period in which the exchange rate changes
   b. Displayed as an extraordinary item in the income statement for the period in which the exchange rate changes
   c. Displayed in the stockholders' equity section of the balance sheet
   d. Displayed as an ordinary item in the income statement for losses, but deferred in the balance sheet for gains
   e. Displayed in none of the foregoing ways

8. In the remeasurement of the trial balance of a foreign branch to its U.S. dollars functional currency, the average exchange rate for the accounting period is applied to the balance of which ledger account?
   a. Sales
   b. Notes Payable
   c. Home Office
   d. Accumulated Depreciation

SHORT EXERCISES

1. In the table below, indicate by placing a check mark in the appropriate column the exchange rate or other amount that is used in the remeasurement of the following financial statement items of a foreign investee to its U.S. dollar functional currency:

Financial statement item	Current rate	Historical rate	Average rate	Other amount
a. Intercompany receivables				
b. Inventories				
c. Additional paid-in capital				
d. Rent revenue				
e. Plant assets				
f. Notes receivable				
g. Salaries payable				
h. Salaries expense				
i. Cost of goods sold				
j. Intercompany sales				
k. Depreciation expense				

2. On April 1, 2005, Morales Corporation, a U.S. multinational enterprise, established a branch in Costa Guinea and shipped to it at a billed price of $220,632 a two month's supply of merchandise. On April 30, 2005, the branch provided Morales with the following trial balance in the local currency unit (LCU), the currency of Costa Guinea:

Morales Corporation
Costa Guinea Branch
Trial Balance
April 30, 2005

	Debit	Credit
Cash	LCU 108,000	
Trade accounts receivable	563,000	
Inventories	318,000	
Home office		LCU 992,000
Sales		844,000
Cost of goods sold	633,000	
Operating expenses	214,000	
Totals	LCU1,836,000	LCU1,836,000

Relevant exchange rates were as follows:

	LCU1 =
April 1, 2005	$0.232
April 30, 2005	0.238

The U.S. dollar is the functional currency of the Costa Guinea Branch. The April 30, 2005, balance of the Investment in Costa Guinea Branch ledger account in the accounting records of Morales Corporation's home office was $232,000.

In the working paper below, remeasure the trial balance of Morales Corporation's Costa Guinea Branch to U.S. dollars.

Morales Corporation
Costa Guinea Branch
Remeasured Trial Balance
April 30, 2005

	Balance (local currency units) dr (cr)	Exchange rates	Balance (U.S. dollars) dr (cr)
Cash	LCU 108,000	$	$
Trade accounts receivable	563,000		
Inventories	318,000		
Home Office	(992,000)		
Sales	(844,000)		
Cost of goods sold	633,000		
Operating expenses	214,000		
Subtotals	LCU -0-		$
Foreign currency transaction (gain) loss			
Totals	LCU -0-		$

CASE

In a classroom discussion of standards for translating foreign currency financial statements to the reporting currency (U.S. dollar) from the foreign functional currency, student Kristen suggested that the foreign currency translation adjustments could have been avoided had the FASB sanctioned use of the end-of-period exchange rate for translating **all** financial statement amounts.

What is your opinion of student Kristen's suggestion? Explain.

SOLUTIONS TO QUESTIONS, SHORT EXERCISES, AND CASE: CHAPTER 12

QUESTIONS

True or False

1. F   2. F   3. T   4. F   5. F   6. T   7. F   8. F

Completion Statements

1. Remeasured.   2. Current, historical.   3. Foreign currency translation adjustments. 4. Historical, current.   5. Loss.   6. Three.

Multiple Choice

1. d   2. b   3. c   4. a   5. d [($240,000 ÷ 1.6) + ($120,000 ÷ 1.8) = $216,667]   6. d   7. e   8. a

SHORT EXERCISES

1.

Financial statement item	Current rate	Historical rate	Average rate	Other amoun
a. Intercompany receivables				√
b. Inventories		√		
c. Additional paid-in capital		√		
d. Rent revenue			√	
e. Plant assets		√		
f. Notes receivable	√			
g. Salaries payable	√			
h. Salaries expense			√	
i. Cost of goods sold		√		
j. Intercompany sales				√
k. Depreciation expense		√		

2.

Morales Corporation
Costa Guinea Branch
Remeasured Trial Balance
April 30, 2005

	Balance (local currency units) dr (cr)	Exchange rates	Balance (U.S dollars) dr (cı
Cash	LCU 108,000	$0.238	$ 25,704
Trade accounts receivable	563,000	0.238	133,994
Inventories	318,000	0.232	73,776
Home Office	(992,000)	Reciprocal Balance	(232,000)
Sales	(844,000)	0.235*	(198,340)
Cost of goods sold	633,000	0.232	146,856
Operating expenses	214,000	0.235*	50,290
Subtotals	LCU -0-		$280
Foreign currency transaction (gain) loss			$ (280)
Totals	LCU -0-		$ -0-

*($0.232 + $0.238) ÷ 2 = $0.235.

CASE

Although attractive in that it would dispose of the theoretically questionable foreign currency translation adjustments, student Kristen's suggestion is impractical. In **FASB Statement No. 52,** "Foreign Currency Translation," the Financial Accounting Standards Board sanctioned the current rate method for translating foreign currency financial statements to the reporting currency from the functional currency so that the latter currency's aspects of the foreign entity's operations would be emphasized. To use the end-of-period current rate to translate income statement amounts and stockholders' equity amounts would distort the functional currency relationships in those areas, which are affected by transactions and events throughout the accounting period, the reporting basis for both income statements and statements of stockholders' equity. In contrast, the end-of-period current rate is appropriate for translating assets and liabilities, which are valued at end-of-period amounts in the balance sheet.

CHAPTER 13
REPORTING FOR COMPONENTS; INTERIM REPORTS; REPORTING FOR THE SEC

HIGHLIGHTS OF CHAPTER

1. According to the FASB, a **component of an entity** comprises operations and cash flows that can be clearly distinguished operationally and for financial reporting purposes.

2. The concept of disaggregated disclosure regarding business components dates back more than 40 years, and is opposed to the philosophy that consolidated financial statements rather than separate ones fairly present the financial position and operations of an economic entity, regardless of its legal or business component structure.

3. In 1976, the FASB required certain information to be disclosed regarding the **industry segments**, foreign operations and export sales, and major customers of segmented business enterprises. Both maximum and minimum limitations were placed on the number of segments or foreign areas for which information was to be provided. Enterprise management was given considerable latitude in identifying segments, allocating nontraceable expenses to them, and disclosing the required information.

4. In 1997, the FASB issued **Statement No. 131,** "Disclosures About Segments . . . ," which provided different standards of disclosure for **operating segments** of a business enterprise. **Statement No. 131** gave far more latitude to enterprise management in identifying segments and measuring the quantitative information to be disclosed for them. The FASB required a **reasonable basis** for procedures for allocating nontraceable expenses to segments.

5. Methods that have been used by business enterprises to allocate nontraceable expenses to operating segments include allocation ratios based on segment revenues, payroll totals, average plant assets and inventories, or a combination thereof.

6. In **Regulation S-K,** the SEC set forth requirements for reporting segment information in filings with it.

7. In **FASB Statement No 144**, the Financial Accounting Standards Board provided standards for disclosure of the disposal of a component such as an operating segment. Income or loss from discontinued operations (net of applicable income taxes), including the gain or loss (net of taxes) from disposal of the segment, is displayed following income from continuing operations in the income statement. This amount is not an extraordinary item.

8. **Interim financial reports** are exemplified by the **quarterly reports** issued by publicly owned companies to their stockholders, the SEC, and the stock exchanges that list their securities. **APB Opinion No. 28,** "Interim Financial Reporting," provides guidelines on accounting and disclosure issues relating to interim financial reports.

9. Revenue from products sold or services rendered is recognized when realized during an interim accounting period on the same basis as followed for the full year. In addition, business enterprises having significant seasonal variations in revenue are to disclose the seasonal nature of their activities.

10. Costs and expenses associated directly with or allocated to products sold, such as material, direct labor, and factory overhead, are accounted for in interim reports as they are in fiscal year financial statements. However, four exceptions are provided in **APB Opinion No. 28** for the measurement of cost of goods sold for interim financial reports. These exceptions cover the gross margin method of estimating cost of goods sold for interim accounting periods; temporary depletion of last-in, first-out inventories layers during interim periods; interim period lower-of-cost-or-market write-downs of inventories; and standard costs variances for interim periods.

11. All costs and expenses other than those associated with revenue are either recognized as expenses in interim accounting periods when incurred, or allocated among interim periods based on an estimate of time expired, benefit received, or activity associated with the period. The procedures adopted for allocating costs and expenses to interim periods should be consistent with allocation procedures for the costs and expenses in annual financial statements. **APB Opinion No. 28** also required that expenses such as inventory shrinkage, doubtful accounts expense, and year-end bonuses be allocated to interim accounting periods in proportion to estimated annual amounts.

12. With respect to income tax provisions in interim reports, **APB Opinion No. 28** required at the end of each interim accounting period an estimate of the expected effective income tax rate for the full year. Income taxes expense for each interim period is based on the estimated effective income tax rate on a year-to-date basis. Estimated effective income tax rates should reflect anticipated foreign tax rates and available tax-planning alternatives.

13. The following items are among the minimum data required by **APB Opinion No. 28** to be reported in interim reports to stockholders: (a) sales or gross revenue, income taxes expense, extraordinary items, cumulative effect of an accounting change, and net income; (b) basic and diluted earnings per share; (c) seasonal revenue, costs, or expenses; (d) significant changes in income tax estimates or provisions; (e) contingent items; and (f) significant changes in financial position. **FASB Statement No. 141**, "Business Combinations," requires substantial disclosures regarding combinations completed in an interim period.

14. The Securities and Exchange Commission (SEC) is an agency of the United States government that oversees interstate issuances and trading of securities. The SEC administers several federal statutes, including the **Securities Act of 1933** (the 1933 Act) and the **Securities Exchange Act of 1934** (the 1934 Act). Throughout its existence, the SEC has had a significant influence on the development of generally accepted accounting principles.

15. With certain exceptions, a **registration statement** must be filed with the SEC, under the **1933 Act**, for all issuances of securities interstate to the public. The purpose of the registration statement is to provide "full and fair" disclosure of all information required by prospective investors in the securities. Although the SEC reviews the registration statement for form and content, it neither approves nor disapproves the registration statement.

16. Under the provisions of the **1934 Act**, companies whose securities are listed on national securities exchanges and many companies whose stock is traded over the counter must register the securities with the SEC and make periodic reports to it. The purpose of the registration and reporting requirements of the **1934 Act** is to keep the SEC, and thus the public, informed as to the current affairs of the reporting companies.

17. The SEC has prescribed a series of Forms (actually formats) for registration statements under the **1933 Act**. Among these are Form S-1, Form S-2, Form S-3, and Form F-1.

18. The principal form for registration of securities under the **1934 Act** is Form 10, which resembles the registration statements under the **1933 Act**. Periodic reports to the SEC by companies subject to the **1934 Act** include Form 10-K, annual report; Form 10-Q, quarterly report; and Form 8-K, current report.

19. The **1934 Act** also governs solicitation of proxies from stockholders. Under certain circumstances, a preliminary proxy statement must be filed with the SEC for review and comment before the definitive proxy statement is issued to stockholders prior to the meeting of stockholders.

20. The SEC is administered by five commissioners and has a headquarters in Washington, D.C., and 15 regional offices and branches.

21. The SEC generally has endorsed pronouncements on accounting principles issued by the FASB and its predecessors, while itself issuing periodic regulations on financial statement disclosures.

The SEC's pronouncements are issued in **Regulation S-X, Regulation S-K, Financial Reporting Releases,** and **Staff Accounting Bulletins.**

22.   **Regulation S-X** of the SEC provides guidance for the form and content of financial statements and schedules required to be filed with the SEC. **Regulation S-K** provides guidance for the completion of nonfinancial statement disclosure requirements in the Forms filed with the SEC.

23.   **Financial Reporting Releases** were initiated by the SEC staff in 1982 to state its views on financial reporting matters. Previously, the SEC's chief accountant had issued **Accounting Series Releases** on such matters.

24.   **Staff Accounting Bulletins** are issued by the SEC staff to disseminate the administrative interpretations and practices used by the SEC's staff in reviewing financial statements filed by companies reporting to the SEC.

25.   The **Sarbanes-Oxley Act of 2002** gave the SEC authority to appoint members of the Public Company Oversight Board.

QUESTIONS

True or False

For each of the following statements, circle the **T** or the **F** to indicate whether the statement is true or false.

T   F   1.   A line of business differs from a business segment.

T   F   2.   Separate financial reporting for operating segments is consistent with the theory of consolidated financial statements.

T   F   3.   **FASB Statement No. 14,** "Financial Reporting for Segments of a Business Enterprise," required the disclosure of information relating to a publicly owned enterprise's foreign operations and major customers.

T   F   4.   **FASB Statement No. 131,** "Disclosures About Segments," adopted the management approach to segment reporting.

T   F   5.   **FASB Statement No. 144,** "Accounting for the…Disposal of Long-Lived Assets," requires that the results of discontinued operations be reported separately from the results of continuing operations.

T   F   6.   According to **APB Opinion No. 28,** "Interim Financial Reporting," revenue from products sold or services rendered is to be recognized during an interim accounting period on the same basis as that followed for the full fiscal year.

T   F   7.   **APB Opinion No. 28** prohibits use of the gross margin method for estimating cost of goods sold for interim accounting periods because that method is not used for measuring cost of goods sold for a full fiscal year.

T   F   8.   Lower-of-cost-or-market write-downs of inventories should not be provided for interim accounting periods if the interim-date market declines are considered to be temporary.

T   F   9.   The anticipated doubtful accounts expense for a full fiscal year is allocated to interim periods so that periods bear a reasonable portion of the anticipated annual amount.

T F 10. Income taxes expense for interim accounting periods is estimated as though each period were a distinct fiscal year.

T F 11. Contingent items are disclosed in interim reports of publicly owned companies.

T F 12. The SEC requires disclosure of financial forecast data in all filings with it.

T F 13. The SEC rarely has used its authority to establish accounting principles underlying financial statements and schedules included in reports filed with the SEC.

T F 14. **Staff Accounting Bulletins** are issued by the SEC to contribute to the development of uniform standards and practices relative to major accounting questions.

T F 15. **Regulation S-X** of the SEC prescribes the form of supporting schedules to accompany financial statements filed with the SEC.

T F 16. Form S-1 of the SEC consists of a number of blanks to be filled in by a company registering securities with the SEC.

T F 17. A Form 10-Q quarterly report is not required for the fourth quarter of the fiscal year of a company subject to the reporting requirements of the **1934 Act.**

T F 18. A preliminary proxy statement must be distributed to stockholders prior to the annual meeting of stockholders for which proxies are solicited.

Completion Statements

Fill in the necessary words or amounts to complete the following statements.

1. A **component of an entity** may be an _____ _____ or a _____ _____.

2. A **Statement** of the FASB replaced the term _____ segment with _____ segment.

3. The FASB **Statement** cited in **2** defined major customers of a business enterprise as those who provide _____% or more of the enterprise's total revenues.

4. Methods that have been used to allocate nontraceable expenses to segments include ratios based on segment _____, _____ _____, _____ _____ _____ and _____, or a combination thereof.

5. Seasonal nature of _____ should be disclosed in publicly owned companies' interim reports to stockholders.

6. The SEC is administered by _____ commissioners appointed for _____-year terms by the president and confirmed by the Senate of the United States.

7. In **Codification of Financial Reporting Policies,** the SEC differentiated between _____ _____ and _____ in financial statements and schedules.

8. The SEC issued _____ to provide guidance for the form and content of financial statements and _____ required to be filed with the SEC.

Multiple Choice

Choose the best answer for each of the following questions and enter the identifying letter in the space provided.

_____ 1.   A component of an entity may include:
   - a. An industry segment
   - b. A business segment
   - c. An operating segment
   - d. A product line

_____ 2.   A **Statement** of the FASB requires measurement of segment profit or loss in accordance with:
   - a. Generally accepted accounting principles
   - b. The enterprise's internal financial reporting system
   - c. The cash basis of accounting
   - d. Guidelines provided by the SEC in **Regulation S-K**

_____ 3.   The **Statement** cited in **2** requires segmentation of business activities based on:
   - a. Product lines
   - b. Lines of business
   - c. Standard Industrial Classifications
   - d. The way a business enterprise is managed

_____ 4.   If planned material price variances and volume or capacity variances are expected to be absorbed by the end of the fiscal year, their treatment for an interim accounting period is:
   - a. Deferral at the end of the interim period
   - b. Inclusion in cost of goods sold for the interim period
   - c. Presentation as an extraordinary item for the interim period
   - d. None of the foregoing

_____ 5.   Which of the following need not be included in publicly owned companies' interim reports to stockholders?
   - a. Cumulative effect of a change in accounting principle
   - b. Significant changes in financial position
   - c. Changes in accounting estimates
   - d. None of the foregoing

_____ 6.   Damon Company plans to dispose of an operating segment. On the planning date, the loss from the disposal is estimated to be $950,000. Included in the $950,000 are severance pay of $100,000 and employee relocation costs of $50,000, both of which are directly associated with the decision to dispose of the segment; but estimated losses of $200,000 from operations of the segment from the beginning of the fiscal year to the planning date are not included in the estimated loss from the disposal. Disregarding income taxes, Damon's income statement includes a loss on discontinued operations (a separate component of income below the caption **income from continuing operations**) of:
   - a. $750,000
   - b. $850,000
   - c. $900,000
   - d. $1,150,000
   - e. Some other amount

7. The United States statute that governs trading of securities over the counter is:
    a. **The Securities Act of 1933**
    b. **The Securities Exchange Act of 1934**
    c. **The Stockbrokers Act of 1936**
    d. **The Corporate Securities Act of 1938**

8. **Staff Accounting Bulletins** issued by the SEC are intended to achieve a wide dissemination of:
    a. Rules of the SEC
    b. Interpretations of the SEC
    c. Publications bearing the SEC's official approval
    d. Practices followed by the chief accountant of the SEC

9. Changes in **Regulation S-X** are the responsibility of the SEC's:
    a. Chief accountant
    b. Division of Enforcement
    c. Division of Corporate Regulation
    d. Division of Corporate Finance

SHORT EXERCISES

1. Fonda Company's accounting records for the fiscal year ended July 31, 2005, included the following information for its two operating segments.

	Operating Segment A	Operating Segment B
Net sales to outsiders	$800,000	$700,000
Intersegment transfers out	50,000	80,000
Traceable expenses	630,000	470,000

    Nontraceable expenses of Fonda were $300,000 for the year ended July 31, 2005. The nontraceable expenses are allocated to the two operating segments on the basis of net segment sales to outsiders.

    In the space below, compute the profit or loss for each of Fonda Company's two operating segments for the year ended July 31, 2005.

    Fonda Company
    Computation of Operating Segment Profit or Loss
    For Year Ended July 31, 2005

	Operating Segment A	Operating Segment B
Revenue:		
Net sales to outsiders	$	$

2. Yebisu Company's accounting records on August 31, 2005, include the following information with respect to its Delta Division (an operating segment):

Net sales, fiscal year ended Aug. 31, 2005	$800,000
Costs and expenses, year ended Aug. 31, 2005	950,000
Estimated operating losses, six months ending Feb. 28, 2006	80,000
Estimated carrying amount of net assets, Feb. 28, 2006	600,000

Disposal of the Delta Division for $500,000 was authorized by Yebisu's board of directors on August 31, 2005. Closing date of the disposal was expected to be February 28, 2006. Yebisu Company's income tax rate is 40%, and its income from continuing operations for the year ended August 31, 2005, was $964,500.

Complete the partial income statement below for the year ended August 31, 2005, to present the foregoing information. Disregard earnings per share data.

Yebisu Company
Partial Income Statement
For Year Ended August 31, 2005

Income from continuing operations	$964,500
Discontinued operations:	
Loss from operations of discontinued Delta Division, including $_____ loss on disposal (less applicable income tax credit of $_____)	
Net income	$_____

3. Kansas Corporation issues financial statements on a quarterly basis. During 2005, its actual quarterly results and its expectations were as follows:

	Actual Taxable Income		Taxable Income Expected for Year
	Quarter	Year to Date	
End of 1st quarter	$20,000	$ 20,000	$ 80,000
End of 2nd quarter	10,000	30,000	60,000
End of 3rd quarter	40,000	70,000	90,000
End of year (Dec. 31, 2005)	30,000	100,000	100,000

Assuming that the corporate income tax rate is 20% on the first $50,000 of taxable income and 40% on any taxable income in excess of $50,000, compute the (a) estimated income tax rate (rounded to the nearest tenth of a percent) for each quarter of 2005, (b) year-to-date income taxes expense as of the end of each quarter of 2005, and (c) income taxes expense for each quarter of 2005. Use the space provided below.

a. Estimated income tax rates for each quarter of 2005:

1st quarter:

2nd quarter:

3rd quarter:

4th quarter:

b. Year-to-date income taxes expense as of the end of each quarter of 2005:

1st quarter:

2nd quarter:

3rd quarter:

4th quarter:

c. Income taxes expense for each quarter of 2005:

1st quarter:

2nd quarter:

3rd quarter:

4th quarter:

CASE

In a classroom discussion of accounting standards for disclosure of discontinued operations, student Colin questions the logic of including net-of-tax operations during the period prior to disposal as a component of the gain or loss on disposal of the segment.

Explain to student Colin the logic behind the disclosure standards described above.

©The McGraw-Hill Companies, Inc., 2006

QUESTIONS

True or False

1. F 2. F 3. T 4. T 5. T 6. T 7. F 8. T 9. T 10. F 11. T 12. F 13. T 14. F 15. T 16. F 17. T 18. F

Completion Statements

1. Operating segment, reportable segment. 2. Industry, operating. 3. 10. 4. Revenues, payroll totals, average plant assets, inventories. 5. Activities. 6. Five, five. 7. Generally accepted accounting principles, disclosures. 8. **Regulation S-X,** schedules.

Multiple Choice

1. c 2. b 3. d 4. a 5. d 6. d ($950,000 + $200,000 = $1,150,000) 7. b 8. d 9. d

SHORT EXERCISES

1.

Fonda Company
Computation of Operating Segment Profit or Loss
For Year Ended July 31, 2005

	Operating Segment A	Operating Segment B
Revenue:		
Net sales to outsiders	$800,000	$700,000
Intersegment transfers out	50,000	80,000
Total revenue	$850,000	$780,000
Cost and expenses:		
Traceable expenses	$630,000	$470,000
Intersegment transfers in	80,000	50,000
Nontraceable expenses (8/15 and 7/15, respectively)	160,000	140,000
Total costs and expenses	$870,000	$660,000
Segment profit (loss)	$ (20,000)	$120,000

2.

Yebisu Company
Partial Income Statement
For Year Ended August 31, 2005

Income from continuing operations	$964,500
Discontinued operations:	
Loss from operations of discontinued Delta Division, including $100,000 loss on disposal (less applicable income tax credit of $132,000†)	(198,000)
Net income	$766,500

*$600,000 – $500,000 = $100,000

†[$950,000 + $80,000 – $800,000 + $100,000] x 0.40 = $132,000

3.   a.   Estimated income tax rates for each quarter of 2005:

1st quarter: $\dfrac{(\$80,000 \times 0.40) - \$10,000^*}{\$80,000} = \underline{27.5\%}$

2nd quarter: $\dfrac{(\$60,000 \times 0.40) - \$10,000^*}{\$60,000} = \underline{23.3\%}$

3rd quarter: $\dfrac{(\$90,000 \times 0.40) - \$10,000^*}{\$90,000} = \underline{28.9\%}$

4th quarter: $\dfrac{(\$100,000 \times 0.40) - \$10,000^*}{\$100,000} = \underline{30.0\%}$

*The $10,000 represents the saving from being taxed at the rate of 20% rather than at the rate of 40% on the first $50,000 of taxable income.

   b.   Year-to-date income taxes expense as of the end of each quarter of 2005:

1st quarter: $20,000 x 0.275 = $5,500
2nd quarter: $30,000 x 0.233 = $6,990
3rd quarter: $70,000 x 0.289 = $20,230
4th quarter: $100,000 x 0.300 = $30,000

   c.   Income taxes expense for each quarter of 2005:

1st quarter: $5,500
    (Same as year-to-date)
2nd quarter: $6,990 - $5,500 = $1,490
    ($5,500 was previously provided)
3rd quarter: $20,230 - $6,990 = $13,240
    ($6,990 was previously provided)
4th quarter: $30,000 - $20,230 = $9,770
    ($20,230 was previously provided)

CASE

Once a decision is made to dispose of an operating segment, it becomes a **quitting concern**; accordingly, any operating gain or loss prior to the actual disposal of the segment is sufficiently related to the gain or loss on disposal of the segment net assets to warrant combining the two amounts in the computation of the overall gain or loss.

CHAPTER 14
BANKRUPTCY: LIQUIDATION AND REORGANIZATION

HIGHLIGHTS OF CHAPTER

1. Business failures are a common occurrence in the U.S. economy. The situation that precedes the typical business failure is inability to pay liabilities at maturity. A business enterprise may be unable to pay its liabilities at maturity even though the current fair value of its assets exceeds its liabilities. However, insolvency is a more typical state of a failing enterprise. **Insolvency** is defined as an excess of liabilities over current fair value of assets.

2. The present U.S. Bankruptcy Code was enacted in 1978 and amended in 1994 to replace the Bankruptcy Act, which with numerous amendments had remained in effect for 80 years. In 1980, the Bankruptcy Tax Act established income tax rules for bankruptcy and insolvency. Important interpretations of the Bankruptcy Code are in the Federal Rules of Bankruptcy Procedure established by the Supreme Court.

3. **Liquidation** under Chapter 7 of the Bankruptcy Code involves the realization (sale) of the assets of an individual or business enterprise and the distribution of the cash proceeds to the creditors. Creditors are ranked in bankruptcy according to whether they have a **security interest** in assets of the debtor or are unsecured. The claims of certain unsecured creditors have **priority** over other unsecured creditors' claims under provisions of the Bankruptcy Code.

4. With certain exceptions, any individual or business enterprise may initiate liquidation proceedings by filing in a federal bankruptcy court a **debtor's petition** for liquidation. Alternatively, under specified conditions creditors of a debtor enterprise may file in a federal bankruptcy court a **creditors' petition** to have the debtor enterprise liquidated. Both types of petitions must be accompanied by extensive supporting data. In addition, a creditors' petition must include a claim that the debtor was not paying debts as they came due, or that recently a custodian had assumed responsibility for the debtor's property.

5. The federal bankruptcy court in which a debtor's or creditors' bankruptcy petition is filed oversees all aspects of the bankruptcy proceedings. One of the court's first acts is to dismiss the petition or to grant an order for relief under the Bankruptcy Code. An **order for relief** acts to stay any suits pending against the debtor until the question of the debtor's **discharge** is determined by the court.

6. Either the creditors or the court may appoint a trustee for the debtor's estate. The trustee realizes the assets of the estate and pays cash to unsecured creditors.

7. Once the debtor's assets have been realized and all possible amounts have been paid to creditors, the debtor may receive from the court a **discharge,** which is a release from all unliquidated debts except those specified in the Bankruptcy Code.

8. The accountant's role in liquidation proceedings is concerned with proper reporting of the financial condition of the debtor and adequate accounting and reporting for the trustee of the debtor's estate. A **statement of affairs** is a financial statement that presents the financial condition of a **quitting concern** entering bankruptcy proceedings. The statement of affairs displays the assets and liabilities of the debtor enterprise from a **liquidation** viewpoint, because liquidation is the outcome of Chapter 7 bankruptcy proceedings. Thus, assets in the statement of affairs are valued at current fair value, and assets and liabilities in the statement are classified according to the rankings and priorities set forth in the Bankruptcy Code. A **contra (offset)** technique is used in the statement of affairs when the legal **right of setoff** exists.

9. Maintenance of the accounting records of a debtor should be continued during the period that a trustee carries on the operations of the debtor's business. An **accountability** technique is used once the trustee begins realization of the debtor's assets. In the accountability method of

accounting, the assets and liabilities for which the trustee is responsible are entered in the trustee's accounting records at their statement-of-affairs valuations. The offset is to a ledger account with a title such as Estate Deficit. Differences between cash receipts and payments and the carrying amounts of assets realized and liabilities paid by the trustee are debited or credited directly to the Estate Deficit ledger account.

10. The periodic and final reports of the trustee to the bankruptcy court are a statement of cash receipts and payments, a statement of realization and liquidation, and for interim reports a supporting exhibit of assets not yet realized and liabilities not yet paid.

11. A **reorganization** under Chapter 11 of the Bankruptcy Code involves such features as reductions of amounts payable to some creditors, issuance of the debtor's equity securities to settle other creditors' claims, and a reduction of the par or stated value of the debtor's common stock.

12. During the process of reorganization, management or owners of the debtor enterprise may continue to operate the enterprise, or the bankruptcy court may appoint a trustee to manage it. The trustee identifies the enterprise's creditors and stockholders and formulates a plan for continuing the enterprise's operations, if management of the enterprise has not done so.

13. The plan of reorganization developed by the trustee or by management is submitted to the bankruptcy court and distributed to other interested parties, including the Secretary of the Treasury and perhaps the Securities and Exchange Commission. The plan must contain a number of provisions, including modifications of the interests and rights of the corporation's creditors and stockholders. The SEC may review, and be heard by the bankruptcy court on, many reorganization plans.

14. In order for a reorganization plan to be confirmed by the court, two-thirds of all stockholders, and a majority of creditors whose claims account for two-thirds of the total liabilities, must accept the plan. Confirmation of a reorganization plan by the court makes it binding on the debtor enterprise and all its creditors and stockholders.

15. Journal entries to record a reorganization typically include (a) exchange of newly authorized common stock for old outstanding common stock and for some liabilities; (b) extension of due dates of other liabilities; (c) payments to other creditors at less than 100 cents for each $1 of debt; and (d) elimination of a retained earnings deficit. Extensive disclosure in a note to the financial statement is essential for the complex provisions of a reorganization.

QUESTIONS

True or False

For each of the following statements, circle the **T** or the **F** to indicate whether the statement is true or false.

T   F   1. A preference in bankruptcy prefers one creditor over other creditors.

T   F   2. A creditors' petition in bankruptcy must state that one or more acts of bankruptcy were committed within the three months preceding the date of filing the petition.

T   F   3. The Bankruptcy Code grants to federal district courts exclusive jurisdiction over bankruptcy proceedings.

T   F   4. The filing of a debtor's petition in bankruptcy does not automatically operate as an order for relief.

T   F   5. A creditors' petition in bankruptcy may be filed only if the debtor has failed to pay debts as they came due.

T F 6. A creditors' petition in bankruptcy must be filed by at least three creditors if the debtor has 12 or more creditors.

T F 7. Federal, state, and local taxes are discharged by bankruptcy.

T F 8. A trustee in bankruptcy usually is elected by the creditors.

T F 9. A priority in a bankruptcy proceeding is given for administration costs, including accountants' and attorneys' fees.

T F 10. A debtor corporation completing a Chapter 11 reorganization should "date" retained earnings in its balance sheets subsequent to the date of the reorganization.

T F 11. All reorganizations under Chapter 11 of the Bankruptcy Code are carried out by a court-appointed trustee.

T F 12. The Securities and Exchange Commission must approve a reorganization in order for it to be confirmed by the bankruptcy court.

T F 13. Certain claims for contributions to employee benefit plans have priority over other unsecured liabilities under the Bankruptcy Code.

T F 14. Amounts payable for alimony or child support may be discharged in bankruptcy.

Completion Statements

Fill in the necessary words or amounts to complete the following statements.

1. The term _____ refers to the financial condition of a person or a business enterprise, and _____ refers to a legal state.

2. Federal Rules of Bankruptcy Procedure are established by the U.S. _____ _____.

3. The bankruptcy process known as _____ involves the _____ of the assets of a debtor and the distribution of the proceeds to creditors.

4. One of the first acts of the bankruptcy court in a Chapter 7 liquidation proceeding is to dismiss the petition or grant an _____ _____ _____.

5. The _____ method of accounting should be used once a trustee begins realization of a debtor's assets.

6. In some bankruptcy reorganizations not involving a trustee, the court may appoint an _____ to investigate possible fraud.

Multiple Choice

Choose the best answer for each of the following questions and enter the identifying letter in the space provided.

_____ 1. A debtor enterprise may be denied a discharge in bankruptcy if:
   a. It has committed an act of bankruptcy within four months prior to the filing of a creditors' petition
   b. It was discharged in bankruptcy five years earlier
   c. It permitted a creditor to obtain a lien on its property three months prior to bankruptcy and did not act to remove the lien
   d. Unsecured, nonpriority creditors with provable claims will be unable to receive more than 10 cents for each $1 of their claims

_____ 2. A statement of financial condition prepared contrary to the going-concern assumption is a :
   a. Statement of realization and liquidation
   b. Statement of affairs
   c. Charge and discharge statement
   d. Statement of liquidation

_____ 3. Which of the following may file a debtor's petition for liquidation in bankruptcy?
   a. An individual person
   b. A savings and loan association
   c. An insurance company
   d. All of the foregoing
   e. None of the foregoing

_____ 4. Which of the following unsecured liabilities does not have priority under the Bankruptcy Code?
   a. Costs incurred by creditors in successfully opposing the discharge of a debtor
   b. Costs of administering a debtor's estate
   c. Claims of governmental entities for various taxes and duties
   d. None of the foregoing

_____ 5. The bankruptcy court's alternative to dismissal of a bankruptcy petition is known as:
   a. Confirmation
   b. Discharge
   c. Order for relief
   d. None of the foregoing

_____ 6. In a statement of affairs (financial statement), a contra (offset) technique is used for:
   a. Free assets
   b. Stockholders' equity
   c. Unsecured liabilities with priority
   d. None of the foregoing

_____ 7. Wrack Company has filed a debtor's bankruptcy petition. In connection with a debt owed to City Finance company, Wrack used a false financial statement to induce City Finance to loan it $5,000. Wrack is seeking a discharge in bankruptcy. Which of the following is a correct statement?

    a. Wrack will be denied a discharge of any of its debts.

    b. Even if it can be proved that City Finance did not rely on the financial statement, Wrack will be denied a discharge either in whole or in part.

    c. Wrack will be denied a discharge of the City Finance debt.

    d. Wrack will be totally discharged despite the false financial statement.

_____ 8. In a bankruptcy liquidation, liabilities with priority are:

    a. Fully secured

    b. Unsecured

    c. Partially secured

    d. Either fully secured or partially secured

    e. Any of the foregoing

SHORT EXERCISES

1. From the following information taken from the December 31, 2005, statement of affairs of Lindee Company, compute in the spaces below (**a**) the estimated deficiency to unsecured, nonpriority creditors and (**b**) the estimated settlement per dollar of unsecured liabilities without priority:

Assets pledged for fully secured liabilities	$50,000
Assets pledged for partially secured liabilities	10,000
Free assets	49,000
Fully secured liabilities	42,500
Partially secured liabilities	25,000
Unsecured liabilities with priority	5,500
Unsecured liabilities without priority	48,750

    a. Estimated deficiency to unsecured, nonpriority creditors:

    b. Estimated settlement per dollar of unsecured liabilities without priority:

2.   Sorrento Company is in the process of completing a reorganization under Chapter 11 of the Bankruptcy Code. All liabilities having priority and cost of the bankruptcy proceeding have been paid by the escrow agent. The stockholders' equity ledger accounts have the following balances on May 31, 2005:

Common stock, $100 par; 600 shares authorized, issues, and outstanding	$ 60,000
Paid-in capital in excess of par	125,000
Retained earnings (deficit)	(275,000)

The confirmed reorganization plan has the following provisions:

(1) A $600,000, 10% unsecured promissory note payable due January 31, 2010, was to be canceled, together with four months' accrued interest. The payee of the note was to accept 5,000 shares of new $100 par, 15% cumulative preferred stock in exchange for the note and accrued interest.

(2) On May 1, 2005, Sorrento's trade creditors had accepted $360,000 in 18% unsecured promissory notes, payable on demand, in settlement of all past-due accounts. No payments of principal or interest had been made on the notes through May 31, 2005. As part of the reorganization, holders of $200,000 face amount of the 18% demand notes were to accept five-year, 19% unsecured promissory notes in exchange for their claims; and the remainder were to accept a reduced cash settlement of 75 cents for each $1 owed.

(3) In an action that was part of the reorganization, stockholders of Sorrento approved the exchange of their present holdings of $100 par common stock for a new issue of 600 shares of $50 par common stock.

In the space on page 170, prepare journal entries for Sorrento Company on May 31, 2005, to record the reorganization, including the new common stock issuance, and the elimination of the deficit in accordance with fresh start reporting. Include explanations for the journal entries. Use a single Paid-in Capital in Excess of Par ledger account.

CASE

In a classroom discussion of accounting procedures for a trustee in a Chapter 7 bankruptcy liquidation, student Amy questions the logic of the trustee's continued use of the debtor enterprise's accounting records during the windup of the debtor's business operations, but the establishment of a separate set of accounting records once the trustee begins realization of the debtor's assets. Amy points out that a business enterprise undergoing liquidation outside of bankruptcy proceedings uses the same set of accounting records for the windup of operations as for the realization of assets.

Are the two sets of accounting records for a trustee in a bankruptcy liquidation really necessary? Explain.

Sorrento Company
Journal Entries

2005			
May 31			

SOLUTIONS TO QUESTIONS, SHORT EXERCISES, AND CASE: CHAPTER 14

QUESTIONS

True or False

1. T   2. F   3. F   4. F   5. F   6. T   7. F   8. T   9. T   10. T   11. F   12. F   13. T   14. F

Completion Statements

1. Insolvent, bankrupt.   2. Supreme Court.   3. Liquidation, realization.   4. Order for relief.
5. Accountability.   6. Examiner.

Multiple Choice

1. b   2. b   3. a   4. a   5. c   6. c   7. c   8. b

SHORT EXERCISES

1.   a.   Estimated deficiency to unsecured, nonpriority creditors:

Excess of assets pledged for fully secured liabilities over related liabilities ($50,000 – $42,500)		$ 7,500
Free assets		49,000
Estimated amount available		56,500
Less: Unsecured liabilities with priority		5,500
Estimated amount available for unsecured, nonpriority creditors		$ 51,000
Less: Unsecured liabilities without priority	$48,750	
Partially secured liabilities ($25,000 – $10,000)	15,000	63,750
Estimated deficiency to unsecured, nonpriority creditors		$(12,750)

b.   Estimated settlement per dollar of unsecured liabilities without priority:

$$\frac{\text{Estimated amount available for unsecured, nonpriority creditors}}{\text{Total unsecured and partially secured liabilities}} = \frac{\$51,000}{\$63,750} = \underline{\$0.80}$$

2.

Sorrento Company
Journal Entries

2005			
May 31	Note Payable (due Jan. 31, 2010)	600,000	
	Interest Payable ($600,000 x 0.10 x 4/12)	20,000	
	15% Cumulative Preferred Stock (5,000 x $100)		500,000
	Paid-in Capital in Excess of Par		120,000
	To record issuance of 5,000 shares of preferred stock for		
	cancellation of note payable and accrued interest.		
31	Notes Payable (due on demand)	360,000	
	Interest Payable ($360,000 x 0.18 x 1/12)	5,400	
	Notes Payable (due May 31, 2010) [$200,000 + ($200,000 x		
	0.18 x 1/12)]		203,000
	Cash [($160,000 + $2,400) x 0.75]		121,800
	Gain from Discharge of Indebtedness in Bankruptcy		40,600
	To record exchange of five-year, 19% promissory notes payable		
	for $200,000 face amount of 18% demand notes payable		
	plus accrued interest, and payment of cash at 75 cents on the		
	dollar for remainder of 18% demand notes payable plus accrued		
	interest.		
31	Common Stock, $100 par	60,000	
	Common Stock, $50 par		30,000
	Paid-in Capital in Excess of Par		30,000
	To record issuance of 600 shares of $50 par common stock in		
	exchange for 600 shares of $100 par common stock.		
31	Paid-in Capital in Excess of Par	234,400	
	Gain from Discharge of Indebtedness in Bankruptcy	40,600	
	Retained Earnings		275,000
	To record elimination of deficit and to close bankruptcy gain to		
	Paid-in Capital in Excess of Par.		

CASE

The differing roles of the trustee in a Chapter 7 bankruptcy liquidation necessitate the trustee's use of two sets of accounting records. During the windup of operations of the debtor's business, the trustee is working with a quitting concern that generates residual revenue and expenses during the windup period. The assets of the debtor's business continue to be carried at amounts based on the going-concern principle. Once operations have ceased, **all** assets and liabilities of the debtor—business and nonbusiness other than exempt property—come under the jurisdiction of the trustee. At that time, current fair values, rather than carrying amounts, of the debtor's business assets are relevant to the trustee, and the accountability technique comes into play. Thus, it would not be appropriate for the trustee to continue to use the accounting records of the debtor's business once it had ceased operations.

CHAPTER 15
ESTATES AND TRUSTS

HIGHLIGHTS OF CHAPTER

1. **Estates** and **trusts** are both accounting and taxable entities. A person acting as a legal representative of an estate or a trust is known as a **fiduciary**. An **executor** of an estate is named in the **will** of the decedent; if the will does not name an executor, a probate court appoints an **administrator**. A **trustee** is the fiduciary of a trust.

2. State laws (known as **probate codes**) regulate the administration of estates. Because these laws differ widely, a **Uniform Probate Code** (Code) has been drafted with the expectation that most states eventually will adopt all or part of it.

3. The Code defines an **estate** as all property of a decedent, trust, or other person whose affairs are subject to the Code. A **person** is deemed to be an individual or organization.

4. All property of a decedent is awarded to **devisees** specified in the decedent's will; in the absence of a will (**intestacy**) the property of the decedent is transferred directly to heirs as specified in the Code.

5. A valid will should be in writing, signed by the **testator** and at least two witnesses. A will is **probated** by a **probate court** (also known as a **surrogate** or **orphan's court**). Probate may be formal or informal. After completion of any hearings, the court issues an order for formal probate of a valid will, or an order that the decedent died **intestate.**

6. The executor or administrator takes possession and control of the decedent's property in trust for the benefit of creditors and devisees. Executors and administrators have the authority to continue a single proprietorship of the decedent for not more than four months, and to allocate cash receipts and payments to **estate principal** (corpus) or to **estate income** pursuant to the provisions of the will or applicable state statutes.

7. Within 30 days after appointment, the personal representative (executor or administrator) must inform the decedent's devisees or heirs of the appointment. A **devisee** is any person or trust named in a will to receive, through a **devise,** property of the decedent. Within three months after appointment, the personal representative prepares an inventory (at current fair value) of the decedent's property and debts on the date of death. No earlier than six months after the date of appointment, the personal representative may close an estate by filing appropriate legal documents and financial statements with the probate court.

8. Certain allowances and exemptions are stipulated for estates by the Code. These are:

    a. **Homestead allowance** The decedent's surviving spouse, or surviving minor and dependent children, are entitled to a total homestead allowance of a specified amount.

    b. **Family allowance** The surviving spouse and minor children of the decedent are entitled to a **reasonable** cash allowance during the administration of the estate.

    c. **Exempt property** the decedent's surviving spouse or children are entitled to an aggregate specified total current fair value of automobiles and household and personal effects.

9. The personal representative is required to publish a notice in a newspaper once a week for three successive weeks requesting creditors of an estate to present their claims within four months after the date of the first publication. Claims not filed within this period are not valid claims against the estate. Payments are made in the following order: (a) costs of administering the estate, (b) decedent's funeral costs and costs of last illness, (c) debts and taxes with preference under federal or state laws, and (d) all other items.

10. After payment of creditors, estate property is distributed in the following order:

a. **Specific devises** (gifts of identifiable objects, such as named paintings, automobiles, or real property)

b. **General devises** (gifts of amounts of money or monetary assets, such as corporate bonds)

c. **Residuary devises** (gifts of all estate property remaining after specific devises and general devises are distributed). If estate property (that is not exempt property) is insufficient to pay estate creditors and the devises, the devises **abate** (are reduced) or are eliminated. Residuary devises are reduced or eliminated first, followed by general devises and specific devises in that order.

11. The federal estate tax assessed against an estate and state inheritance taxes levied against devisees sometimes are called **death taxes.** These taxes either are apportioned against the various devises according to the provisions of the will or are prorated according to provisions of the Code.

12. The allocation of revenue and expenses of the estate between **principal** and **income** is important because the **income beneficiary** and the **principal beneficiary** (or **remainderman)** may be different persons. If the will does not provide specific instructions for such allocation, provisions of the Revised Uniform Principal and Income Act or state laws would apply.

13. Following are some general guidelines of the Revised Uniform Principal and Income Act for allocation of revenue and expenses to principal and income:

a. **Income** is the return derived from the use or investment of the principal assets and includes rent, interest, cash dividends, and revenue received during administration of the estate.

b. **Principal** consists of property to be held in trust for delivery to a devisee remainderman. Principal includes proceeds of insurance on principal property, stock dividends, and liquidating dividends. Any accrued revenue on the date of the decedent's death is considered principal.

c. Premium or discount on investments in bonds included in principal is not amortized. All proceeds from disposal of bonds are principal. Depreciation on all property except property used by a beneficiary as a residence is charged against income. Income is also charged for costs of administering income-producing estate property. Principal is charged with expenditures incurred in preparing property for sale or rent, extraordinary repairs to principal property, and income taxes on gains allocable to principal. Administrative and other costs for periodic reporting to the probate court are apportioned between principal and income.

14. The accounting records of an estate are opened to record the inventory of estate property by debits to Principal Cash and other appropriate asset ledger accounts; liability accounts for liens on estate property and Estate Principal Balance are credited. Property subsequently discovered is recorded by a debit to an asset account and a credit to Property Discovered. Receipts of income are debited to Income Cash, and distributions of income are debited to Distributions to Income Beneficiaries and credited to Income Cash. Distributions to devisees are debited to Devises Distributed and credited to Principal Cash or other asset accounts. Payments of decedent's debts, illness costs, and funeral costs are recorded by a debit to Liabilities Paid and a credit to Principal Cash.

15. A charge and discharge statement may be prepared by the executor or administrator periodically and on closing of the estate. This statement, prepared from a trial balance, consists of two sections—**principal** and **income.** The "charges" include, for example, the inventory of principal property, property discovered, gains on disposal of principal property, and receipts of income; "credits" consist essentially of losses on disposal of principal property, liabilities paid, devises and income distributed, and administrative costs. Appropriate exhibits in support of the "charges" and "credits" accompany the charge and discharge statement.

16. The charge and discharge statement summarizes the accountability of the personal representative of the decedent. Once the probate court accepts the final charge and discharge statement, the accounting records for the estate may be closed.

17. A **trust** created by a will is termed a **testamentary trust.** A trust created by a living person is known as an **inter vivos** or **living trust.** A trust is created by the **settlor** (also known as **donor** or **trustor**); it is administered by a **trustee** for the benefit of **income beneficiaries** and **principal beneficiaries.**

18. The trustee must comply fully with the provisions established by the settlor during the stated term of the trust and must maintain accounting records for both trust principal and trust income. Such accounting records usually are maintained on the **cash basis.**

19. There is no need to accrue revenue or expenses for a trust because a balance sheet and an income statement generally are not prepared. The periodic financial report prepared by the trustee is a charge and discharge statement.

20. A closing journal entry is required for a trust at the end of each reporting period for which a charge and discharge statement is prepared, to clear the revenue, expense, and distributions ledger accounts for the next reporting period.

QUESTIONS

True or False

For each of the following statements, circle the **T** or the **F** to indicate whether the statement is true or false.

T F 1. Under the provisions of the Revised Uniform Principal and Income Act, a reasonable amount of depreciation on estate property is charged against the income of an estate.

T F 2. The Internal Revenue Code does not consider estates and trusts to be taxable entities.

T F 3. State inheritance taxes and the federal estate tax generally are allocated to devisees in accordance with the instructions of a decedent's will.

T F 4. The personal representative of an estate has the authority to use estate property to invest in a new business enterprise.

T F 5. The Uniform Probate Code has been adopted in its entirety by all 50 states.

T F 6. An administrator is a personal representative named in the decedent's will, but an executor is appointed by the probate court as the personal representative of an intestate decedent.

T F 7. The property of an estate is entered in the accounting records of the personal representative at carrying amount to the decedent.

T F 8. If the property of an estate not exempt under the Uniform Probate Code is insufficient to pay claims against the estate in full, taxes with preference under federal and state laws must be paid before costs of administering the estate are paid.

T F 9. If estate property is insufficient to distribute the devises listed in a will, the general devises are the first to be abated, followed by specific devises and residuary devises.

T F 10. Because a charge and discharge statement is not prepared in accordance with generally accepted accounting principles, it is not appropriate for an independent CPA to attest to the fairness of the statement.

T F   11. If the principal and income beneficiaries of an estate or a trust are the same person, there is no need to differentiate between principal and income in the accounting records of the estate or trust.

T F   12. The proceeds from the disposal of shares of stock received as a 10% stock dividend and proceeds from the disposal of warrants for stock rights are credited to revenue ledger accounts of estates and trusts.

T F   13. The debts of a decedent on the date of death generally are recorded, together with the inventory of property on the date of death, in the accounting records of the personal representative.

T F   14. Administrative costs are displayed under the "I credit myself as follows" section of a charge and discharge statement.

T F   15. A testamentary trust is created by an executor of an estate pursuant to authority granted to the executor by the testator.

T F   16. The accrual basis of accounting is used for testamentary trusts.

T F   17. A debit to the Trust Principal Balance ledger account in a closing journal entry for a trust indicates that a portion of the trustee's administrative costs was allocated to the principal of the trust or that a loss was incurred on the disposal of principal property.

Completion Statements

Fill in the necessary words or amounts to complete the following statements.

1. The individuals or corporations that manage the property of estates and trust are known as _____; when a decedent does not leave a valid will, he or she is said to have died _____.

2. A probate court sometimes is referred to as _____ or _____ court.

3. A _____ is a person or trust named in a will to receive property of the decedent in a transfer known as a _____.

4. The _____ tax is assessed by the federal government against the net property of an estate, and _____ taxes are assessed by the various _____ against the devisees or _____ of the decedent.

5. The accountability of the personal representative of a decedent generally is reported in a _____ _____ _____.

6. The _____ _____ ledger account is _____ in the accounting records of the personal representative when estate property is transferred to devisees and the _____ _____ _____ _____ ledger account is _____ when the income of an estate is paid to income beneficiaries.

7. A trust created by the act of a living person is known as an _____ _____ or _____ trust. The three parties to a trust are the _____, _____, and _____.

8. A principal beneficiary of a trust also is known as a _____.

Multiple Choice

Choose the best answer for each of the following questions and enter the identifying letter in the space provided.

_____ 1. The personal representative of an estate may not:
   a. Take possession and control of the decedent's property
   b. Obtain title to the decedent's property in trust for the benefit of creditors and devisees
   c. Operate a single proprietorship of the decedent indefinitely if the proprietorship is profitable
   d. Allocate revenue and expenses of the estate to principal and income as provided by the will or by law

_____ 2. Which of the following procedures is acceptable in accounting for an estate of a decedent?
   a. Funeral costs are charged to income of the estate.
   b. The cash basis of accounting is adopted by the executor.
   c. Liens against real property on the date of death of the testator are recorded in the accounting records of the estate.
   d. None of the foregoing

_____ 3. Household furniture and personal effects with a specified aggregate value are classified under the Uniform Probate Code as:
   a. Family allowance
   b. Exempt property
   c. Residuary devise
   d. Homestead allowance

_____ 4. The Kathy Moody Trust was established on March 1, 2005. The property of the trust included interest receivable of $2,400. During the remainder of 2005, interest and dividends received amounted to $36,000, and expenses chargeable to income were $6,200. In addition, bonds were disposed of at a gain of $6,800, common stocks were disposed of at a loss of $2,700, and common stock received as an 8% stock dividend was disposed of for $3,220. The income of the trust for 2005 was:

   a. $34,720

   b. $31,500

   c. $29,800

   d. $27,400

   e. Some other amount

_____ 5. Which of the following is appropriately charged against the principal of an estate?
   a. Depreciation of real property of the estate
   b. Property taxes
   c. Special assessment taxes for installation of sewage system
   d. Amortization of discount on corporate bonds owned by the estate

_____ 6. If estate property that is not exempt is insufficient to cover creditors' claims and all devises, which of the following is least threatened by the possibility of abatement?
   a. Property not disposed of by the will
   b. Specific devises
   c. Residuary devises
   d. General devises

_____ 7.   The settlor of a trust is most likely to instruct the trustee to record depreciation on trust property if the settlor:

    a.   Intended for the trustee to distribute all cash receipts less cash expenditures to the beneficiaries

    b.   Created a trust of short duration and intended for the trustee to transfer title to depreciable property to a nonprofit organization

    c.   Intended for the trustee to maintain the principal of the trust intact

    d.   Wanted to maintain intact the purchasing power of the trust

_____ 8.   In the charge and discharge statement prepared by the executor of the will of Julio Chan, the total "charges" were listed at $120,000 and total "credits" were listed at $105,000. Which of the following is correct?

    a.   The income of the estate was $15,000 for the period covered by the charge and discharge statement.

    b.   Administrative costs for the period were $15,000.

    c.   Property discovered subsequent to the filing of the inventory of estate property with the probate court amounts to $15,000.

    d.   The undistributed property of the estate amounted to $15,000 on the date the charge and discharge statement was prepared.

SHORT EXERCISES

1.   The following trial balance was prepared by George Saunders, executor of the will of Alan Beel, who died April 1, 2005:

George Saunders, Executor
Of the Will of Alan Beel, Deceased
Trial Balance
September 30, 2005

Principal:	Dr (Cr)
Estate principal balance	$(142,000)
Property discovered	(1,500)
Principal cash	45,000
Marketable securities	55,000
Interest receivable	3,000
Loss on disposal of principal property	1,600
Administrative costs	3,900
Liabilities paid	5,000
Devises distributed	30,000
Total	$ -0-
Income:	
Dividend and interest revenue	$ (4,150)
Expenses chargeable to income	310
Distributions to income beneficiaries	2,690
Income cash	1,150
Total	$ -0-

Complete the charge and discharge statement below. Supporting exhibits are not required.

George Saunders, Executor
Of the Will of Alan Beel, Deceased
Charge and Discharge Statement
For period April 1 through September 30, 2005

First, as to Principal

 I charge myself as follows:

  Inventory of estate property, Apr. 1, 2005 $142,000

2. Edward Kane died, leaving an estate valued at $225,000. Kane's will listed the following devises:

Specific devise to daughter Lilly Kane Cole, automobile included in inventory of estate property		$ 5,000
Specific devise to son John Kane, 200 shares of Quaid Company common stock included in inventory of estate property		12,000
General devises to grandchildren:		
Riley Cole	$125,000	
Julie Kane	75,000	200,000
Residuary devise to friend:		
Georgia Piney		if any remainder

Noncash property of the estate, other than the specific devises, was disposed of at a loss of $10,000. Funeral and administrative costs of $4,000 and debts of $12,000 were paid. The remainder of the estate property was distributed.

Assuming that devises abate according to the Uniform Probate Code in the event that all devises cannot be paid, prepare a summary in the space on page 180 showing how the remainder of the estate property would be distributed to the various beneficiaries. Disregard death taxes.

Estate of Edward Kane
Summary of Distribution to Beneficiaries

Property of estate, per inventory on date of death $225,000
Less:

3.   The following selected transactions and events were completed during the month of June by Robin Lee, executor of the will of Margo Loo, deceased:

    (1) Filed the inventory of estate property, as follows:

Bank checking account	$ 4,260
Savings account	20,410
Signal, Inc., common stock (500 shares)	8,000
Data-Max Company 12 1/2% bonds, face amount of $10,000	10,750
Accrued interest on Data-Max Company bonds	156
Residence (subject to mortgage note payable of $15,000)	36,000
Personal effects	14,200

    (2) Discovered a savings account of $3,500 in the name of Margo Loo.

    (3) Disposed of Signal, Inc., common stock for $8,310.

    (4) Received interest of $625 on Data-Max Company bonds.

    (5) Paid the following:

Funeral costs	$ 1,600
Debts incurred by Margo Loo prior to her death	2,350
Administrative costs ($100 is allocable to income)	1,600

    (6) Distributed the residence and personal effects to the devisees, along with cash of $5,000.

    In the space on page 181, prepare journal entries in the executor's accounting records to record the foregoing transactions or events. (Record all securities in a Marketable Securities controlling account.)

Robin Lee, Executor of Will of Margo Loo, Deceased
Journal Entries

(1)			
(2)			
(3)			
(4)			
(5)			
(6)			

4. The following transactions or events were completed by Hubert Caspers during the first year as trustee of the John Roman Trust:

(1) The trust was established with the following principal property:

Cash	$12,500
Marketable securities	40,000
Apartment building	80,000

(2) Bonds were acquired for $8,200, including accrued interest of $180.

(3) Cash receipts for the year were rents, $9,200; dividends and interest, $2,700 (including $180 accrued interest acquired).

(4) Depreciation of $2,000 was recorded. The trust indenture provided that depreciation was to be deducted in measuring the amount of income to be distributed to the income beneficiary.

(5) Cash payments for the year were as follows:

Costs of operating the apartment building	$5,150
Trustee's fees (all applicable to income)	1,200
Payments to income beneficiary	3,370

In the space below, prepare journal entries to record the transactions or events of the trustee.

Hubert Caspers, Trustee of John Roman Trust
Journal Entries

(1)

(2)

(3)

(4)

(5)

CASE

You have been appointed as accountant for the estate of Minnie Martin, deceased. The executor of the estate informs you, by showing you Minnie Martin's will, that Minnie Martin's surviving spouse, Willard Martin, is both the income beneficiary and the remainderman of the testamentary trust established in a residuary devise by Minnie Martin's will. The executor asks you why it is necessary for you to account separately for estate principal and estate income prior to the trustee's assumption of responsibility for the Minnie Martin trust, given that Willard Martin is both income beneficiary and remainderman of the trust.

Write a reply to the executor's question.

SOLUTIONS TO QUESTIONS, SHORT EXERCISES, AND CASE: CHAPTER 15

QUESTIONS

True or False

1. T   2. F   3. T   4. F   5. F   6. F   7. F   8. F   9. F   10. F   11. F   12. F   13. F   14. T   15. F   16. F   17. T

Completion Statements

1. Fiduciaries, intestate.   2. Surrogate, orphan's.   3. Devisee, devise. 4. Estate, inheritance, states, heirs. 5. Charge and discharge statement.   6. Devises Distributed, debited, Distributions to Income Beneficiaries, debited.   7. Inter vivos, living, settlor (also donor or trustor), trustee, beneficiary. 8. Remainderman.

Multiple Choice

1. c   2. a   3. b   4. d ($36,000 – $2,400 – $6,200 = $27,400)   5. c   6. b   7. c   8. d

SHORT EXERCISES

1.

George Saunders, Executor
Of the Will of Alan Beel, Deceased
Charge and Discharge Statement
For period April 1 through September 30, 2005

First, as to Principal

I charge myself as follows:

Inventory of estate property, Apr. 1, 2005	$142,000	
Property discovered	1,500	$143,500

I credit myself as follows:

Loss on disposal of principal property	$ 1,600	
Liabilities paid	5,000	
Devises distributed	30,000	
Administrative costs	3,900	40,500
Balance, Sept. 30, 2005		$103,000

Second, as to Income

I charge myself as follows:

Dividend and interest revenue		$4,150

I credit myself as follows:

Distributions to income beneficiaries	$ 2,690	
Expenses chargeable to income	310	3,000
Balance, Sept. 30, 2005		$ 1,150

2.

Estate of Edward Kane
Summary of Distribution to Beneficiaries

Property of estate, per inventory on date of death		$225,000
Less: Loss on disposal of property	$10,000	
Funeral and administrative costs	4,000	
Debts paid	12,000	26,000
Property of estate available for distribution		$199,000
Less: Specific devise to Lilly Cole	$ 5,000	
Specific devise to John Kane	12,000	17,000
Available for general devises		$182,000
Distributions to general devisees:		
Riley Cole: $182,000 x 125/200		$113,750
Julie Kane: $182,000 x 75/200		68,250
Total		$182,000

(Nothing is available for the residuary devisee.)

3.

Robin Lee, Executor of Will of Margo Loo, Deceased
Journal Entries

(1)	Principal Cash	4,260	
	Savings Account	20,410	
	Marketable Securities ($8,000 + $10,750)	18,750	
	Interest Receivable	156	
	Residence	36,000	
	Personal Effects	14,200	
	Mortgage Note Payable		15,000
	Estate Principal Balance		78,776
	To record inventory of property owned by Margo Loo on the date		
	of her death.		
(2)	Savings Account	3,500	
	Property Discovered		3,500
	To record property discovered subsequent to filing of original		
	inventory.		
(3)	Principal Cash	8,310	
	Marketable Securities		8,000
	Gain on Disposal of Principal Property		310
	To record disposal of 500 shares of Signal, Inc., common stock.		
(4)	Income Cash	469	
	Principal Cash	156	
	Interest Receivable		156
	Interest Revenue		469
	To record interest on Data-Max Company bonds.		

(continued)

(5)	Liabilities Paid ($1,600 + $2,350)	3,950	
	Administrative Costs—Principal	1,500	
	Administrative Costs—Income	100	
	Principal Cash		5,450
	Income Cash		100
	To record cash payments.		
(6)	Devises Distributed	40,200	
	Mortgage Note Payable	15,000	
	Principal Cash		5,000
	Residence		36,000
	Personal Effects		14,200
	To record distributions to devisees.		

4.

Hubert Caspers, Trustee of John Roman Trust
Journal Entries

(1)	Principal Cash	12,500	
	Marketable Securities	40,000	
	Apartment Building	80,000	
	Trust Principal Balance		132,500
	To record establishment of John Roman Trust.		
(2)	Marketable Securities	8,020	
	Interest Receivable	180	
	Principal Cash		8,200
	To record acquisition of bonds with accrued interest of $180.		
(3)	Income Cash	11,720	
	Principal Cash	180	
	Interest Receivable		180
	Rent Revenue		9,200
	Dividend and Interest Revenue		2,520
	To record cash receipts.		
(4)	Depreciation Expense	2,000	
	Principal Cash	2,000	
	Accumulated Depreciation		2,000
	Income Cash		2,000
	To record depreciation and transfer of corresponding amount from income cash to principal cash.		
(5)	Operating Expenses	5,150	
	Administrative Costs	1,200	
	Distributions to Income Beneficiary	3,370	
	Income Cash		9,720
	To record cash payments.		

CASE

The need to differentiate between income and principal of a trust is established either by the trust document or by the Revised Uniform Principal and Income Act, irrespective of the identity of income beneficiary and remainderman of the trust. Typically, trust income is distributed periodically, while trust principal is distributed at the end of the trust term. Although theoretically it would be possible to maintain a single set of accounting records with trust principal and income amounts commingled, the need for the trustee to carry out terms of the trust document or of the Revised Uniform Principal and Income Act indicates the prudence of maintaining separate accounts for trust principal and trust income. The maintenance of separate ledger accounts for principal cash and income cash does not preclude the use of a single bank account for the trust, however.

HIGHLIGHTS OF CHAPTER

1. A **nonprofit** (or **not-for-profit**) **organization** is an entity that is operated for the benefit of society as a whole. Examples of nonprofit organizations include colleges and universities, health and welfare organizations, some hospitals, philanthropic foundations, professional societies, and most fraternal and cultural organizations.

2. For many years, generally accepted accounting principles for business enterprises were not considered to be entirely applicable to nonprofit organizations. In the 1970s, the AICPA issued four **Audit and Accounting Guides** or **Industry Audit Guides** for 21 types of nonprofit organizations. Because of inconsistencies among the four **Guides,** the FASB has issued four **Statements of Financial Accounting Standards** and the AICPA has issued an **Audit and Accounting Guide,** "Not-for-Profit Organizations," to provide greater uniformity in accounting for various types of nonprofit organizations.

3. Nonprofit organizations have some characteristics comparable with those of governmental entities described in Chapter 17 of the textbook, and other characteristics similar to those of profit-oriented business enterprises.

4. For example, characteristics of nonprofit organizations that resemble those of governmental entities include service to society, absence of the profit motive, financing by citizenry, stewardship for resources, and extensive use of the budgetary process. Characteristics of nonprofit organizations that resemble those of business enterprises include governance by a board of directors, measurement of cost expirations, and use of the accrual basis of accounting.

5. The basic internal accounting unit for many nonprofit organizations is the **fund.** Separate funds generally are established for resources that may be used at the discretion of the board of directors and for restricted gifts that must be expended pursuant to instructions of donors. The following funds generally are used by nonprofit organizations:

   a. Unrestricted fund (also called unrestricted current fund, general fund, or unrestricted operating fund)

   b. Restricted fund (also called restricted specific-purpose fund or restricted operating fund)

   c. Endowment fund

   d. Agency or custodian fund

   e. Annuity and life income funds (sometimes called split-interest funds)

   f. Loan fund

   g. Plant fund (also called land, building, and equipment fund)

6. The **unrestricted fund** of a nonprofit organization is **residual** in nature because it includes all resources of a nonprofit organization not earmarked for specific purposes.

7. Revenues and gains of an unrestricted fund may be derived from numerous sources. For example, revenues for a hospital may result from patient services, educational programs, research and other grants, and contributions of cash, goods, or services. Revenues for a university may include tuition, fees, governmental grants and contracts, private unrestricted income from endowment funds, and revenue from auxiliary enterprises such as student residences and athletic programs. Different sources of revenues are recorded in separate ledger accounts.

8. Revenues of nonprofit organizations may be in the form of material, facilities, or services, rather than in cash. Significant contributed material and facilities are recognized as revenues at current fair value, offset by a debit to an asset or an expense ledger account, as appropriate. Contributed

services are recognized as revenues if they meet certain criteria set forth in **FASB Statement No. 116,** "Accounting for Contributions Received and Contributions Made."

9. A **pledge** is a promise by a donor to contribute a specified amount of cash or property to a nonprofit organization. Pledges generally are recognized as receivables and revenue, with appropriate provision for doubtful amounts.

10. The various funds of nonprofit organizations may pool resources for investment purposes. The pooling of investment resources requires a careful allocation of investment revenues, gains, and losses among the participating funds. The allocation is made on the basis of the current fair value of assets invested by each fund and subsequently is revised when funds enter or withdraw from the investment pool.

11. The expenses and losses of unrestricted funds of a nonprofit organization are similar to those of a business enterprise. Depreciation must be recognized by nonprofit organizations as required by the Financial Accounting Standards Board.

12. Expenses unique to some nonprofit organizations include fund-raising expense, grants, and income taxes on certain unrelated business income. **Fund-raising costs** generally are recognized as expenses when incurred.

13. Some nonprofit organizations make **grants** to individuals or other organizations. Generally, such grants are recognized as expenses when approved by the governing board of the nonprofit organizations. However, **conditional** grants are not recognized as expenses until they become unconditional.

14. Income taxes expense incurred on **unrelated business income** by some nonprofit organizations is subject to the interperiod tax allocation requirements for business enterprises.

15. Most assets and liabilities of a nonprofit organization's unrestricted fund are similar to the current assets and liabilities of a business enterprise. Health care entities account for plant assets in the general fund, but most other nonprofit organizations have separate plant funds. Collections of some nonprofit organizations such as museums are not recognized as assets; they are disclosed in a note to the organizations' financial statements.

16. The net assets of a nonprofit organization's unrestricted fund are represented by a **fund balance.** The board of directors of a nonprofit organization may **designate** a portion of an unrestricted fund's resources for a specific purpose. This portion of the fund is a **designated portion of the unrestricted fund,** rather than a restricted fund. The designation is recorded by a journal entry as follows:

Undesignated Fund Balance	XXX	
Designated Fund Balance		XXX

17. **Restricted funds** are established by nonprofit organizations to account for resources available for current use but expendable only as authorized by donors. Resources of restricted funds are not obtained from the operations of the nonprofit organization. For example, the restricted funds for a hospital include funds for specific operating purposes, funds for additions to plant assets, and endowment funds.

18. Resources of a restricted fund are transferred to the unrestricted fund as net assets released from restrictions of that fund at the time the designated expenditure authorized by the donor is made.

19. An endowment fund of a nonprofit organization is similar to a nonexpendable private-purpose trust fund of a governmental entity, as described in Chapter 19. The three types of endowment funds are as follows:

    a. **Permanent endowment fund,** in which the principal must be maintained indefinitely in revenue-producing investments, and only the revenues may be spent.

    b. **Term endowment fund,** in which the principal may be spent after a specified number of years or after the occurrence of an event specified by the donor.

c. **Quasi-endowment fund,** which is created by the board of directors of a nonprofit organization. The principal of the quasi-endowment fund may be expended at a later date.

20. An **agency fund** of a nonprofit organization is established to account for resources belonging to other parties. The nonprofit organization acts as a custodian, and resources are expended pursuant to the instructions of the owner. The net assets of an agency fund are offset by a liability of the nonprofit organization.

21. An **annuity fund** is established by a nonprofit organization to receive resources and pay periodic fixed amounts to named recipients for a fixed period of time. At the end of the fixed time period, the remaining assets of the annuity fund are transferred to the unrestricted fund, or to another fund specified by the donor.

22. A **life income fund** is used to account for specified payments of income to a named beneficiary during his or her lifetime. The principal of a life income fund remains intact.

23. A **loan fund** may be established by nonprofit organizations, particularly colleges and universities. Loan funds usually are **revolving** because new loans are made as outstanding loans are repaid. Ordinarily, provisions for doubtful loans and other expenses are debited directly to the Fund Balance ledger account, and interest received on loans is credited to the Fund Balance ledger account.

24. **Plant funds** serve varying functions in different nonprofit organizations. In addition to plant assets, plant funds may include cash and investments earmarked for additions to plant assets, mortgage notes payable and other liabilities collateralized by the plant assets, and sinking fund assets set aside for retirement of debt incurred to acquire plant assets.

25. In **FASB Statement No. 117,** "Financial Statements of Not-for-Profit Organizations," the Financial Accounting Standards Board established guidelines for the following financial statements of nonprofit organizations: statement of financial position, statement of activities, and statement of cash flows.

QUESTIONS

True or False

For each of the following statements, circle the **T** or the **F** to indicate whether the statement is true or false.

T F 1. Some characteristics of nonprofit organizations that resemble those of business enterprises are the use of the accrual basis of accounting, measurement of cost expirations, and governance by a board of directors.

T F 2. The concept of **net income** is applicable to many types of nonprofit organizations.

T F 3. The **Industry Audit Guides** issued by various committees of the AICPA have the substantial authoritative support required for generally accepted accounting principles.

T F 4. Service to society and financing by the citizenry are among the characteristics of nonprofit organizations that resemble those of governmental entities.

T F 5. Nonprofit organizations seldom use program or performance budgets in controlling expenditures.

T F 6. An annuity fund of a nonprofit organization also is known as an endowment fund.

T F 7. The unrestricted fund of a nonprofit organization is residual in nature.

T F 8. Some of the revenues of the unrestricted fund of a nonprofit organization may be derived from the sale of goods and services

T F 9. In the statement of activity of a nonprofit health care organization, the balance of the Contractual Adjustments ledger account is deducted from the balance of the Patient Service Revenue account.

T F 10. The revenues, gains, and losses of an investment pool operated by a nonprofit organization generally are allocated to the various participating funds on the basis of the original cost of the securities contributed to the pool.

T F 11. The Financial Accounting Standards Board requires that depreciation be recognized by nonprofit colleges and universities.

T F 12. The principal of a term endowment fund may be spent at any time at the option of the board of directors of the nonprofit organization.

T F 13. If assets amounting to $100,000 are contributed to an annuity fund, and the estimated present value of the annuity to be paid is $88,000, the difference of $12,000 is credited to the Contributions Revenue ledger account of the annuity fund.

T F 14. Payments to beneficiaries from a life income fund vary from period to period, but payments to beneficiaries from an annuity fund are made in fixed periodic amounts.

T F 15. Interest on loans made from resources of a nonprofit organization's loan fund ordinarily is credited to the Fund Balance ledger account of the loan fund.

T F 16. The plant fund of a nonprofit organization may include resources set aside for interest payments and for the retirement of long-term debt issued to acquire plant assets.

T F 17. A statement of cash flows is appropriate for **all** types of nonprofit organizations.

T F 18. All contributed services are recognized as revenues by nonprofit organizations.

T F 19. If a donor's pledge is payable over a future period, it is recognized as revenue by the nonprofit organization over that future period.

T F 20. Fund-raising costs of nonprofit organizations are recognized as expenses when incurred.

T F 21. Collections of nonprofit organizations may not have a value assigned in the organization's balance sheet.

Completion Statements

Fill in the necessary words or amounts to complete the following statements.

1. An **Audit and Accounting Guide** issued by the AICPA to improve accounting practices for nonprofit organizations is titled _____ _____.

2. The citizenry's contributions to nonprofit organizations are _____ _____.

3. The stewardship requirement makes _____ _____ appropriate for nonprofit organizations.

4. In addition to the unrestricted fund and restricted funds, the following funds commonly are used by nonprofit organizations:

    a. _____

    b. _____

    c. _____

    d. _____

    e. _____

5. Contributed merchandise received by a nonprofit organization is recorded in the _____ ledger account at the _____ _____ _____ of the merchandise.

6. Resources available for investment may be _____ and administered by a single _____ _____.

7. A permanent endowment fund is one for which the principal must be maintained indefinitely in _____ _____. A _____ _____ may be _____ by the board of directors of a nonprofit organization.

8. Resources of a student organization are accounted for in an _____ _____; however, the net assets of such an organization are reported as a _____ of the school because the school has no _____ in the organization's resources.

9. Unpaid amounts of conditional grants that may be _____ by a nonprofit organization are not recorded as expenses until they are _____.

Multiple Choice

Choose the best answer for each of the following questions and enter the identifying letter in the space provided.

_____ 1. Resources of a nonprofit organization's unrestricted fund that have been set aside for a specific purpose by the board of directors of the organization are accounted for in:

   a. The unrestricted fund
   b. A term endowment fund
   c. A restricted operating fund
   d. An annuity fund
   e. None of the foregoing

2. The fund used to record resources contributed to a nonprofit organization on the condition that the organization pay a fixed periodic amount to a named individual for a fixed time period is:
   a. Loan fund
   b. Agency fund
   c. Life income fund
   d. Annuity fund
   e. None of the foregoing

3. The cash basis of accounting is appropriate for a nonprofit organization's:
   a. Pledges received from potential donors
   b. Contributions of goods and services
   c. Interest on loans made to students
   d. Salaries expense

4. Nonprofit organizations recognize pledges as receivables and revenues if the pledges are:
   a. Received in cash
   b. Deemed collectible
   c. Unconditional
   d. Legally enforceable

5. The AICPA's "Hospital Audit Guide" was replaced by:
   a. "Health Care Organizations"
   b. "Not-for-Profit Organizations"
   c. "Financial Reporting by Not-for-Profit Organizations: . . ."
   d. "Nonprofit Accounting Guide"

6. Nonprofit organizations that do not depend on the general population for a substantial portion of their revenues include:
   a. Political parties
   b. Professional associations
   c. Research and scientific organizations
   d. None of the foregoing

7. Is a revenues valuation account used for:

	Contractual adjustments?	Tuition remissions?
a.	Yes	Yes
b.	Yes	No
c.	No	Yes
d.	No	No

8. Are contributions of services recognized as revenues by a nonprofit organization if the services:

	Create nonfinancial assets?	Require specialized skills?
a.	Yes	Yes
b.	Yes	No
c.	No	Yes
d.	No	No

SHORT EXERCISES

1. Early in 2005, the four funds of Colorado Aid Society, a voluntary health and welfare organization, pooled their investments, consisting of stocks and bonds, as follows:

	Cost	Current fair value
Gaston Endowment Fund	$125,000	$180,000
Plant Fund	233,000	240,000
Unrestricted Current Fund	147,000	150,000
Restricted Current Fund	45,000	30,000
Totals	$550,000	$600,000

    At the end of the year, the manager of the pool reported the following results for 2005:

Dividends and interest revenue	$38,400
Realized and unrealized gains on disposal of investments	36,000
Realized and unrealized losses on disposal of investments	16,600

    Complete the following analysis, allocating the net earnings and gains or losses for 2005 to the four funds.

	Equity percentages	Realized and unrealized gains (net)	Dividends and interest
Gaston Endowment Fund	%	$	$
Plant Fund			
Unrestricted Current Fund			
Restricted Current Fund			
Totals	%	$	$

    Computations:

2. The following selected transactions and events were completed during 2005 by the Axel Cooper Annuity Fund of State University.

    a. Received $80,000 cash from Axel Cooper for an annuity of $7,200 a year to be paid to him in monthly installments during his lifetime. The actuarially computed present value of the annuity based on Cooper's life expectancy and an 8% rate of interest was $57,750.

    b. Invested all but $1,000 of the cash received from Cooper in corporate bonds.

    c. Paid first monthly annuity check to Cooper.

    d. Revenue from investments amounted to $2,450.

    e. Received actuaries' report that the gain for 2005, based on a revised life expectancy for Cooper and actual earnings on investments, was $1,210. (Debit the Annuity Payable ledger account.)

    In the space on page 195, prepare journal entries to record the above transactions and events in the accounting records of the Axel Cooper Annuity Fund.

Axel Cooper Annuity Fund
Journal Entries

2005			
a.			
b.			
c.			
d.			
e.			

3. The following events or transactions occurred for two separate nonprofit organizations:

    a. Eagle Elementary School received rent-free use of new school premises, beginning on July 1, 2005, the start of a fiscal year. Current fair rental value of the premises is $3,000 a month.

    b. Classical Performing Arts Organization made on July 1, 2005, the beginning of a fiscal year, the first payment on a $15,000 conditional grant to a musician to help with music study. The grant was payable $5,000 a year on July 1, 2005, 2006, and 2007, unless revoked.

In the space provided below, prepare journal entries for the foregoing transactions or events. In a brief explanation, indicate in what fund, if any, each entry is recorded.

Journal Entries

	2005			
a.				
b.	2005			

CASE

Nonprofit organizations recognize revenues for all contributed goods and facilities. However, the Financial Accounting Standards Board, in **FASB Statement No. 116**, "Accounting for Contributions Received and Contributions Made," limited the recognition of revenues for services contributed to nonprofit organizations to services meeting specified criteria. Is this inconsistency justified? Explain.

SOLUTIONS TO QUESTIONS, SHORT EXERCISES, AND CASE: CHAPTER 16

QUESTIONS

True or False

1. T 2. F 3. T 4. T 5. F 6. F 7. T 8. T 9. T 10. F 11. T 12. F 13. T 14. T 15. T 16. T 17. T 18. F 19. F 20. T 21. T

Completion Statements

1. "Not-for-Profit Organizations." 2. Voluntary donations. 3. Fund accounting. 4. a. Endowment, b. Agency, c. Annuity and Life Income, d. Loan, e. Plant. 5. Inventories, current fair value. 6. Pooled, portfolio manager. 7. Revenue-producing investments, quasi-endowment fund, expended. 8. Agency fund, liability, equity. 9. Revoked, unconditional.

Multiple Choice

1. a 2. d 3. c 4. d 5. a 6. b 7. b 8. a

SHORT EXERCISES

1.

	Equity percentages	Realized and unrealized gains (net)	Dividends and interest
Gaston Endowment Fund	30%	$ 6,000	$11,520
Plant Fund	40	8,000	15,360
Unrestricted Current Fund	25	5,000	9,600
Restricted Current Fund	5	1,000	1,920
Totals	100%	$20,000	$38,400

2.

Axel Cooper Annuity Fund
Journal Entries

2005			
a.	Cash	80,000	
	Annuity Payable		57,750
	Contributions Revenue		22,250
	To establish Axel Cooper Annuity Fund.		
b.	Investments	79,000	
	Cash		79,000
	To record acquisition of corporate bonds.		
c.	Annuity Payable	600	
	Cash		600
	To record first monthly payment to Axel Cooper.		
d.	Cash	2,450	
	Annuity Payable		2,450
	To record revenue on investments.		
e.	Annuity Payable	1,210	
	Contributions Revenue		1,210
	To record actuarial gain for 2005.		

3.

Journal Entries

a.

	2005			
	July 1	Rent Expense	3,000	
		Contributions Revenue		3,000
		To record current fair value of July, 2005, rental of		
		school building whose use was contributed.		

b.

	2005			
	July 1	Grants Expense	5,000	
		Cash		5,000
		To record payment of first annual installment of a		
		conditional grant.		

CASE

The inconsistency in the accounting for contributed goods, facilities, and services by nonprofit organizations is justified by the differences among the three types of contributions. The current fair values of goods and facilities contributed to a nonprofit organization generally can be measured without undue difficulties. In contrast, the current fair values attributable to many services contributed to nonprofit organizations are impossible to measure, especially services of members of the organization. For example, many members of professional associations contribute substantial hours of service to boards of directors, officerships, committees, etc., of the associations. Volunteer fund-raisers for nonprofit organizations, often on their own, give significant amounts of time to the organizations. Members of the congregations of churches and related private schools contribute services to their organizations. In recognition of these facts, the Financial Accounting Standards Board, in **FASB Statement No. 116,** "Accounting for Contributions Received and Contributions Made," placed significant restrictions on the recognition of revenue for services contributed to nonprofit organizations.

HIGHLIGHTS OF CHAPTER

1.   Governmental entities in the United States consist of the federal government, states, territories, counties, townships, municipalities, school districts, and special districts (such as port authorities, airports, public buildings, libraries, and others).

2.   Some characteristics of governmental entities are:

   Organization to serve the citizenry

   General absence of the profit motive

   Taxation as the principal source of revenue

   Impact of the legislative process

   Stewardship for resources

3.   For many years, neither the AICPA nor the FASB gave attention to the accounting problem of governmental entities.

4.   The National Council on Governmental Accounting (NCGA), an organization of 21 local, state, and national governmental financial officers, had established accounting principles for governmental entities for many years. In 1984, the GASB was established as an arm of the Financial Accounting Foundation with the authority to establish accounting standards for state and local governmental entities.

5.   Shortly after its establishment in 1984, the Governmental Accounting Standards Boards (GASB) issued **GASB Concepts Statement No. 1,** "Objectives of Financial Reporting," in which it set forth three reporting standards for state and local governmental entities.

6.   One of the first acts of the GASB was to codify governmental accounting and financial reporting standards in effect in 1984. Subsequently, the GASB issued a number of **Statements** on governmental accounting standards and revised codifications.

7.   The GASB provided that the **governmental financial reporting entity** was to consist of the **primary** (state or local) **government** and **component units.**

8.   The primary accounting unit for governmental entities is the **fund.** A fund is a fiscal and accounting entity with a self-balancing set of accounts recording cash and other financial resources, together with all related liabilities and residual equities or balances, and changes therein, that are segregated for the purpose of carrying on specific activities or attaining certain objectives in accordance with specific regulations, restrictions, or limitations.

9.   The **funds** recommended for governmental entities are:

   General fund

   Special revenue funds

   Capital projects funds

   Debt service funds

   Permanent funds

   Enterprise funds

   Internal service funds

   Trust and agency funds (four types)

   In addition, self-balancing **account groups** for **general capital assets** and **general long-term debt** are often used voluntarily by governmental entities.

10. Except for the two proprietary funds (enterprise funds and internal service funds), governmental accounting does not emphasize the results of operations. Financial reporting for governmental entities focuses on the stewardship of fund resources. As a result, the accrual basis of accounting is used for many operating funds of a governmental entity.

11. Because of the lack of emphasis on operating results in funds other than the two proprietary funds (enterprise funds and internal service funds), **expenditures** rather than expenses are recorded in the accounting records of most governmental funds. Consequently, depreciation expense generally is recognized only in enterprise funds and internal service funds.

12. **Annual budgets** and **capital budgets** are a means of exercising legislative control over governmental entities. Annual budgets generally are used for the general and special revenue funds; capital budgets are appropriate for capital projects funds. The budgets for general and special revenue funds generally are recorded in their accounting records. Annual budgets as a rule are not recorded in the accounting records of enterprise funds and internal service funds.

13. Several types of annual budgets may be used by a governmental entity. Among these are the following:

    a. An **object budget,** which classifies authorized expenditures by department and by object

    b. A **program budget,** which stresses the measurement of total cost of a program, regardless of how many departments (or funds) are involved in the program

    c. A **performance budget,** which attempts to relate input of resources to output of services

14. The annual budget for a **general fund** (which includes all transactions not recorded in another fund) is recorded as follows:

Estimated Revenues	XXX	
Estimated Other Financing Sources	XXX	
Appropriations		XXX
Estimated Other Financing Uses		XXX
Budgetary Fund Balance		XXX

If estimated revenues and estimated other financing sources exceed appropriations and other financing uses, the **budgetary surplus** is credited to the Budgetary Fund Balance ledger account; if appropriations and estimated other financing uses exceed estimated revenues and other financing sources, the **budgetary deficit** is debited to the Budgetary Fund Balance ledger account.

15. Purchase orders for nonrecurring acquisitions of goods and services by a general fund may require a debit to Encumbrances and a credit to Fund Balance Reserved for Encumbrances to ensure that total expenditures for a fiscal year do not exceed appropriations. When the invoice is received, the foregoing journal entry is reversed and the actual amount of the invoice is recorded as a debit to Expenditures and a credit to Vouches Payable.

16. Other typical transactions for a general fund are illustrated in Chapter 17 of the textbook. Students should study these pages carefully. At the end of a fiscal year, a trial balance is prepared as a preliminary step to the preparation of the following general fund financial statements: (a) the statement of revenues, expenditures, and changes in net assets and (b) the balance sheet, and the preparation of closing entries.

17. Closing entries for a general fund consist of (a) a journal entry to close the Encumbrances ledger account; (b) an entry to close the budgetary ledger accounts; and (c) an entry to close the Revenues, Expenditures, and Other Financing Sources and Uses ledger accounts.

QUESTIONS

True or False

For each of the following statements, circle the **T** or the **F** to indicate whether the statement is true or false.

T F 1. The profit motive is among the objectives of the two proprietary funds (enterprise funds and internal service funds) of a governmental entity.

T F 2. The recognition of expenses and the matching of expenses and revenues are among the characteristics of accounting systems for governmental entities.

T F 3. The accrual basis of accounting is appropriate for a governmental entity's general fund, special revenue funds, capital projects funds, and debt service funds.

T F 4. Encumbrance journal entries are not required for recurring expenditures such as salaries, utilities, and rent.

T F 5. The Estimated Revenues ledger account of a general fund may be considered a **pseudo liability** account.

T F 6. Because a general fund records only transactions not recorded in one of the other ten types of funds, it may be considered a **residual** fund.

T F 7. The Unreserved and Undesignated Fund Balance ledger account shows the ownership equity of a governmental entity in the general fund.

T F 8. The Budgetary Fund Balance ledger account of a general fund is debited when the Revenues and Estimated Revenues accounts are closed a the end of a fiscal year if actual revenues exceed estimated revenues.

T F 9. Both outstanding encumbrances and inventory of supplies may be displayed in the balance sheet for a general fund prepared at the end of a fiscal year.

T F 10. The Governmental Accounting Standards Board has established standards of accounting for the federal government.

T F 11. In a **program budget,** there is an attempt to relate the input of governmental resources to the output of governmental services.

T F 12. Amounts transferred as subsidies to the general fund from other funds represent revenues to the general fund.

Completion Statements

Fill in the necessary words or amounts to complete the following statements.

1. The primary accounting unit for governmental entities is the _____. A _____ _____ fund is used to account for the payment of interest and principal on general long-term debt of a governmental entity.

2. A _____ _____ fund is used to account for financial resources to be used for the acquisition or construction of facilities other than those financed by _____ funds and _____ funds.

3. If the Fund Balance Reserved for Encumbrances ledger account of a general fund is debited or credited, the _____ ledger account generally is credited or debited.

4. A _____ _____ attempts to relate the input of governmental resources to the output of governmental services.

5. A statement of revenues, expenditures, and changes in fund balance usually is prepared in a three-column format: one column for _____, one for _____, and the final column showing the _____, favorable and unfavorable.

6. The _____ _____ _____ _____ ledger account includes budgeted amounts of transfers out to other funds.

Multiple Choice

Choose the best answer for each of the following questions and enter the identifying letter in the space provided.

Questions **1** and **2** are based on the following related journal entries that were recorded in chronological sequence in the general fund of a governmental entity:

Entry A	Encumbrances	15,000	
	Fund Balance Reserved for Encumbrances		15,000
Entry B	Fund Balance Reserved for Encumbrances	15,000	
	Encumbrances		15,000
Entry C	Expenditures	15,150	
	Vouchers Payable		15,150

____ 1. The sequence of these journal entries indicates that:
   a. An adverse event was foreseen and a reserve of $15,000 was created; later the reserve was canceled and a liability for the unfavorable event was recorded.
   b. An order was placed for goods or services estimated to cost $15,000; the actual cost was $15,150, for which a liability was recorded when the goods or services were received.
   c. Encumbrances were anticipated but later failed to materialize and were reversed; a liability of $15,150 was incurred.
   d. Entry A was erroneous and was reversed; a liability of $15,150 was incurred.

____ 2. Immediately after journal entry **A** was recorded, the general fund had a balanced annual budget for all transactions. Recording entries **B** and **C** would:
   a. Not change the balanced condition of the budget
   b. Cause the general fund to show a budgetary surplus
   c. Cause the general fund to show a budgetary deficit
   d. Not affect the current fiscal year budget but would affect the budget of the following fiscal year

_____ 3. A city's general fund budget for the forthcoming fiscal year shows estimated revenues in excess of appropriations. The recording of this budget results in an increase in the ledger account:

a. Taxes Receivable—Current
b. Budgetary Fund Balance
c. Fund Balance Reserved for Encumbrances
d. Encumbrances
e. Unreserved and Undesignated Fund Balance

_____ 4. Which of the following types of revenues generally is recognized in the general fund of a governmental entity?

a. Receipts from a city-owned parking structure
b. Interest earned on investments held for retirement of employees
c. Revenues of internal service funds
d. Property taxes

_____ 5. Authority granted by a governmental entity's legislative body to make general fund expenditures and to incur obligations during a fiscal year is the definition of an:

a. Appropriation
b. Authorization
c. Encumbrance
d. Expenditure

_____ 6. When goods that previously were approved for purchase are received by a general fund but not yet paid for, what ledger account is credited?

a. Fund Balances Reserved for Encumbrances
b. Vouchers Payable
c. Expenditures
d. Appropriations
e. Some other account

_____ 7. What ledger account might be credited to record a general fund's obligation for goods ordered but not yet received?

a. Appropriations
b. Encumbrances
c. Obligations
d. Fund Balance Reserved for Encumbrances

_____ 8. A credit to the Budgetary Fund Balance ledger account in a journal entry to record the budget of a governmental entity's general fund indicates that:

a. Estimated expenses exceed actual revenues
b. Actual expenses exceed estimated expenses
c. Estimated revenues exceed appropriations
d. Appropriations exceed estimated revenues

_____ 9. Billings for goods and services to the general fund from other funds of a governmental entity are debited to the ledger account:

a. Interfund Expenditures
b. Other Financing Uses
c. Interfund Obligations
d. Expenditures

SHORT EXERCISES

1. The trial balance for the General Fund of the City of Colima on June 30, 2005, follows. There were no budgeted or actual other financing sources or other financing uses.

City of Colima General Fund
Trial Balance
June 30, 2005

	Debit	Credit
Cash	$ 35,500	
Taxes receivable—delinquent	14,250	
Allowances for uncollectible delinquent taxes		$ 250
Inventory of supplies (balance on June 30, 2004, $10,000)	12,500	
Vouchers payable		17,500
Fund balance reserved for encumbrances		1,250
Fund balance reserved for inventory of supplies		12,500
Unreserved and undesignated fund balance		17,500
Budgetary fund balance		10,000
Estimated revenues	200,000	
Appropriations		190,000
Revenues		202,000
Expenditures	187,500	
Encumbrances	1,250	
Totals	$451,000	$451,000

a. Complete the following statement of revenues, expenditures, and changes in net assets of the General Fund for the year ended June 30, 2005:

City of Colima General Fund
Statement of Revenues, Expenditures, and
Changes in Fund Balance
For Year Ended June 30, 2005

	Budget	Actual	Variance favorable (unfavorable)
Revenues	$	$	$

b. Complete the following balance sheet of the General Fund on June 30, 2005:

City of Colima General Fund
Balance Sheet
June 30, 2005
Assets

Cash	$

(continued)

©The McGraw-Hill Companies, Inc., 2006

Liabilities & Fund Balance

Liabilities: $
   Vouchers payable

c. In the space below, prepare closing entries for the City of Colima General Fund on June 30, 2005. Omit explanations.

City of Colima General Fund
Closing Entries

2005			
June 30			

2. The following transactions and events took place for the City of Roverton General Fund for the fiscal year ended June 30, 2005:

  a. The City Council of Roverton adopted the annual budget for the general operations of the government during the year ending June 30, 2005. Revenues were estimated at $985,000. Legal authorization for budgeted expenditures was $970,000. There were no estimated other financing sources or other financing uses.

  b. Property taxes of $750,000 were levied. Uncollectible property taxes were estimated at 2%.

  c. (1) On July 20, 2004, office furniture estimated to cost $20,000 was ordered for the city manager's office. The city records encumbrances for nonrecurring commitments for expenditures such as the acquisition of plant assets.

     (2) The furniture ordered July 20, 2004, was received on August 19, 2004, accompanied by an invoice for $20,600.

For each transaction or event, prepare a journal entry (or entries) in the General Fund, including a brief explanation for each entry. Use the space below.

City of Roverton General Fund
Journal Entries

a.			
b.			
c. (1)			
(2)			

CASE

In a classroom discussion of accounting standards for the general fund of a governmental entity, student Ralph questions the need to differentiate **quasi-external transactions** from **transfers in** or **out.** Ralph points out that both types of activities are between the general fund and another fund; he likens them to the intercompany transactions between parent company and subsidiaries. Ralph recommends a **transfers in (out) from (to) other funds** category in the statement of revenues, expenditures, and changes in fund balance for a general fund to include both quasi-external transactions and regular transfers in or out.

Do you agree with student Ralph? Explain.

QUESTIONS

True or False

1. F   2. F   3. F   4. T   5. F   6. T   7. F   8. F   9. T   10. F   11. F   12. F

Completion Statements

1. Fund, debt service.   2. Capital projects, proprietary, trust.   3. Encumbrances.   4. Performance budget.
5. Budget, actual, variance.   6. Estimated Other Financing Uses.

Multiple Choice

1. b   2. c   3. b   4. d   5. a   6. b   7. d   8. c   9. d

SHORT EXERCISES

1.   a.

City of Colima General Fund
Statement of Revenues, Expenditures, and
Changes in Fund Balance
For Year Ended June 30, 2005

	Budget	Actual	Variance favorable (unfavorable)
Revenues	$200,000	$202,000	$2,000
Expenditures	190,000	187,500	2,500
Excess of revenues over expenditures	$ 10,000	$ 14,500	$4,500
Fund balance, beginning of year	30,000	30,000 (1)	
Fund balance, end of year	$ 40,000	$ 44,500	$4,500

(1) $17,500 + $2,500 + $10,000 = $30,000

b.

City of Colima General Fund
Balance Sheet
June 30, 2005
Assets

Cash	$35,500
Taxes receivable, net of allowance for estimated uncollectible amounts, $250	14,000
Inventory of supplies	12,500
Total assets	$62,000

Liabilities & Fund Balance

Liabilities:		
Vouchers payable		$17,500
Fund balance:		
Reserved for encumbrances	$ 1,250	
Reserved for inventory of supplies	12,500	
Unreserved and undesignated	30,750 (1)	44,500
Total liabilities		$62,000

(1) $17,500 – $1,250 + $14,500 = $30,750

City of Colima General Fund
Closing Entries

2005			
June 30	Unreserved and Undesignated Fund Balance	1,250	
	Encumbrances		1,250
30	Appropriations	190,000	
	Budgetary Fund Balance	10,000	
	Estimated Revenues		200,000
30	Revenues	202,000	
	Expenditures		187,500
	Unreserved and Undesignated Fund Balance		14,500

2.
City of Roverton General Fund
Journal Entries

a.	Estimated Revenues	985,000	
	Appropriations		970,000
	Budgetary Fund Balance		15,000
	To record annual budget adopted for fiscal year ending June 30, 2005.		
b.	Taxes Receivable—Current	750,000	
	Allowance for Uncollectible Current Taxes ($750,000 x 0.02)		15,000
	Revenues		735,000
	To accrue property taxes billed and to provide for estimated uncollectible portion.		
c. (1)	Encumbrances	20,000	
	Fund Balance Reserved for Encumbrances		20,000
	To record encumbrance for office furniture.		
(2)	Fund Balance Reserved for Encumbrances	20,000	
	Encumbrances		20,000
	To record cancellation of encumbrance for office furniture on receipt of invoice.		
	Expenditures	20,600	
	Vouchers Payable		20,600
	To record expenditure for office furniture encumbered for $20,000.		

CASE

Given the importance of the annual budget for a governmental entity's general fund, student Ralph's recommendation may not be feasible. Quasi-external transactions of a general fund do differ significantly from the fund's transfers in or out; the former resemble transactions that the general fund has with outside entities, while the latter are related strictly to activities within the governmental entity itself. The distinction between the two may be significant in the budgetary process.

CHAPTER 18

GOVERNMENTAL ENTITIES: OTHER GOVERNMENTAL FUNDS AND ACCOUNT GROUPS

HIGHLIGHTS OF CHAPTER

1. **Special revenue funds** account for the proceeds of specific revenue sources, such as certain taxes and special assessments, to finance specified activities. The journal entries and financial statements for special revenue funds are similar to those for a general fund.

2. **Capital projects funds** account for the receipt and payment of cash expended for the acquisition or construction of facilities other than those financed by proprietary funds or trust funds. The resources of a capital projects fund generally are derived from proceeds of general obligation bonds. Resources also may be received from tax revenues or from grants from other governmental entities.

3. The opening journal entry for a capital projects fund financed with the proceeds of general obligation bonds issued at face amount is as follows:

Cash	XXX	
Other Financing Sources		XXX

    Any premium or discount on the bonds is recorded in a separate ledger account.

    The proceeds of the bond issue do not represent revenues to the capital projects fund. The liability for the bonds might be recorded in a voluntarily maintained general long-term debt account group until the bonds mature. On the maturity date, the bond liability is moved to the appropriate debt service fund, if any.

4. Journal entries to record encumbrances and expenditures in a capital projects fund are similar to those for a general fund; expenditures recorded might be accompanied by an end-of-year journal entry debit to Construction Work in Progress and a credit to Investment in Capital Assets from Capital Projects Fund a voluntarily maintained general capital assets account group. The revenues, expenditures, and encumbrances accounts of a capital projects fund are closed at the end of the fiscal year, and the capital projects fund itself is closed upon completion of the project by transfer of any unused cash to either a debt service fund or the general fund. A deficiency normally would be covered by a transfer of cash from the general fund.

5. The financial statements for a capital projects fund are a statement of revenues, expenditures, and changes in fund balance and a balance sheet.

6. **Debt service funds** account for the payments of interest and principal on long-term debt other than special assessment bonds, revenue bonds, and general obligation bonds serviced by an enterprise fund. The liabilities for bonds and interest to be paid by a debt service fund are not recorded in the fund until the obligations mature. Prior to the maturity date, the bond liabilities might be recorded a voluntarily maintained general long-term debt account group.

7. Cash received by a debt service fund from the general fund is credited to the Other Financing Sources ledger account. On the due date for any principal and interest payments, the Expenditures ledger account is debited and related Matured Bonds Payable and Matured Interest Payable accounts are credited.

8. The financial statements for a debt service fund are a statement of revenues, expenditures, and changes in fund balance and a balance sheet.

9. A **general capital assets account group** and a **general long-term debt account group** are not funds. Their purpose is to provide a memorandum record of plant assets and debt that are not recorded in funds.

10. Plant assets in the general capital assets account group are recorded at their cost, or at current fair value if donated to the governmental entity. The offsetting credit is to one of several Investment in General Capital Assets ledger accounts.

11. Depreciation may be recorded in a general capital assets account group with a debit to the appropriate Investment in General Capital Assets ledger account and a credit to an Accumulated Depreciation account. When a plant asset carried in a general capital assets account group is disposed of by the governmental entity, the carrying amount of the asset is removed from the memorandum ledger accounts in the general capital assets account group, and any disposal proceeds are recognized as revenues or other financing sources in the general fund.

12. An analysis of changes in general capital assets is included in a governmental entity's comprehensive annual financial report by means of a note to the financial statements.

13. General obligation bonds and other long-term debt of a governmental entity that are not accounted for in an enterprise fund might be recorded in a general long-term debt account group with a debit to the Amount to Be Provided ledger account and a credit to an appropriate liability account.

14. When cash or other assets have been accumulated in a debt service fund for the ultimate payment of a bond issue or other long-term liabilities, a journal entry debiting Amount Available in Debt Service Fund and crediting Amount to Be Provided is recorded in a general long-term debt account group (if one is used). When the bonds or other liabilities are accrued by the debt service fund, the memorandum ledger accounts are reversed in the general long-term debt account group at the end of the fiscal year.

15. An analysis of changes in general long-term debt is included in a governmental entity's comprehensive annual financial report by means of a note to the financial statements.

16. If a capital lease is executed for property of a governmental entity not recorded in a proprietary fund, the property might be recorded in a general capital assets account group, and the noncurrent potion of the lease liability might be recorded in a general long-term debt account group. The periodic lease payments typically are included in the expenditures of the general fund.

17. **Special assessment bonds,** which sometimes are issued by a governmental entity to finance construction projects pending receipt of special assessments payable in annual installments, might be recorded in a general long-term debt account group under the following circumstances: (a) if the governmental entity is obligated for the bonds in some manner; or (b) if no portion of the bonds is a direct obligation of an enterprise fund or is expected to be repaid from operating revenues of an enterprise fund.

QUESTIONS

True or False

For each of the following statements, circle the **T** or the **F** to indicate whether the statement is true or false.

T   F   1.   A general capital assets account group and a general long-term debt account group do not fit the definition of **funds.**

T   F   2.   The proceeds from the issuance of general obligation bonds for a school district might be recorded in a general long-term debt account group.

T   F   3.   Generally, there is no unreserved fund balance in the balance sheet of a debt service fund.

T F 4. Depreciation on assets constructed through activities of a capital projects fund is included among the expenses of that fund.

T F 5. Depreciation **expense** may be recorded in a general capital assets account group.

T F 6. A special revenue fund may be established for the proceeds of special assessments.

T F 7. Proceeds from the issuance of general obligation bonds for a construction project represent revenues to the capital projects fund established for the project.

T F 8. Despite the absence of legal requirements or a formal plan for accumulations of a sinking fund, a debt service fund should be established for all general long-term bonds of a governmental entity other than those to be repaid by an enterprise fund.

T F 9. An Investment in General Capital Assets ledger account in a governmental entity's voluntarily maintained general capital assets account group is an asset account.

T F 10. Journal entries related to a capital lease executed by a governmental entity are prepared for a general capital assets account group and a general long-term debt account group if they are used, and the general fund.

T F 11. Special assessment debt for which a governmental entity is not obligated in any manner is disclosed in a note to the governmental entity's financial statements.

Completion Statements

Fill in the necessary words or amounts to complete the following statements.

1. Revenue bonds and other long-term borrowings by enterprise funds are not recorded in a
    _____ _____ _____ _____ _____.

2. Because a debt service fund does not issue _____ _____,
    encumbrance accounting is not required.

3. Account titles, budgetary processes, and financial statements for _____ _____
    _____ are similar to those for general funds.

4. The assets constructed with resources of a capital projects funds are sometimes recorded in the
    governmental entity's _____ _____ _____ _____
    _____.

5. The journal entry to record depreciation in a governmental entity's general capital assets account
    group includes a debit to the appropriate _____ _____ _____ _____
    _____ ledger account.

Multiple Choice

Choose the best answer for each of the following questions and enter the identifying letter in the space provided.

_____ 1.   In order to provide for the retirement of general obligations bonds, a governmental entity invested a portion of its cash receipts for revenues in marketable securities. This investment activity may be accounted for in:
a.   A trust fund
b.   An enterprise fund
c.   A debt service fund
d.   A special revenue fund
e.   Some other fund

_____ 2.   The proceeds of a federal grant made to assist in financing the construction of an adult education center by a governmental entity are recorded in:
a.   The general fund
b.   A special revenue fund
c.   A capital projects fund
d.   An internal service fund
e.   Some other fund

_____ 3.   The liability for special assessment bonds that carry a secondary pledge of the State of Texas general credit might be recorded in:
a.   An enterprise fund
b.   A special revenue fund and a general long-term debt account group
c.   A general long-term debt account group
d.   A special assessment fund and disclosed in a note to the statement of changes in general long-term debt
e.   Some other manner

_____ 4.   Which of the following types of bonds of a governmental entity is never recognized as a liability of a debt service fund?
a.   Serial bonds
b.   Revenue bonds
c.   Term bonds
d.   General obligation bonds
e.   None of the foregoing

_____ 5.   Might a general capital assets account group of a governmental entity be used to account for the plant assets of?

	Governmental Funds?	Proprietary Funds?
a.	No	Yes
b.	No	No
c.	Yes	No
d.	Yes	Yes

_____ 6.   The governmental funds category of a governmental entity includes all the following except:
   a.   General fund
   b.   Agency fund
   c.   Capital projects fund
   d.   Debt service fund

_____ 7.   Is an Expenditures ledger account included in the accounting records of a governmental entity's:

	Special Revenue Fund?	Capital Projects Fund?	Debt Service Fund?
a.	Yes	Yes	Yes
b.	Yes	No	Yes
c.	No	Yes	No
d.	No	Yes	Yes

_____ 8.   An Amount to Be Provided ledger account is included in the accounting records of a governmental entity's:
   a.   Debt service fund only
   b.   General long-term debt account group only
   c.   Debt service fund and general long-term debt account group
   d.   Special revenue fund only

SHORT EXERCISE

1.   The four independent transactions or events described below were completed by four different governmental entities:

   a.   The City of Keene General Fund transferred $108,000 to the Debt Service Fund for maturing principal and interest ($8,000) on 8% serial bonds.

   b.   A citizen devised 20 acres of land to Ryan City for a future school site. The donor's cost of the land was $100,000. The current fair value of the land was $175,000.

   c.   (1) On March 31, 2005, Dana City issued 6% general obligation term bonds payable March 31, 2010, at face amount of $100,000. Interest was payable each March 31 and September 30. Dana City was to use the proceeds to finance a street-widening project.

      (2) On November 1, 2005, the full $97,000 cost of the completed street-widening project was accrued. Also, appropriate closing entries were made with regard to the project.

   d.   The General Fund of Welby Village billed the Special Revenue Fund $60,000 for expenditures that were reimbursable to the General Fund by the Special Revenue Fund.

In the spaces provided below and on page 215, prepare journal entries in the appropriate fund or account group for each transaction or event. Include a brief explanation for each entry, and indicate the fund, or account group (assuming used) in which it is recorded.

Journal Entries

a.

b.

c. (1)

(2)

Journal Entries (concluded)

d.			

CASE

You are an audit manager of the CPA firm Rand & Stole LLP assigned to conduct a staff training program on accounting for governmental entities. An area you intend to emphasize is the interrelationship among three funds and the optional two account groups when general obligation bonds are issued by a governmental entity to finance the construction of a plant asset that will provide services to all citizens of the entity.

Write a paragraph describing the journal entries in the funds and account groups affected by the construction of a plant asset funded by general obligation bonds by a governmental entity.

SOLUTIONS TO QUESTIONS, SHORT EXERCISE, AND CASE: CHAPTER 18

QUESTIONS

True or False

1. T 2. F 3. T 4. F 5. F 6. T 7. F 8. F 9. F 10. T 11. F

Completion Statements

1. General long-term debt account group. 2. Purchase orders. 3. Special revenue funds. 4. General capital assets account group. 5. Investment in General Capital Assets.

Multiple Choice

1. c 2. c 3. c 4. b 5. c 6. b 7. a 8. b

SHORT EXERCISE

1.

	Journal Entries		
a.	Other Financing Uses	108,000	
	Cash		108,000
	To record transfer by **general fund** to debt service fund for maturing principal and interest on 6% serial bonds.		
	Cash	108,000	
	Other Financing Sources		108,000
	To record in **debt service fund** receipt of cash from general fund for payment of maturing principal and interest on 6% serial bonds.		
	Amount Available in Debt Service Fund	100,000	
	Amount to Be Provided		100,000
	To record amount available for maturing 6% serial bonds principal in **general long-term debt account group.**		
b.	Land	175,000	
	Investment in General Capital Assets from Donation		175,000
	To record donated land in **general capital assets account group.**		
c. (1)	Cash	100,000	
	Other Financing Sources		100,000
	To record issuance of bonds for street-widening project in **capital projects fund.**		
	Amount to Be Provided	100,000	
	Term Bonds Payable		100,000
	To record issuance of 6% general obligation term bonds for street-widening project in **general long-term debt account group.**		

(2)	Expenditures	97,000	
	Vouchers Payable		97,000
	To record expenditures for street-widening project in **capital projects fund.**		
	Unreserved and Undesignated Fund Balance	97,000	
	Expenditures		97,000
	To close expenditures in **capital projects fund.**		
	Improvements Other than Buildings	97,000	
	Investment in General Capital Assets from Capital Projects Fund		97,000
	To record cost of street-widening project in **general capital assets account group.**		
d.	Receivable from Special Revenue Fund	60,000	
	Expenditures		60,000
	To record in **general fund** billing to special revenue fund for reimbursable expenditures.		
	Expenditures	60,000	
	Payable to General Fund		60,000
	To record in **special revenue fund** billing from general fund for reimbursable expenditures.		

CASE

When general obligation bonds are issued by a governmental entity to finance the construction of a plant asset, the proceeds of the bonds are recorded in a capital projects fund with a debit to Cash, a credit to Other Financing Sources for the face amount of the bonds, and a debit to a discount account or a credit to a premium account, as required. A the same time, the liability for the bonds might be recorded in a general long-term debt account group with a debit to Amount to Be Provided and a credit to Bonds Payable for the face amount of the bonds. Assuming the construction project is completed during the same fiscal year that the bonds were issued, upon completion the appropriate plant asset ledger account might be debited in a general capital assets account group, with a credit to Investment in General Capital Assets from Capital Projects Funds. When the general fund transfers cash to a debt service fund established for the bonds, the general fund accountant debits Other Financing Uses and credits Cash; the debt service fund accountant debits Cash and credits Other Financing Sources; and the general long-term debt account group accountant debits Amount Available in Debt Service Fund and credits Amount to Be Provided. The debt service fund accountant accrues bond principal and interest on the maturity date with a debit to Expenditures and credits to Matured Bonds Payable and Matured Interest Payable; the accountant for the general long-term debt account group debits Bonds Payable and credits Amount Available in Debt Service Fund for the principal to be paid.

CHAPTER 19
GOVERNMENTAL ENTITIES: PROPRIETARY FUNDS, FIDUCIARY FUNDS, AND COMPREHENSIVE ANNUAL FINANCIAL REPORT

HIGHLIGHTS OF CHAPTER

1. Enterprise funds account for the operations of commercial-type activities of a governmental entity such as utilities, airports, seaports, and recreational facilities, which sell services to the public, and perhaps to other funds of the governmental entity, at a profit. Because of their similarity to business enterprises, enterprise funds of a governmental entity use the accrual basis of accounting, with short-term prepayments, depreciation expense, and doubtful accounts expense included in the funds' accounting records.

2. Among the ways in which financial statements of an enterprise fund of a governmental entity differ from financial statements of a business enterprise are the following:

   a. Enterprise funds have no income taxes expense; however, the operating expenses of an enterprise fund may include a **payment in lieu of property taxes** to the general fund of the governmental entity.

   b. Instead of capital stock, the statement of net assets of an enterprise fund includes contributed capital from general fund in the net assets section.

   c. Following current assets in the statement of net assets of an enterprise fund is a **restricted assets** section—typically cash and short-term investments—in the total amount of cash deposits made by customers and unexpended proceeds of revenue bonds issued to finance construction of plant assets for the enterprise fund.

   d. Following current liabilities in the statement of net assets of an enterprise fund is a section for **liabilities payable from restricted assets,** which includes accrued interest and current maturities of revenue bonds as well as customers' deposits.

   e. A **restricted net assets category** of an enterprise fund typically is provided in an amount equal to the cash and short-term investments of the enterprise fund that are restricted to payment of interest and principal of revenue bonds.

   f. Subsidy-type transfers to the general fund from an enterprise fund are reported in the transfers section of the enterprise fund's statement of revenues, expenses, and changes in net assets.

   g. The statement of cash flows for a governmental entity's enterprise fund has **four** categories of cash flows: from **operating** activities, from **noncapital financing** activities, from **capital and related financing** activities, and from **investing** activities. In the indirect method, **operating income,** rather than **increase (decrease) in net assets,** is reconciled to net cash provided by operating activities.

3. An internal service fund of a governmental entity sells supplies and services to other funds of the governmental entity but not to the public. Except for the lack of a profit motive, the operations of an internal service fund resemble those of a business enterprise. The revenues of an internal service fund generally are adequate to cover the fund's operating costs and expenses, with perhaps a modest increase in net assets.

4. Because internal service funds do not issue revenue bonds and do not receive contributions or deposits from customers, their financial statements are nearly identical in form and content to the financial statements of business enterprises, except for four categories of cash flows. Similar to

the statement of net assets of an enterprise fund, the statement of net assets of an internal service fund includes contributed capital from general fund in the net assets section.

5. In **GASB Statement No. 20,** "Accounting and Financial Reporting for Proprietary Funds," the GASB provided temporary guidance for governmental entities for applying business enterprise-type accounting standards, as appropriate, to their proprietary funds.

6. Agency funds, expendable and nonexpendable private-purpose trust funds, investment trust funds, and pension trust funds constitute the fiduciary funds category of a governmental entity. The position of the governmental entity with respect to such funds is that of a **custodian** or **trustee** rather than an **owner.**

7. Agency funds, which are of short duration, are established by a governmental entity to account for sales taxes, payroll taxes, other deductions withheld from salaries and wages payable to governmental entity employees, and amounts set aside as deferred compensation for such employees.

8. Because agency funds do not have operations during a fiscal year, the only financial statements for such funds are a statement of assets and liabilities showing cash or receivables and amounts payable to other funds or governmental entities or to outsiders, and a statement of changes in assets and liabilities.

9. An **expendable private-purpose trust fund** is one whose principal and income both may be expended to achieve the objectives of the trust. A **nonexpendable private-purpose trust fund** is one whose principal remains intact; only the revenues of such a fund are expended to carry out the objectives of the trust. A nonexpendable trust fund requires two separate accounting entities: one for principal and one for revenues. Because the governmental entity acts as a custodian for a private-purpose trust fund, accounting for such a trust fund should comply with the trust indenture.

10. The financial statements for both expendable trust funds and nonexpendable trust funds are a statement of changes in fiduciary net assets and a statement of fiduciary net assets. Trust indentures may provide that there is to be no unreserved and undesignated net assets balance for a trust fund.

11. Pension trust funds involve accounting for liabilities and net assets reserves that are computed on the basis of actuarial assumptions regarding such matters as life expectancies of governmental entity employees and rates of earnings on pension trust fund assets. Pension trust funds are accounted for in essentially the same manner as proprietary funds; thus, the accounting records of pension trust funds are maintained under the accrual basis.

12. The statement of changes in fiduciary net assets of a governmental entity's pension trust fund has additions such as employee contributions, employer (governmental entity) contributions, and investment net gains; and deductions such as annuity benefits, disability benefits, refunds of contributions, and administrative expenses. Typical assets and liabilities of a pension trust fund include cash, interest and dividends receivable, investments, plant assets, refunds payable, and other liabilities. The net assets of a pension trust fund are held in trust for pension benefits.

13. **Sponsoring governments** are required by **GASB Statement No. 31,** "Accounting and Financial Reporting for . . . External Investment Pools," to establish investment trust funds for investments of smaller governmental entities entrusted to the sponsoring government for investments in higher-yielding financial instruments than the smaller governmental entities have the capacity to acquire. Financial statements for the investment pools are the same as for pension trust funds: a statement of fiduciary net assets and a statement of changes in fiduciary net assets.

14. The Governmental Accounting Standards Board requires state and local governmental entities to prepare a comprehensive annual financial report (CAFR) as a matter of record. Components of a CAFR are an introductory section; management's discussion and analysis; basic financial statements; required supplementary information other than management's discussion and

analysis; and a combining and individual fund statements, schedules, narrative explanations, and statistical section.

QUESTIONS

True or False

For each of the following statements, circle the **T** or the **F** to indicate whether the statement is true or false.

T F 1. Internal service funds sell services to the public as well as to agencies of the governmental entity.

T F 2. The caption **net income** is included in a statement of revenues, expenses, and changes in net assets of an internal service fund.

T F 3. Revenues such as those realized by a governmental entity's motor vehicle pool are accounted for in an enterprise fund.

T F 4. A trust indenture is a legal document that creates either an expendable private-purpose trust fund or a nonexpendable private-purpose trust fund of a governmental entity.

T F 5. Both types of proprietary funds (enterprise funds and internal service funds) of a governmental entity issue income statements.

T F 6. Payments in lieu of property taxes, made by an enterprise fund to the general fund of a governmental entity, are displayed in the transfers section of the enterprise fund's statement of revenues, expenses, and changes in net assets.

T F 7. Because agency funds of a governmental entity do not have operations during a fiscal year, no financial statements are issued for such funds.

T F 8. Two separate accounting units are required for a governmental entity's expendable private-purpose trust fund.

T F 9. The final amount in the statement of fiduciary net assets of a governmental entity's pension trust fund is captioned **net assets available for benefits.**

T F 10. In a statement of cash flows for a governmental entity's enterprise fund, operating income is reconciled to net cash provided by operating activities.

Completion Statements

Fill in the necessary words or amounts to complete the following statements.

1. Services sold to the general public by a governmental entity are accounted for in _____ funds; and assets held by a governmental entity as custodian are accounted for in _____ funds and _____ funds.

2. Restricted assets are typical of _____ funds.

3. A statement of revenues, expenditures or expenses, and changes in net assets is not issued for _____ funds.

4. A _____ of net assets typically is included in the statement of net assets of an _____ fund.

5. The _____ of a nonexpendable private-purpose trust fund remains _____.

6. Transfers to or from other funds of the governmental entity are displayed in the _____ _____ _____ section of the statement of cash flows of an enterprise fund.

Multiple Choice

Choose the best answer for each of the following questions and enter the identifying letter in the space provided.

_____ 1. A government entity recognizes depreciation as an expense in its:
   a. Enterprise funds and internal service funds
   b. Internal service funds and general capital assets account group
   c. General fund and enterprise funds
   d. Enterprise funds and capital projects funds

_____ 2. A governmental entity realized gains and losses on securities in its library private-purpose trust fund. In the absence of specific instructions from the donor or state statutory requirements, these amounts are accounted for in:
   a. The general fund
   b. The debt service fund
   c. The library principal nonexpendable private-purpose trust fund
   d. The library revenues expendable private-purpose trust fund

_____ 3. The activities of a motor vehicle pool that provides and services vehicles for the official use of a governmental entity's employees are accounted for in:
   a. An agency fund
   b. The general fund
   c. An internal service fund
   d. A special revenue fund
   e. Some other fund

_____ 4. The activities of a governmental entity's employee pension plan that is financed by both employer and employee contributions are accounted for in:
   a. An agency fund
   b. An internal service fund
   c. A special revenue fund
   d. A private-purpose trust fund
   e. Some other fund

_____ 5.   The City of Medina collects property taxes for the benefit of the local sewer, park, and school districts and periodically remits collections to those governmental entities. This activity is accounted for in:
a.   An agency fund
b.   The general fund
c.   An internal service fund
d.   A special revenue fund
e.   Some other fund

_____ 6.   Customers' deposits that may not be expended for operating purposes are displayed as restricted assets in the statement of net assets of a governmental entity's:
a.   Internal service fund
b.   Trust fund
c.   Agency fund
d.   Enterprise fund

_____ 7.   In the statement of cash flows for a governmental entity's enterprise fund, temporary investments of funds received from borrowings for plant assets construction are reported with cash flows from:
a.   Capital and related financing activities
b.   Operating activities
c.   Noncapital financing activities
d.   Investing activities

Questions **8** through **10** are based on the following data relating to Lely Township:

Printing and binding equipment used for servicing all of Lely's departments and agencies, on a cost-reimbursement basis	$100,000
Equipment used for supplying water to Lely's residents	900,000
Amounts receivable for completed sidewalks to be paid for in installments by affected property owners	950,000
Cash received from federal government, restricted to highway maintenance, which must be accounted for in a separate fund	995,000

_____ 8.   What amount **must** be accounted for in a special revenue fund or funds?
a. $995,000
b. $1,050,000
c. $1,095,000
d. $1,945,000

_____ 9.   What amount **might** be accounted for in an internal service fund?
a. $100,000
b. $900,000
c. $950,000
d. $995,000

_____ 10.   What amount **might** be accounted for in an enterprise fund?
a. $100,000
b. $900,000
c. $950,000
d. $995,000

SHORT EXERCISE

1. The four independent transactions or events described below were completed by four different governmental entities.

   a. The Kopper City General Fund repaid to the Enterprise Fund a loan of $100,000 plus $8,000 interest. The loan had been made earlier in the fiscal year.

   b. A citizen of Lane City transferred common stock with a current fair value of $140,000 to the city under a trust indenture that required the trust principal to be maintained intact and the trust revenues to be used for financing scholarships for university students. During the same fiscal year, dividends totaling $5,300 were received on the common stock.

   c. The Town of Morey Internal Service Fund billed supplies shipments to other funds as follows:

General Fund	$12,000
Special Revenue Fund	3,000
Enterprise Fund	8,000

   d. The Logan City Pension Trust Fund received the city's pension fund contribution of $30,000 and the city's employee's pension fund contribution of $22,000, which had been withheld from employees' salaries and accounted for in the Logan City Agency Fund.

   In the space provided on page 224, prepare journal entries in the appropriate funds for each transaction or event. Include a brief explanation for each entry, and indicate the fund in which it is recorded. Record the receipt of the dividend in **b** only in an endowment revenues expendable private-purpose trust fund.

Journal Entries

a.			
b.			
c.			
d.			

CASE

Prior to the issuance of **GASB Statement No. 34**, "Basic Financial Statements . . . ," in 1999, enterprise funds of governmental entities issued **statements of revenues, expenses, and changes in retained earnings**, which included captions for "net income" and beginning and ending "retained earnings." However, **GASB Statement No. 34** changed the operating statements of enterprise funds to **statements of revenues, expenses, and changes in net assets**, with captions for "increase in net assets" and beginning and ending "net assets."

What support do you find for the GASB's action? Explain.

QUESTIONS

True or False

1. F 2. F 3. F 4. T 5. F 6. F 7. F 8. F 9. F 10. T

Completion Statements

1. Enterprise, agency, trust. 2. Enterprise. 3. Agency. 4. Segregation, enterprise. 5. Principal, intact. 6. Noncapital financing activities.

Multiple Choice

1. a 2. d 3. c 4. e (A pension trust fund) 5. a 6. d 7. a 8. d ($950,000 + $995,000 = $1,945,000) 9. a 10. b

SHORT EXERCISE

1.

	Journal Entries		
a.	Payable to Enterprise Fund	100,000	
	Expenditures	8,000	
	Cash		108,000
	To record repayment by **General Fund** of a loan from the enterprise fund.		
	Cash	108,000	
	Interest Revenue		8,000
	Receivable from General Fund		100,000
	To record in **Enterprise Fund** the repayment of a loan by the general fund.		
b.	Investments	140,000	
	Revenues		140,000
	To record in **Endowment Principal Private-Purpose Nonexpendable Trust Fund** the current fair value of common stock donated by a citizen.		
	Cash	5,300	
	Other Financing Sources		5,300
	To record in **Endowment Revenues Expendable Private-Purpose Trust Fund** the dividends on investments.		

c.	Receivable from General Fund	12,000	
	Receivable from Special Revenue Fund	3,000	
	Receivable from Enterprise Fund	8,000	
	Charges for Services		23,000
	To record billings for supplies in **Internal Service Fund.**		
	Inventory of Supplies	12,000	
	Payable to Internal Service Fund		12,000
	To record supplies received in **General Fund.**		
	Inventory of Supplies	3,000	
	Payable to Internal Service Fund		3,000
	To record supplies received in **Special Revenue Fund.**		
	Inventory of Supplies	8,000	
	Payable to Internal Service Fund		8,000
	To record supplies received in **Enterprise Fund.**		
d.	Cash	52,000	
	Member Contributions		22,000
	Employer Contributions		30,000
	To record pension fund contributions in **Pension Trust Fund.**		
	Expenditures	30,000	
	Cash		30,000
	To record pension fund contributions in **General Fund.**		
	Vouchers Payable	22,000	
	Cash		22,000
	To record pension fund contributions in **Agency Fund.**		

CASE

One reason for GASB's action might be the need for consistency in the terminology for operating statements of both proprietary funds and fiduciary funds of governmental entities. Further, "net income" and "retained earnings" are terms generally associated with for-profit enterprises; although enterprise funds generally operate with the expectations that their revenues will exceed their expenses, such excesses often are transferred to the general fund as either payments in lieu of property taxes or subsidies. In contrast, the retained earnings of business enterprises are the source of distributions to their owners (stockholders).

Working Papers

		OSCAR, PAUL & QUINN LLP																								
		Journal Entries																								
20	05																									

		Gee, Hawe & Ivan LLP			
		Journal Entries			

a.

20	05				

b.

20	05				

a.

Ross & Saye LLP			
Income Statement			
For Year Ended February 28, 2005			

Exhibit A—Division of net income:	Ross	Saye	Combined

b.

Ross & Saye LLP			
Statement of Partners' Capital			
For Year Ended February 28, 2005			
	Ross	Saye	Combined

Lucas & May LLP

Division of Net Income

For Year Ended December 31, 2005

	Lucas	May	Combined
a.			
b.			
c.			
d.			

	Capital account balance	Fraction of year unchanged	Average capital account balance
Exhibit A—Computation of average capital account balances			

a.

Alex, Baron & Crane LLP
Salaries and Division of Net Income
For Year Ended December 31, 2005

	Alex	Baron	Crane	Combined

Exhibit A—Computation of interest on average capital account balances:

b.

Alex, Baron & Crane LLP
Statement of Partners' Capital
For Year Ended December 31, 2005

	Alex	Baron	Crane	Combined

Chu, Dow & Eng LLP
Journal Entries

a.

20	05			
July	10			

b.

20	05			
July	10			

c.

20	05			
July	10			

d.

20	05			
July	10			

a.

		Yee & Zane LLP			
		Journal Entry			

20	05			
Dec	31			

b.

		Yee Zane & Arne LLP			
		Journal Entry			

20	05			
Dec	31			

Alef, Beal & Clarke LLP				
Statements of Cash Flows				
For Year Ended December 31, 2005				
Net cash provided by operating activities (**Exhibit 1**)				

Southwestern Enterprises (a limited partnership)

Income Statement

For Year Ended December 31, 2005

Southwestern Enterprises (a limited partnership)

Statement of Partners' Capital

For Year Ended December 31, 2005

	General Partner		Limited Partners		Combined	
	Units	Amount	Units	Amount	Units	Amount

Southwestern Enterprises (a limited partnership)

Balance Sheet

December 31, 2005

Assets		
Liabilities & Partners' Capital		

Southwestern Enterprises (a limited partnership)				
Statement of Cash Flows				
For Year Ended December 31, 2005				
Net cash provided by operating activities (Exhibit 1)				

Exhibit 1 Cash flows from operating activities:				

Noble & Roland LLP
Correcting Journal Entries
a.   **June 30, 2005**

Noble & Roland LLP
Corrected Balance Sheet
b.   **June 30, 2005**

Current Assets

Liabilities & Partners' Capital

			Doris, Elsie & Frances Partnership										
			Journal Entries										
			·										
20	05												
Jan.	17												

		Olmo, Perez & Quinto LLP			
		Journal Entries			

20	05				
Feb.	1				

Exhibit 1	Olmo, Perez & Quinto LLP			
	Cash Distribution Program			
	January 31, 2005			
	Creditors	Olmo	Perez	Quinto

Olmo, Perez & Quinto LLP			
Working Paper for Cash Distributions to Partners during Liquidation			
January 31, 2005			
	Olmo	Perez	Quinto

	Creditors	Hal	Ian	Jay	Kay
Hal, Ian, Jay & Kay LLP					
Cash Distribution Program					
September 25, 2005					
First					
Next					
Next					
All over					

	Hal	Ian	Jav	Kav
Hal, Ian, Jay & Kay LLP				
Working Paper for Cash Distributions to Partners during Liquidation				
September 25, 2005				

a.

				Creditors	Carson	Worden
		First				
		Next				
		All over				

Carson & Worden LLP

Cash Distribution Program

September 23, 2005

Carson & Worden LLP

Working Paper for Cash Distribution to Partners during Liquidation

September 23, 2005

b.

Carson & Worden LLP

Journal Entries

20 05				
Sept.	23			

			Luke, Mayo & Nomura LLP																						
			Journal Entries																							
20	05																									
May	9																									

a.

Luna, Nava & Ruby LLP

Computation of Loss from Liquidation

December 31, 2005

b.

Luna, Nava & Ruby LLP

Statement of Realization and Liquidation

December 31, 2005

	Assets		Liabilities	Partners' Capital (net of drawings)		
	Cash	Other		Luna (50%)	Nava (30%)	Ruby (20%)

c.

Luna, Nava & Ruby LLP

Journal Entries

20	05				
Dec.	31				

		Haye & Lee LLP																		
		Journal Entries																		
20	05																			
Apr.	1																			

a.

Adams, Barna & Coleman LLP

Statement of Realization and Liquidation

June 4, 2005

	Assets		Liabilities	Partners' Capital		
	Cash	Other		Adams (40%)	Barna (40%)	Coleman (20%)
Balances before liquidation						

b.

Adams, Barna & Coleman LLP

Journal Entries

20	05				
June	4				

c.

Smith, Jones & Webb LLP

Statement of Realization and Liquidation

May through July, 2005

	Assets		Liabilities	Partners' Capital		
	Cash	Other		Smith (1/3)	Jones (1/3)	Webb (1/3)
Balances before liquidation						

Exhibit 1	Smith, Jones & Webb LLP			
	Cash Distribution Program			
	April 30, 2005			
	Creditors	Smith	Jones	Webb
First				
Next				
Next				
All over				

	Smith, Jones & Webb		
	Working Paper for Cash Distributions to Partners during Liquidation		
	April 30, 2005		
	Smith	Jones	Webb
Capital account balances before liquidation			

Densen, Eastin & Feller LLP							
Cash Distribution Program							
December 31, 2005							
	Creditors		Denson		Eastin		Feller
First							
Next							
Next							
All over							

Densen, Eastin & Feller LLP			
Working Paper for Cash Distributions to Partners during Liquidation			
December 31, 2005			
	Denson	Eastin	Feller

Pr. 3–10

Lord-Lee Corporation
Balance Sheet
January 2, 2006

Assets					

Liabilities & Stockholders' Equity					

b.

Lord-Lee Corporation
Journal Entries

20	06						
Jan.	2						

Lord-Lee Corporation				
Balance Sheet				
January 2, 2006				
Assets				

Hartman, Inc.						
Reno Branch						
Journal Entries						

Hartman, Inc.						
Home Office						
Journal Entries						

a.

Lobo Company

Home Office and Wade Branch

Reconciliation of Reciprocal Accounts

January 31, 2005

				Investment in Wade Branch ledger account (in home office accounting records)							Home Office ledger account (in Wade Branch accounting records)						
		Balances before adjustments		$	4	8	5	0	0	dr	$	3	5	7	0	0	cr

b. (1)

Lobo Company

Journal Entries in Accounting Records of Home Office

20	05																		
Jan.	31																		

b. (2)

Lobo Company

Journal Entries in Accounting Records of Wade Branch

20	05																		
Jan.	31																		

Styler Corporation			
Data Relating to Merchandise at Branch			
January 1 through March 10, 2005			
		Billed prices, 120% of home office cost	Selling prices, 110% of billed prices
	Home office cost		

a.

Styler Corporation		
Journal Entries in Accounting Records of Branch		
March 10, 2005		

b.

Styler Corporation		
Journal Entries in Accounting Records of Home Office		
March 10, 2005		

a.

Yugo Company

Computation of Unadjusted Balance of Home Office Account

December 31, 2005

		Balance of investment in Ryble Branch ledger account of home office, before adjustment					$ 5 5 5 5 0 0	

b.

Yugo Company

Journal Entries in Accounting Records of Home Office

December 31, 2005

	(1)			

c.

		Yugo Company		
		Journal Entries in Accounting Records of Ryble Branch		
		December 31, 2005		

d.

	Yugo Company	
	Reconciliation of Reciprocal Ledger Accounts	
	December 31, 2005	
	Investment in Ryble Branch (In home office accounting records)	Home Office (in Ryble Branch accounting records)
Balances before adjustments (see a)	$ 5 5 5 0 0 dr	$ 4 9 6 8 0 cr

a.

		Trudy Company																					
		Journal Entries for First Year of Operations																					
		(Perpetual Inventory System)																					
	(1)	In accounting records of Savoy Branch:																					
	(2)	In accounting records of home office:																					

Trudie Company				
Journal Entries for First Year of Operations (concluded)				
(Perpetual Inventory System)				

b.	Trudie Company			
	Journal Entries for First Year of Operations			
	(Periodic Inventory System)			
(1)	In accounting records of Savoy Branch:			

		Trudy Company																							
		Journal Entries for First Year of Operations (concluded)																							
		(Periodic Inventory System)																							
	(2)	In accounting records of home office:																							
	(2)																								

a.

Kosti-Marian Company

Journal Entries in Accounting Records of Home Office

20 05				
Dec.	31			

b.

Kosti-Marian Company

Journal Entries in Accounting Records of Branch

20 05				
Dec.	31			

c.

	Kosti-Marian Company							
	Working Paper for Combined Financial Statements of Home Office and Branch							
	For Year Ended December 31, 2005							
	(Periodic Inventory System: Billings above Cost)							
	Adjusted trial balances				Eliminations	Combined	
	Home office dr (cr)		Branch dr (cr)		dr (cr)		dr (cr)	
Income statement								
Sales								
Inventories, Jan. 1, 2005								
Purchases								
Shipments to branch								
Shipments from home office								
Freight-in from home office								
Inventories, Dec. 31, 2005								
Operating expenses								
Net income (to statement of								
retained earnings below)								
Totals								
Statement of retained earnings								
Retained earnings, Jan. 1, 2005								
Net (income) (from income								
statement above)								
Dividends declared								
Retained earnings, Dec. 31,								
(to balance sheet below)								
Totals								
Balance sheet								
Cash								
Inventories, Dec. 31, 2005								
Investment in branch								
Allowance for overvaluation								
of branch inventories								
Other assets (net)								
Current liabilities								
Common stock, $2.50 par								
Retained earnings (from								
statement of retained								
earnings above)								
Home office								
Totals								

a.

Solis Company
Working Paper for Combined Financial Statements of Home Office and Branch
For Year Ended December 31, 2005
(Period Inventory System: Billings at Cost)

	Adjusted trial balances		Eliminations	Combined
	Home office dr (cr)	Branch dr (cr)	dr (cr)	dr (cr)
Income statement				
Sales				
Cost of goods sold				
Operating expenses				
Net income (loss) (to				
statement of retained				
earnings below)				
Totals				
Statement of retained earnings				
Retained earnings, Dec. 31, 05				
Net (income) loss (from				
income statement above)				
Dividends declared				
Retained earnings, Dec. 31, 05				
(to balance sheet below)				
Totals				
Balance sheet				
Cash				
Notes receivable				
Trade accounts receivable				
(net)				
Inventories				
Investment in branch				
Furniture and equipment				
(net)				
Trade accounts payable				
Common stock, $2 par				
Retained earnings (from				
statement of retained				
earnings above				
Home Office				
Totals				

b.

Solis Company

Closing Entries for Branch

20 05					
Dec.	31				

c.

Solis Company

Adjusting and Closing Entries for Home Office

20 05					
Dec.	31				

a.

Calco Corporation

Journal Entries in Accounting Records of Home Office

20 05					
Dec.	31				

b.

Calco Corporation

Journal Entries in Accounting Records of Branch

20 05					
Dec.	31				

c.	Calco Corporation						
	Working Paper to Summarize Operations						
	For Year Ended December 31, 2005						
Revenue and Expenses		Home Office			Branch		Combined
Sales							
Cost of goods sold:							
Inventories, Jan. 1, 2005 (at cost)							
Purchases							
Shipments to branch (at cost)							
Cost of goods available for sale							
Less: Inventories, Dec. 31, 2005							
Cost of goods sold							
Gross margin on sales							
Operating expenses							
Net income							

a.

	Kreshek Company				

Kreshek Company

Reconciliation of Investment in Lee Branch Ledger Account and Home Office Account

For Quarter Ended April 30, 2005

	Investment in Lee Branch ledger account (home office accounting records)		Home Office ledger account (branch accounting records)	
	Debit	**Credit**	**Debit**	**Credit**
Balances before adjustments	$1 3 3 9 7 0			$1 4 3 0 4 0

b.

Kreshek Company

Correcting Entries in Accounting Records of Lee Branch

20	05				
Apr.	30				

c.

Kreshek Company
Correcting Entries in Accounting Records of Home Office

	20	05							
Apr.	30								

Name_____Section_____Date_____

Pr. 4–10

a.   **Arnie's**

Journal Entries in Accounting Records of Home Office

20	05				
Dec.	31				

b.   **Arnie's**

Journal Entries in Accounting Records of Vida Branch

20	05				
Dec.	31				

c.

	Arnie's							
	Working Paper for Combined Financial Statements of Home Office and Branch							
	For Year Ended December 31, 2005							
	(Periodic Inventory System: Billings above Cost)							
	Adjusted trial balances		**Eliminations**	**Combined**
	Home office dr (cr)	**Vida Branch** dr (cr)	dr (cr)	dr (cr)
Income statement				
Sales				
Cost of goods sold				
Operating expenses				
Net income (to statement of				
proprietor's capital below)				
Totals				
Statement of proprietor's capital				
Arnold Nance, capital Jan. 1, 05				
Net (income) (from				
income statement above)				
Arnold Nance, drawing				
Arnold Nance, capital Dec. 31,				
2005 (to balance sheet below)				
Totals				
Balance sheet				
Cash				
Trade accounts receivable (net)				
Inventories				
Investment in Vida Branch				
Allowance for overvaluation of				
Inventories: Vida Branch				
Equipment (net)				
Trade accounts payable				
Accrued liabilities				
Note payable, due 2008				
Home office				
Arnold Nance, capital (from				
statement of proprietor's				
capital above)				
Totals				

d.

Arnie's

Adjusting and Closing Entries in Accounting Records of Home Office

	20 05			
Dec.	31			

		La Salle Corporation																									
		Journal Entries																									
20	05																										
Jan.	31																										

Name_____Section_____Date_____

Pr. 5–2

		Lionel Corporation				
		Journal Entries				
20	05					
Aug.	31					

		Wabash Corporation																												
		Journal Entries																												
20	05																													
Dec.	31																													

		Combinor Corporation				
		Journal Entries				
20 05						
Oct.	31					

		Consol Corporation																							
		Journal Entries																							
20	05																								
July	31																								

		Silva Corporation																										
		Journal Entries																										
20	05																											
Mar.	1																											

			Solomon Corporation						
			Journal Entries						
20	05								
Oct.	31								

		Value Corporation				
		Journal Entries				
20	05					
Apr.	1					

		Stave Corporation																								
		Journal Entries																								
20	05																									
Apr.	30																									

		Coolidge Corporation				
		Journal Entries				
a.						
20	05					
Sept.	30					

Coolidge Corporation							
Journal Entries							

b.

	20	06				
Sept.	30					

Name_____Section_____Date_____

a.

Solo Corporation				
Net Income and Earnings per Share				
For Year Ended October 31, 2005				

b.

Solo Corporation				
Net Income and Earnings per Share				
For Year Ending October 31, 2006				

Solo Corporation			
Pro Forma Combined Balance Sheets			
c. October 31, 2005			
Assets			
Liabilities & Stockholders' Equity			

a.

Parr Corporation
Journal Entries

20	05				
Sept.	30				

b.

Parr Corporation and Subsidiary
Working Paper Elimination
September 30, 2005

a.

		Philly Corporation																																	
		Journal Entries																																	
20	05																																		
Sept.	30																																		
b.																																			

		Philly Corporation and Subsidiary																																	
		Working Paper Elimination																																	
		September 30, 2005																																	
	(a)																																		

Pr. 6–2

	Philly Corporation	Stype Corporation	Eliminations increase (decrease)	Consolidated
Assets				
Cash		1 0 0 0 0 0		
Trade accounts receivable (net)		2 0 0 0 0 0		
Inventories (net)		3 0 0 0 0 0		
Investment in Stype Company common stock				
Plant assets (net)		1 0 0 0 0 0 0		
Goodwill				
Total assets		1 6 0 0 0 0 0		
Liabilities & Stockholders' Equity				
Current liabilities		4 0 0 0 0 0		
Long-term debt		1 0 0 0 0 0		
Discount on long-term debt				
Common stock, no par				
Common stock, $20 par		4 0 0 0 0 0		
Minority interest in net assets of subsidiary				
Retained earnings		7 0 0 0 0 0		
Total liabilities & stockholders' equity		1 6 0 0 0 0 0		

Philly Corporation and Subsidiary
Working Paper for Consolidated Balance Sheet
September 30, 2005

a.

Pellman Corporation

Journal Entries

	20 05				
May	31				

b.

Pellman Corporation and Subsidiary

Working Paper Elimination

May 31, 2005

	(a)				

Pellman Corporation and Subsidiary
Working Paper for Consolidated Balance Sheet
May 31, 2005

	Pellman Corporation	Shire Corporation	Eliminations increase (decrease)	Consolidated
Assets				
Cash		1 0 0 0 0		
Trade accounts receivable (net)		6 0 0 0 0		
Inventories (net)		1 2 0 0 0 0		
Investment in Shire Company common stock				
Plant assets (net)		6 1 0 0 0 0		
Total assets		8 0 0 0 0 0		
Liabilities & Stockholders' Equity				
Current liabilities		8 0 0 0 0		
Long-term debt		4 0 0 0 0 0		
Premium on long-term debt				
Common stock, $10 par		1 0 0 0 0 0		
Additional paid-in capital		4 0 0 0 0		
Retained earnings		1 8 0 0 0 0		
Total liabilities & stockholders' equity		8 0 0 0 0 0		

a.

		Seaver Company				
		Journal Entries				
20	05					
Apr.	30					

b.

		Powell Corporation				
		Journal Entries				
20	05					
Apr.	30					

Pr. 6–4

	Powell Corporation	Seaver Corporation	Eliminations increase (decrease)	Consolidated
c. Powell Corporation and Subsidiary				
Working Paper for Consolidated Balance Sheet				
April 30, 2005				
Assets				
Cash				
Trade accounts receivable (net)				
Intercompany receivables (payables)				
Inventories				
Investment in Seaver Company common stock				
Plant assets (net				
Goodwill				
Total assets				
Liabilities & Stockholders' Equity				
Current liabilities				
Long-term debt				
Premium on long-term debt				
Common stock, no par				
Common stock, $10 par				
Additional paid-in capital				
Minority interest in net assets of subsidiary				
Retained earnings (deficit)				
Total liabilities & Stockholders' equity				

		Powell Corporation and Subsidiary																													
		Working Paper Elimination																													
		April 30, 2005																													
	(a)																														

a.

		Pyr Corporation						
		Journal Entries						
20 05								
July	31							
b.								

		Pyr Corporation and Subsidiary				
		Working Paper Elimination				
		July 31, 2005				
	(a)	Common Stock-Soper		2 5 0 0 0		

b.

Pyr Corporation and Subsidiary
Working Paper for Consolidated Balance Sheet
July 31, 2005

	Pyr Corporation	Soper Corporation	Eliminations increase (decrease)	Consolidated
Assets				
Current assets		150 000		
Investment in Soper Company common stock				
Plant assets (net)		300 000		
Goodwill		20 000		
Total assets		470 000		
Liabilities & Stockholders' Equity				
Current liabilities		120 000		
Long-term debt		200 000		
Discount on long-term debt				
Common stock, $2 par				
Common stock, $5 par		25 000		
Additional paid-in capital		50 000		
Retained earnings		75 000		
Total liabilities & stockholders' equity		470 000		

Pali Corporation and Subsidiary

Working Paper Elimination

August 31, 2005

	(a)			

a.

		Pagel Corporation						
		Journal Entries						
20 05								
Oct.	31							

b.

		Pagel Corporation and Subsidiary						
		Working Paper Elimination						
		October 31, 2005						
	(a)							

b.

Pagel Corporation and Subsidiary

Working Paper for Consolidated Balance Sheet

October 31, 2005

	Pagel Corporation	Sayre Corporation	Eliminations increase (decrease)	Consolidated
Assets				
Cash		150000		
Inventories		600000		
Other current assets		260000		
Investment in Sayre Company common stock				
Plant assets (net)		1500000		
Patents (net)		80000		
Goodwill				
Total assets		2590000		
Liabilities & Stockholders' Equity				
Income taxes payable		60000		
Other current liabilities		854000		
Long-term debt		1240000		
Discount on long=term debt				
Common stock, $2 stated value				
Common stock, $10 par		100000		
Additional paid-in capital				
Minority interest in net assets of subsidiary				
Retained earnings		336000		
Total liabilities & stockholders' equity		2590000		

Name_____Section_____Date_____

Pr. 6–8

a.

Porcino Corporation
Journal Entries

	20	05						
	Jan.	31						

b.

Porcino Corporation and Subsidiary
Working Paper Elimination
January 31, 2005

	(a)				

b.	Porcino Corporation and Subsidiary			
	Working Paper for Consolidated Balance Sheet			
	January 31, 2005			
	Porcino Corporation	Secor Corporation	Eliminations increase (decrease)	Consolidated

a.

Singh Company

Correcting Entries

June 30, 2005

b.

Pandit Corporation and Subsidiary
Working Paper Elimination
June 30, 2005

(a)

Pandit Corporation and Subsidiary
Working Paper for Consolidated Balance Sheet
June 30, 2005

	Pandit Corporation	Singh Corporation	Eliminations increase (decrease)	Consolidated
Assets				
Cash				
Income tax refund receivable				
Trade accounts receivable (net)				
Inventories				
Investment in Singh Company common stock				
Plant assets (net)				
Goodwill				
Total assets				
Liabilities & Stockholders' Equity				
Trade accounts payable				
Income taxes payable				
15% note payable				
Common stock, $10 par				
Additional paid-in capital				
Minority interest in net assets of subsidiary				
Retained earnings				
Total liabilities & stockholders' equity				

a.

		Pliny Corporation					
		Journal Entries					

20 05							
Dec.	31						

b.

		Pliny Corporation and Subsidiary				
		Working Paper Elimination				
		December 31, 2005				

b.

	Pliny Corporation	Sylia Corporation	Eliminations increase (decrease)	Consolidated
Assets				
Inventories		3 0 0 0 0 0		
Other current assets		5 0 0 0 0 0		
Investment in Sylla Company common stock				
Long-term investments in marketable securities		2 0 0 0 0 0		
Plant assets (net)		9 0 0 0 0 0		
Intangible assets (net)		2 0 0 0 0 0		
Goodwill				
Bond issue costs				
Total assets		2 1 0 0 0 0 0		
Liabilities & Stockholders' Equity				
Current liabilities		3 0 0 0 0 0		
10% note payable				
Bonds payable		5 0 0 0 0 0		
Discount on bonds payable				
Common stock, $1 par		2 0 0 0 0 0		
Additional paid-in capital		4 0 0 0 0 0		
Retained earnings		7 0 0 0 0 0		
Total liabilities & stockholders' equity		2 1 0 0 0 0 0		

Pliny Corporation and Subsidiary
Working Paper for Consolidated Balance Sheet
December 31, 2005

a.

		Parthenia Corporation				
		Correcting Journal Entry				
		June 30, 2005				

b.

		Parthenia Corporation and Subsidiary				
		Working Paper Elimination				
		June 30, 2005				

b.

Parthenia Corporation and Subsidiary

Working Paper for Consolidated Balance Sheet

June 30, 2005

	Parthenia Corporation	Storey Corporation	Eliminations increase (decrease)	Consolidated
Assets				
Cash		50 000		
Trade accounts receivable (net)		90 000		
Inventories		160 000		
Investment in Storey Company common stock				
Plant assets (net)		500 000		
Goodwill				
Total assets		800 000		
Liabilities & Stockholders' Equity				
Current liabilities		280 000		
Long-term debt		300 000		
Discount on long-term debt				
Common stock, $5 par				
Common stock, $10 par		50 000		
Additional paid-in capital		70 000		
Minority interest in net assets of subsidiary				
Retained earnings		100 000		
Total liabilities & stockholders' equity		800 000		

a. | Investment in Supp Company Stock

Date		Explanation	Debit	Credit	Balance
20 05					
Dec.	31	Balance			
20 06					
Dec.	8				

b. | Prem Corporation and Subsidiary

Working Paper Elimination

December 31, 2006

	(a)			

Pro Corporation
Journal Entries

20 06				
Sept.	5			

a. | **Promo Corporation**

Journal Entries

20 06					
Mar.	1				

b. **Investment in Sanz Company Common Stock**

Date		Explanation	Debit	Credit	Balance
20 05					
Mar	3	Balance			
20 06					

Intercompany Investment Income

Date		Explanation	Debit	Credit	Balance
20 06					
Mar	31				

c.

Promo Corporation

Working Paper Elimination

March 31, 2006

(a)

		Penn Corporation and Subsidiary					
		Working Paper Eliminations					
		October 31, 2006					
	(a)						

a.

		Pewter Corporation						
		Journal Entries						
		(1)						
20	06							
Jan	2							

b.

		Pewter Corporation		Stewart Company		Skate Company	
		Computation of Minority Interest in Net Assets of Subsidiaries					
		December 31, 2006					

c.	Pewter Corporation																								
	Computation of Consolidated Retained Earnings																								
	December 31, 2006																								
Mav	31																								

a.

Parks Corporation

Journal Entries

20	06				

b.	Parks Corporation and Subsidiary																										
		Working Paper Eliminations																									
		May 31, 2006																									
	(a)																										

a.

			Paseo Corporation					
			Journal Entries					

20	06						
Mar	31						

b.	Paseo Corporation and Subsidiary
	Working Paper Eliminations
	March 31, 2006

a.

Pavich Corporation
Journal Entries

20 06				
Sept.	30			

20 07				
Sept	30			

b.		(a)	Pavich Corporation and Subsidiary																							
			Working Paper Eliminations																								
			September 30, 2006																								

Pavich Corporation and Subsidiary																						
Working Paper Eliminations																						
September 30, 2007																						
	(a)																					

c.

Retained Earnings of Subsidiary

Date		Explanation		Debit	Credit	Balance
20 06						
Sept	30					

a. **Plumm Corporation**

Journal Entries

20	06			
Nov	30			

b. **Plumm Corporation and Subsidiary**

Working Paper Eliminations

November 30, 2006

	(a)			

Plumm Corporation and Subsidiary

Working Paper for Consolidated Financial Statements

November 30, 2006

	Plumm Corporation	Stamm Company	Eliminations increase (decrease)	Consolidated
Income Statement				
Revenue:				
Sales	800000	415000		
Intercompany investment income	70000			
Total revenue	870000	415000		
Costs and expenses:				
Cost of goods sold	500000	110000		
Operating expenses	233333	155000		
Income taxes expense	26667	60000		
Total costs and expenses	760000	325000		
Net income	110000	90000		
Statement of Retained Earnings				
Retained earnings, beginning of year	640000	220000		
Net income	110000	90000		
Subtotals	750000	310000		
Dividends declared	60000	30000		
Retained earnings, end of year	690000	280000		
Balance Sheet				
Assets				
Investment in Stamm Company common stock	600000			
Other	1840000	960000		
Goodwill				
Total assets	2440000	960000		
Liabilities & Stockholders' Equity				
Liabilities	650000	400000		
Common stock, $1 par	500000	80000		
Additional paid-in capital	600000	200000		
Retained earnings	690000	280000		
Total liabilities & stockholders' equity	2440000	960000		

a.

		Ping Corporation and Subsidiary		
		Adjusting Entries		
		December 31, 2006		

		(1)		
		(2)		

b.

Ping Corporation and Subsidiary
Working Paper for Consolidated Financial Statements
December 31, 2006

	Ping Corporation	Stang Corporation	Eliminations increase (decrease)	Consolidated
Income Statements				
Revenue:				
Net sales		300000		
Intercompany investment income				
Total revenue		300000		
Cost and expenses:				
Cost of goods sold		240000		
Other expenses		35000		
Minority interest in net income of subsidiary				
Total costs and expenses		275000		
Net income		25000		
Statement of Retained Earnings				
Retained earnings, beginning of year		59000		
Net income		25000		
Subtotals		84000		
Dividends declared		9000		
Retained earnings, end of year		75000		
Balance Sheet				
Assets				
Current assets		199100		
Intercompany dividends receivable (payable)		(7200)		
Investment in Stang Company common stock				
Land		10500		
Building and equipment		40000		
Accumulated depreciation		(7000)		
Signboard leases (net)		8400		
Total assets		243800		
Liabilities & Stockholders' Equity				
Dividends payable		1800		
Other current liabilities		67000		
Common stock, no par		100000		
Retained earnings		75000		
Minority interest in net assets of subsidiary				
Retained earnings of subsidiary				
Total liabilities & stockholders' equity		243800		

Name_____Section_____Date_____

Pr. 7–10

		Ping Corporation and Subsidiary				
		Working Paper Eliminations				
		December 31, 2006				
	(a)					

Name_____Section_____Date_____

Pr. 7–11

Petal Corporation and Subsidiary																		
Consolidated Balance Sheet																		
December 31, 2006																		
Assets																		
Liabilities & Stockholders' Equity																		
*Computation of goodwill																		

a.

Prentiss Corporation

Journal Entries

20 06					
Oct.	21				

b.

Scopes Company

Journal Entries

20 06					
Oct.	21				

a.

			Pillsbury Corporation																										
			Journal Entries																											
20	06																													
May	1																													

b.

		Sarpy Company			
		Journal Entries			
20	06				
May	1				

a.

		Pittsburgh Corporation (parent company)						
		Correcting Entries						
		July 31, 2005						

b.

| Syracuse Company (subsidiary company) |
| Correcting Entries |
| July 31, 2005 |

(1)

(2)

(3)

(4)

c.

| Pittsburgh Corporation and Subsidiary |
| Partial Working Paper for Consolidated Financial Statements |
| July 31, 2005 |

	Pittsburgh Corporation	Syracuse Company	Eliminations Increase (decrease)	Consolidated

		Parley Corporation and Subsidiary				
		Working Paper Eliminations				
		February 28, 2008				
	(a)					

Peke Corporation and Subsidiary

Working Paper Eliminations

June 30, 2007

	(a)				

Padua Corporation and Subsidiary					
Working Paper Eliminations					
April 30, 2006					
(a)					

a.

		Pacific Corporation																												
		Journal Entries																												
20	05																													
July	1																													

b.		Pacific Corporation and Subsidiary																														
		Working Paper Eliminations																														
		June 30, 2006																														
	(a)																																

a.

Pollard Corporation
Ledger Accounts

Investment in Silver Company Bonds				
Date	Explanation	Debit	Credit	Balance
20 07				
Aug 31				
20 08				
Feb 28				
Aug 31				

Intercompany Interest Revenue				
Date	Explanation	Debit	Credit	Balance
20 08				
Feb 28				
Aug 31				

Silver Company
Ledger Accounts

Intercompany Bonds Payable				
Date	Explanation	Debit	Credit	Balance
20 07				
Aug 31				

Discount on Intercompany Bonds Payable				
Date	Explanation	Debit	Credit	Balance
20 07				
Aug 31				
20 08				
Feb 28				
Aug 31				

Intercompany Interest Expense				
Date	Explanation	Debit	Credit	Balance
20 08				

b.

		Pollard Corporation and Subsidiary
		Working Paper Eliminations
		August 31, 2007 and 2008

20	07					
Aug	31					
	(a)					
20	08					
Aug	31					
	(a)					

a.

Procus Corporation
Ledger Accounts

Intercompany Lease Receivables

Date		Explanation	Debit	Credit	Balance
20 06					
Dec	31				

Unearned Intercompany Interest Revenue

Date		Explanation	Debit	Credit	Balance
20 06					
Dec	31				

Intercompany Interest Revenue

Date		Explanation	Debit	Credit	Balance
20 07					
Dec	31				

Stoffer Company
Ledger Accounts

Leased Equipment—Capital Lease				
Date	Explanation	Debit	Credit	Balance
20 06				
Dec 31				

Intercompany Liability under Capital Lease				
Date	Explanation	Debit	Credit	Balance
20 06				
Dec 31				

Intercompany Interest Expense				
Date	Explanation	Debit	Credit	Balance
20 07				
Dec 31				

b.		Procus Corporation and Subsidiary					
		Working Paper Eliminations					
		December 31, 2006 and 2007					
20	06						
Dec	31						
	(a)						
20	07						
Dec	31						
	(a)						

		Patrick Corporation and Subsidiary																								
		Working Paper Eliminations																								
		December 31, 2005																								
	(a)																									

	Patrick Corporation	Shannon Company	Eliminations increase (decrease)	Consolidated
Assets				
Cash		300000		
Trade accounts receivable (net)		450000		
Intercompany receivables (payables)		300000		
Inventories		950000		
Investment in Shannon Company common stock				
Investment in Shannon Company bonds				
Plan assets (net)		2000000		
Other assets		350000		
Total assets		4350000		
Liabilities & Stockholders' Equity				
Other current liabilities		945000		
Bonds payable		950000		
Intercompany bonds payable		250000		
Common stock, $10 par		900000		
Additional paid-in capital		175000		
Retained earnings		1130000		
Total liabilities & stockholders' equity		4350000		

Patrick Corporation and Subsidiary
Working Paper for Consolidated Balance Sheet
December 31, 2005

Power Corporation and Subsidiary
Working Paper for Consolidated Financial Statements (concluded)
For Year Ended December 31, 2005

	Power Corporation	Snyder Company	Eliminations increase (decrease)	Consolidated
Balance Sheet				
Assets				
Intercompany receivables (payables)	100	(100)		
Inventories	300000	75000		
Investment in Snyder Company common stock	164680			
Investment in Snyder Company bonds	40000			
Plant assets	794000	280600		
Accumulated depreciation of plant assets	(260000)	(30000)		
Other assets	610900	73400		
Goodwill				
Total assets	1649680	398900		
Liabilities & Stockholders' Equity				
Dividends payable		1600		
Bonds payable	600000	45000		
Intercompany bonds payable		40000		
Other liabilities	376340	114300		
Common stock, $100 par	360000	125000		
Additional paid-in capital	49000	12000		
Minority interest in net assets of subsidiary				
Retained earnings	264340	61000		
Total liabilities & stockholders' equity	1649680	398900		

Power Corporation and Subsidiary					
Working Paper Eliminations					
December 31, 2005					

Power Corporation and Subsidiary
Working Paper Eliminations
December 31, 2005

Power Corporation and Subsidiary
Working Paper Eliminations (concluded)
December 31, 2005

a.

		Pritchard Corporation		
		Adjusting Entries		
		December 31, 2005		

		Spangler Company		
		Adjusting Entries		
		December 31, 2005		

b.

Pritchard Corporation and Subsidiary

Working Paper for Consolidated Financial Statements

For Year Ended December 31, 2005

	Pritchard Corporation	Spangler Company	Eliminations increase (decrease)	Consolidated
Income Statement				
Revenue:				
Net sales				
Intercompany sales				
Intercompany revenue				
(expenses)				
Intercompany investment				
income				
Intercompany gain on sale of				
equipment				
Total revenue				
Cost and expenses:				
Cost of goods sold				
Intercompany cost of				
goods sold				
Operating expenses and				
income taxes expense				
Total costs and expenses				
Net income				
Statement of Retained Earnings				
Retained earnings, beginning				
of year				
Net income				
Subtotal				
Dividends declared				
Retained earnings, end of year				

	Pritchard Corporation	Spangler Company	Eliminations increase (decrease)	Consolidated

Pritchard Corporation and Subsidiary

Working Paper for Consolidated Financial Statements (concluded)

For Year Ended December 31, 2005

Balance Sheet				
Assets				
Intercompany receivables				
(payables)				
Inventories				
Investment in Spangler				
Company common stock				
Plant assets				
Accumulated depreciation of				
plant assets				
Other assets				
Total assets				
Liabilities & Stockholders' Equity				
Liabilities				
Common stock, $10 par				
Common stock, $20 par				
Additional paid-in capital				
Retained earnings				
Total liabilities &				
stockholders' equity				

Pritchard Corporation and Subsidiary
Working Paper Eliminations
December 31, 2005

(a)

a.

Pro Corporation and Subsidiaries

Working Paper Eliminations

October 31, 2006

	(b)			

b.

Primrose Corporation and Subsidiary

Working Paper Eliminations

October 31, 2006

	(b)			

a.

		Pullet Corporation					
		Journal Entry					
20 07							
Nov	30						

		Sagehen Company					
		Journal Entry					
20 07							
Nov	30						

b.

		Pullet Corporation and Subsidiary					
		Working Paper Eliminations					
		November 30, 2007					
	(b)						

		Presto Corporation				
		Journal Entries				
20	05					
Jan	2					

Pellerin Corporation
Journal Entries

20 05							
Dec	31						

Porcelain Corporation and Subsidiary					
Consolidated Statement of Cash Flows (indirect method)					
For Year Ended December 31, 2006					
Net cash provided by operating activities (Exhibit 1)					

		Parkhurst Corporation and Subsidiary					
		Working Paper Eliminations					
		March 31, 2006					
	(b)						

		Parkhurst Corporation and Subsidiary			
		Working Paper Eliminations (concluded)			
		March 31, 2006			

a.

Paine Corporation

Journal Entries

20	06				
June	30				

		Paine Corporation				
		Journal Entries (concluded)				
20	06					
June	30					

b.

Paine Corporation and Subsidiaries
Working Paper for Consolidated Financial Statements
For Year Ended June 30, 2006

	Paine Corporation	Spilberg Company	Sykes Company	Eliminations increase (decrease)	Consolidated
Income Statement					
Revenue:					
Net sales		5 5 0 0 0 0	2 2 0 0 0 0		
Intercompany sales					
Intercompany investment income					
Total revenue		5 5 0 0 0 0	2 2 0 0 0 0		
Cost and expenses and minority interest:					
Cost of goods sold		3 5 7 5 0 0	1 4 3 0 0 0		
Intercompany cost of goods sold					
Operating expenses		1 2 5 8 3 3	4 3 6 6 7		
Interest expense		2 6 6 6 7	1 3 3 3 3		
Income taxes expense					
Minority interest in net income of subsidiaries					
Total costs and expenses and minority interest		5 1 0 0 0 0	2 0 0 0 0 0		
Net income		4 0 0 0 0	2 0 0 0 0		
Statement of Retained Earnings					
Retained earnings, beginning of year		3 0 0 0 0 0	1 5 0 0 0 0		
Net income		4 0 0 0 0	2 0 0 0 0		
Subtotal		3 4 0 0 0 0	1 7 0 0 0 0		
Dividends declared		2 0 0 0 0	1 0 0 0 0		
Retained earnings, end of year		3 2 0 0 0 0	1 6 0 0 0 0		

b.

Paine Corporation and Subsidiaries
Working Paper for Consolidated Financial Statements (concluded)
For Year Ended June 30, 2006

Balance Sheet	Paine Corporation	Spilberg Company	Sykes Company	Eliminations increase (decrease)	Consolidated
Assets					
Intercompany dividends receivable (payable)		(1 9 8 0 0)	(9 0 0 0)		
Inventories		8 0 0 0 0 0	7 0 0 0 0 0		
Investment in Spilberg Company common stock					
Investment in Sykes Company common stock					
Goodwill					
Other assets		1 2 6 0 0 0 0	7 9 0 0 0 0 0		
Total assets		2 0 4 0 2 0 0	1 4 8 1 0 0 0		
Liabilities & Stockholders' Equity					
Other liabilities		1 0 2 0 2 0 0	8 9 1 0 0 0		
Common stock, $1 par		5 0 0 0 0 0	3 0 0 0 0 0		
Additional paid-in capital		2 0 0 0 0 0	1 3 0 0 0 0		
Minority interest in net assets of subsidiaries					
Retained earnings		3 2 0 0 0 0	1 6 0 0 0 0		
Total liabilities & stockholders' equity		2 0 4 0 2 0 0	1 4 8 1 0 0 0		

	(a)					

Paine Corporation and Subsidiary

Working Paper Eliminations

June 30, 2006

Pickens Corporation and Subsidiary
Working Paper for Consolidated Financial Statements
December 31, 2005

	Pickens Corporation	Skiffen Company	Eliminations increase (decrease)	Consolidated
Income Statement				
Revenue:				
Net sales	8 4 0 0 0 0	3 6 0 0 0 0		
Intercompany sales	8 0 6 0 0	6 5 0 0 0		
Gain on extinguishment of bonds				
Intercompany gain on sale of equipment	9 5 0 0			
Intercompany interest revenue	2 7 0 2			
Intercompany investment income	4 4 8 0 0			
Total revenue	9 7 7 6 0 2	4 2 5 0 0 0		
Costs & expenses & minority interest:				
Cost of goods sold	5 4 6 0 0 0	2 5 2 0 0 0		
Intercompany cost of goods sold	5 6 4 2 0	4 8 7 5 0		
Interest expense	3 2 0 0 0	9 1 0 6		
Intercompany interest expense		2 2 7 6		
Other operating expenses and income taxes expense	2 7 0 7 5 2	5 6 8 6 8		
Minority interest in net income of subsidiary				
Total cost and expenses and minority interest	9 0 5 1 7 2	3 6 9 0 0 0		
Net income	7 2 4 3 0	5 6 0 0 0		
Statement of Retained Earnings				
Retained earnings, beginning of year	5 9 5 0 0 0	1 3 6 0 0 0		
Net income	7 2 4 3 0	5 6 0 0 0		
Subtotal	6 6 7 4 3 0	1 9 2 0 0 0		
Dividends declared	2 0 0 0 0	1 1 0 0 0		
Retained earnings, end of year	6 4 7 4 3 0	1 8 1 0 0 0		

Pickens Corporation and Subsidiary
Working Paper for Consolidated Financial Statements (concluded)
December 31, 2005

	Pickens Corporation	Skiffen Company	Eliminations increase (decrease)	Consolidated
Balance Sheet				
Assets				
Intercompany receivables (payables)	3 5 8 0 0	(3 5 8 0 0)		
Inventories	1 8 0 0 0 0	9 6 0 0 0		
Investment in Skiffen Company common stock	3 9 3 2 0 0			
Investment in Skiffen Company bonds	2 7 9 1 8			
Plant assets	7 8 1 5 0 0	5 1 0 0 0 0		
Accumulated depreciation	(8 7 0 0 0)	(8 5 0 0 0)		
Other assets	3 3 3 7 8 2	1 4 6 5 0 0		
Goodwill				
Total assets	1 6 6 5 2 0 0	6 3 1 7 0 0		
Liabilities & Stockholders' Equity				
Dividends payable	2 0 0 0 0	2 2 0 0		
Bonds payable	4 0 0 0 0 0	1 2 0 0 0 0		
Intercompany bonds payable		3 0 0 0 0		
Discount on bonds payable		(4 2 8 1)		
Discount on intercompany bonds payable		(1 0 7 0)		
Deferred income tax liability	1 5 8 0 0			
Other liabilities	1 6 4 4 7 0	2 4 8 5 1		
Common stock, $2.50 par	4 0 0 0 0 0	2 5 0 0 0 0		
Additional paid-in capital	1 4 0 0 0	2 9 0 0 0		
Minority interest in net assets of subsidiary				
Retained earnings	6 4 7 4 3 0	1 8 1 0 0 0		
Retained earnings of subsidiary	3 5 0 0			
Total liabilities & stockholders' equity	1 6 6 5 2 0 0	6 3 1 7 0 0		

Pickens Corporation and Subsidiary

Working Paper Eliminations (concluded)

December 31, 2005

(a)

		Pickens Corporation and Subsidiary																										
		Working Paper Eliminations (concluded)																										
		December 31, 2005																										

a.

		Plummer Corporation			
		Adjusting Entry			
		December 31, 2005			

b.

Plummer Corporation and Subsidiary

Working Paper for Consolidated Financial Statements

December 31, 2005

	Plummer Corporation	Sinclair Company	Eliminations increase (decrease)	Consolidated
Income Statement				
Revenue:				
Net sales		426 000		
Intercompany sales				
Dividends revenue		750		
Intercompany gain on sale of				
machinery		800		
Intercompany investment				
income				
Other revenue		2 900		
Total revenue		534 450		
Costs & expenses & minority interest:				
Cost of goods sold		301 200		
Intercompany cost of goods				
sold		72 800		
Depreciation expense		11 200		
Other operating expenses		84 667		
Income taxes expenses		25 833		
Minority interest in net				
income of subsidiary				
Total costs and expenses				
and minority interest		495 700		
Net income		38 750		
Statement of Retained				
earnings				
Retained earnings, beginning				
of year		112 000		
Net income		38 750		
Subtotal		150 750		
Dividends declared		4 000		
Retained earnings, end of year		146 750		

Plummer Corporation and Subsidiary
Working Paper for Consolidated Financial Statements (concluded)
December 31, 2005

	Plummer Corporation	Sinclair Company	Eliminations increase (decrease)	Consolidated
Balance Sheet				
Assets				
Short-term investments		18 0 0 0		
Intercompany receivables				
(payables)		(16 0 0 0)		
Inventories		135 0 0 0		
Other current assets		106 7 5 0		
Deferred income tax asset				
Investment in Sinclair				
Company common stock				
Plant assets		279 0 0 0		
Accumulated depreciation		(196 7 0 0)		
Total assets		326 0 5 0		
Liabilities & Stockholders' Equity				
Dividends payable				
Income taxes payable		25 8 3 3		
Other current liabilities		123 4 6 7		
Deferred income tax liability				
Common stock, $10 par				
Common stock, $5 par		20 0 0 0		
Additional paid-in capital		10 0 0 0		
Minority interest in net assets				
of subsidiary				
Retained earnings		146 7 5 0		
Total liabilities &				
stockholders' equity		326 0 5 0		

Plummer Corporation and Subsidiary
Working Paper Eliminations
December 31, 2005

		Plummer Corporation and Subsidiary				
		Working Paper Eliminations (concluded)				
		December 31, 2005				

Pinch Corporation and Subsidiary						
Working Paper Eliminations						
March 31, 2006						

a.

		Prime Corporation						
		Journal Entries						

20	05				
Dec.	29				

b.

		Prime Corporation and Subsidiary						
		Working Paper Eliminations						
		December 31, 2005						

a.

		Pumble Corporation					
		Journal Entries					

20	07			
Oct	31			

b.

		Pumble Corporation		
		Working Paper Eliminations		
		October 31, 2007		

	(a)			

a.

			Speedy Company					
			Journal Entry					
20	06							
Mar	1							

b.

			Pronto Corporation			
			Computation of Balance of Investment in Speedy Company Common Stock			
			Ledger Account			
			March 1, 2006			

c.

		Pronto Corporation and Subsidiary			
		Working Paper Elimination			
		March 1, 2006			
	(a)				

	Pun Corporation and Subsidiary				
	Working Paper Eliminations				
	November 1, 2006				
(a)					

Name_____Section_____Date_____

Pr. 10–6

		Peterson Corporation and Subsidiary				
		Working Paper Eliminations				
		May 31, 2007				
	(a)					

a.

		Pomerania Corporation					
		Adjusting Entries					
		December 31, 2005					

b.

Pomerania Corporation and Subsidiaries

Working Paper for Consolidated Financial Statements

For Year Ended December 31, 2005

	Pomerania Corporation	Slovakia Company	Sylvania Company	Eliminations increase (decrease)	Consolidated

b.

Pomerania Corporation and Subsidiaries
Working Paper for Consolidated Financial Statements (concluded)
For Year Ended December 31, 2005

Balance Sheet	Pomerania Corporation	Slovakia Company	Sylvania Company	Eliminations increase (decrease)	Consolidated
Assets					
Intercompany receivables (payables)		(4 1 0 0 0)	(2 4 0 0 0)		
Inventories		9 0 0 0 0	1 1 5 0 0 0		
Investment in Slovakia Company common stock					
Investment in Slovakia Company bonds					
Investment in Sylvania Company preferred stock					
Investment in Sylvania Company common stock					
Other assets		5 5 5 0 0 0	5 1 0 0 0 0		
Total assets		6 0 4 0 0 0	6 0 2 6 0 0		
Liabilities & Stockholders' Equity					
Dividends payable		6 0 0 0 0			
Bonds payable		1 2 5 0 0 0	1 2 5 0 0 0		
Intercompany bonds payable		2 5 0 0 0			
Discount on bonds payable		(1 0 0 0 0)			
Discount on intercompany bonds payable		(2 0 0 0)			
Other liabilities		7 8 0 0 0	1 0 7 6 0 0		
Preferred stock, $20 par			5 0 0 0 0		
Common stock, $10 par		2 5 0 0 0 0	2 0 0 0 0 0		
Minority interest in net assets of subsidiaries					
Retained earnings		1 3 2 0 0 0	1 2 0 0 0 0		
Total liabilities & stockholders' equity		6 0 4 0 0 0	6 0 2 6 0 0		

Pomerania Corporation and Subsidiary

Working Paper Eliminations

December 31, 2005

(a)

		Pomerania Corporation and Subsidiary																						
		Working Paper Eliminations (concluded)																						
		December 31, 2005																						

a.

		Plover Corporation and Starling Company				
		Analysis of Intercompany Receivables (Payables) Accounts				
		December 31, 2006				
				Plover Corporation	Starling Company	

b.

		Plover Corporation		
		Adjusting Entry		
		December 31, 2006		

c.

Plover Corporation and Subsidiary
Working Paper for Consolidated Financial Statements
For Year Ended December 31, 2006

	Plover Corporation	Starling Company	Eliminations increase (decrease)	Consolidated
Income Statement				
Revenue:				
Net sales				
Intercompany sales				
Contract revenue		1 210 000		
Intercompany contract revenue		79 000		
Interest revenue				
Intercompany investment income				
Intercompany dividend revenue				
Intercompany gain on sale of land				
Intercompany interest revenue (expense)		(851)		
Total revenue		1 288 149		
Costs and expenses and minority interest:				
Cost of goods sold				
Intercompany cost of goods sold				
Cost of contract revenue		789 500		
Intercompany cost of contract revenue		62 500		
Operating expenses and income taxes expense		360 000		
Interest expense		31 149		
Minority interest in net income of subsidiary				
Total costs and expenses and minority interest		1 243 149		
Net income		45 000		
Statement of Retained Earnings				
Retained earnings, beginning of year		49 500		
Net income		45 000		
Subtotal		94 500		
Dividends declared		2 500		
Retained earnings, end of year		92 000		

Name_____Section_____Date_____

	Plover Corporation	Starling Company	Eliminations increase (decrease)	Consolidated
Balance Sheet				
Assets				
Intercompany receivables				
(payables)		2 1 1 8 9		
Costs and estimated earnings				
in excess of billings on				
uncompleted contracts		3 0 1 0 0		
Inventories		1 1 7 5 0 0		
Investment in Starling Company				
common stock				
Land		4 2 0 0 0		
Other plant assets (net)		4 0 8 0 0 0		
Other assets		8 4 2 1 1		
Total assets		7 0 3 0 0 0		
Liabilities & Stockholders' Equity				
Dividends payable		2 0 0 0		
Mortgage notes payable		3 8 9 0 0 0		
Other liabilities		7 0 0 0 0		
5% noncumulative,				
nonparticipating preferred				
stock, $1 par		5 0 0 0 0		
Common stock, no par		1 0 0 0 0 0		
Minority interest in net assets				
of subsidiary				
Retained earnings		9 2 0 0 0		
Retained earnings of subsidiary				
Total liabilities &				
stockholders' equity		7 0 3 0 0 0		

Plover Corporation and Subsidiary
Working Paper Eliminations
December 31, 2006

(a)

Pullard Corporation and Subsidiary

Working Paper for Consolidated Financial Statements

For Period Ended October 31, 2005

	Pullard Corporation	Staley Company	Eliminations increase (decrease)	Consolidated
Income Statement				
Revenue:				
Net sales	18 0 4 2 0 0 0	5 5 3 0 0 0 0		
Intercompany sales	1 5 8 0 0 0	2 3 0 0 0 0		
Intercompany investment income	5 0 5 1 5 0			
Interest revenue	2 6 2 5 0	1 7 0 0		
Intercompany interest revenue (expense)	7 8 7 5 0	(7 8 7 5 0)		
Total revenue	18 8 1 0 1 5 0	5 6 8 2 9 5 0		
Costs and expenses:				
Cost of good sold	10 4 4 2 0 0 0	3 0 1 0 5 0 0		
Intercompany cost of goods sold	1 5 8 0 0 0	1 4 9 5 0 0		
Depreciation expense	1 1 0 3 0 0 0	5 8 8 7 5 0		
Operating expenses and income taxes expense	3 4 4 8 5 0 0	1 0 6 3 9 0 0		
Interest expense	8 0 6 0 0 0	1 9 0 6 5 0		
Total costs and expenses	15 9 5 7 5 0 0	5 0 0 3 3 0 0		
Net income	2 8 5 2 6 5 0	6 7 9 6 5 0		
Statement of Retained Earnings				
Retained earnings, beginning of period	12 6 8 3 5 0 0	1 0 0 6 0 0 0		
Net income	2 8 5 2 6 5 0	6 7 9 6 5 0		
Retained earnings, end of period	15 5 3 6 1 5 0	1 6 8 5 6 5 0		

Pullard Corporation and Subsidiary
Working Paper for Consolidated Financial Statements (concluded)
For Period Ended October 31, 2005

	Pullard Corporation	Staley Company	Eliminations increase (decrease)	Consolidated
Balance Sheet				
Assets				
Cash	822000	530000		
Notes receivable		85000		
Trade accounts receivable (net)	2723700	1346400		
Intercompany receivables (payables)	12300	(12300)		
Inventories	3204000	1182000		
Investment in Staley Company common stock	6355150			
Investment in Staley Company preferred stock	150000			
Investment in Staley Company bonds	1500000			
Land	4000000	1560000		
Other plant assets	17161000	7850000		
Accumulated depreciation	(6673000)	(3838750)		
Other assets	263000	140000		
Goodwill				
Total assets	29518150	8842350		
Liabilities & Stockholders' Equity				
Notes payable		115000		
Trade accounts payable	1342000	169700		
7% bonds payable		3500000		
Intercompany 7% bonds payable		1500000		
Long-term debt	10000000			
Preferred stock, $5 par		750000		
Common stock, $10 par	2400000	1000000		
Additional paid-in capital	240000	122000		
Minority interest in net assets of subsidiary				
Retained earnings	15536150	1685650		
Total liabilities & stockholders' equity	29518150	8842350		

Pullard Corporation and Subsidiary					
Working Paper Eliminations					
October 31, 2005					

Caribbean Company

Journal Entries

a.

20 05					
Aug	1				

b.

20 05					
Aug	1				

a.   **U.S. Company**

Journal Entries

20	05															
June	27															

b.   **Spheric Company**

Journal Entries

Mar	31															

a.

		Zonal Corporation																										
		Journal Entries																										
20	05																											
Nov	19																											

b.

		Iberia Company																										
		Journal Entries																										
20	05																											
Jun	30																											

Imex Company

Journal Entries

a.

	20	05				
Mar		6				

b.

		Impo Company				
		Journal Entries				
20	05					
June	30					

		Allison Company				
		Adjusting Entries				
		Sept. 30, 2005				

Transcontinent Company
Remeasurement of Mideastia Branch Trial Balance
March 31, 2005

	Balance (LCUs) dr (cr)	Exchange rates	Balance (U.S. dollars) dr (cr)
Cash	LCU 2 0 0 0		
Trade accounts receivable	5 8 0 0 0		
Allowance for doubtful accounts	(1 0 0 0)		
Inventories	1 2 6 0 0 0		
Home office	(2 2 0 0 0 0)		
Sales	(1 8 4 0 0 0)		
Cost of goods sold	1 6 0 0 0 0		
Operating expenses	5 9 0 0 0		
Subtotals	LCU - 0 -		
Foreign currency transaction loss	- 0 -		
Totals	LCU - 0 -		

Sarasota Company
Remeasurement of Foreign Branch Trial Balance
April 30, 2005

	Balance (LCUs) dr (cr)	Exchange rates	Balance (U.S. dollars) dr (cr)
Cash	LCU 10000		
Trade accounts receivable	50000		
Inventories	124375		
Home office	(104565)		
Sales	(279300)		
Cost of goods sold	152289		
Operating expenses	47201		
Subtotals	-0-		
Foreign currency transaction loss	-0-		
Totals	LCU -0-		

Pan-Europe Corporation
Remeasurement of Amounts in Foreign Subsidiary's Trial Balances
November 30, 2007 and 2006

	Nov. 30, 2007			Nov. 30, 2006		
	LCUs	Exchange rates	U.S. dollars	LCUs	Exchange rates	U.S. dollars
Trade accounts receivable (net)	LCU 40000			LCU 35000		
Allowance for doubtful accounts	2200			2000		
Inventories	80000			75000		
Plant assets (net):						
Dec. 1, 2005 acquisition	136000			150000		
June 4, 2007 acquisition	27000					
Total plant assets (net)	LCU 163000			LCU 150000		
Accumulated depreciation:						
Dec. 1, 2005 acquisition (164,000)	LCU 28000			LCU 14000		
June 4, 2007 acquisition (30,000)	3000					
Total accumulated depreciation	LCU 31000			LCU 14000		
Long-term debt	LCU 100000			LCU 120000		
Common stock	LCU 50000			LCU 50000		

Westpac Corporation					
Journal Entries					
August, 2005					
Home Office Accounting Records ($)			Branch Accounts Records (S$)		

	Sudamerica Corporation																						
	Remeasurement of Trial Balance																						
	December 31, 2006																						
	Nicaduran							Exchange						U.S. dollars									
	pesos							rates						dr (cr)									
	dr (cr)																						
Cash	$N		2	5	0	0	0																
Trade accounts receivable			2	0	0	0	0																
Allowance for doubtful accounts			(	5	0	0	)																
Receivable from Portero Corporation			3	3	0	0	0																
Inventories	1	1	0	0	0	0																	
Plant assets	2	1	0	0	0	0																	
Accumulated depreciation of plant assets		(	7	9	9	0	0	)															
Notes payable		(	6	0	0	0	0	)															
Trade accounts payable		(	2	2	0	0	0	)															
Income taxes payable		(	4	0	0	0	0	)															
Common stock		(	5	0	0	0	0	)															
Retained earnings	(	1	0	0	6	0	0	)															
Sales—local	(	1	7	0	0	0	0	)															
Sales—foreign	(	2	0	0	0	0	0	)															
Cost of goods sold		2	0	7	6	0	0																
Depreciation expense			2	2	4	0	0																
Other operating expenses			6	0	0	0	0																
Income taxes expense			4	0	0	0	0																
Gain on disposal of plant assets			(	5	0	0	0	)															
Subtotals	$N			-	0	-																	
Foreign currency transaction loss																							
Totals	$N			-	0	-																	

a. (1)

Hightower Company Home Office				
Journal Entry (U.S. dollars)				
December 31, 2005				

(2)

Hightower Company Branch				
Journal Entries (Brazentina pesos)				
December 31, 2005				

Hightower Company

Working Paper for Combined Financial Statements of Home Office and Branch

For Year Ended December 31, 2005

	Home office adjusted trial balance (U.S. dollars) dr (cr)	Branch adjusted trial balance			Eliminations (U.S. dollars) dr (cr)	Home office and branch combined dr (cr)
		In Brazentina pesos dr (cr)	Exchange rates (remeasurement)	In U.S. dollars dr (cr)		
Income Statement:						
Sales						
Intracompany sales						
Inventories, beginning of year						
Purchases			(1)			
Intracompany purchases						
Inventories, end of year			(2)			
Depreciation expense						
Franchise fee expense						
Other operating expenses and income taxes expense						
Foreign currency transaction gain						
Net income						
Statement of Retained Earnings:						
Retained earnings, beginning of year						
Net income						
Retained earnings, end of year						

b.

b.

Hightower Company
Working Paper for Combined Financial Statements of Home Office and Branch (concluded)
For Year Ended December 31, 2005

	Home office adjusted trial balance (U.S. dollars) dr (cr)	Branch adjusted trial balance			Eliminations (U.S. dollars) dr (cr)	Home office and branch combined dr (cr)
		In Brazentina pesos dr (cr)	Exchange rates (remeasurement)	In U.S. dollars dr (cr)		
Balance Sheet:						
Cash						
Trade accounts receivable (net)						
Inventories, end of year						
Short-term prepayments						
Investment in Brazentina Branch						
Branch market research						
Plant assets						
Accumulated depreciation of plant assets						
Current liabilities						
Long-term debt						
Home office						
Common stock						
Retained earnings, end of year						
Totals						

Hightower Company				
Analysis of Intracompany Sales, Cost of Goods Sold, and Unrealized Profit in Inventories				
Home Office to Branch				
For Year Ended December 31, 2005				
	Selling Price		Cost	Markup
	Brazentina pesos	U.S. dollars	U.S. dollars	U.S. dollars
Beginning inventories				
Add: Shipments				
Subtotals				
Less: Ending inventories				
Cost of goods sold				

a.

Mapleleaf Corporation
Translated of Financial Statements
For Year Ended December 31, 2005

	Canadian dollars	Exchange rates	U.S. dollars
Income Statement			
Total revenue	$C 800 000		
Total costs and expenses	700 000		
Net income	$C 100 000		
Statement of Retained Earnings			
Retained earnings, beginning of year			
Net income	$C 100 000		
Subtotal	$C 100 000		
Dividends declared			
Retained earnings, end of year	$C 100 000		
Balance Sheet			
Assets			
Current assets	$C 400 000		
Plant assets (net)	500 000		
Total assets	$C 900 000		
Liabilities & Stockholder's Equity			
Current liabilities	$C 200 000		
Long-term debt	400 000		
Common stock	200 000		
Retained earnings	100 000		
Foreign currency translation adjustments			
Total liabilities & stockholder's equity	$C 900 000		

b.

Eagle Corporation
Journal Entries
December 31, 2005

c.	Eagle Corporation and Subsidiary																														
	Working Paper for Consolidated Financial Statements																															
	For Year Ended December 31, 2005																															
		Eagle Corporation							Mapleleaf Company							Eliminations increase (decrease)							Consolidated								
Income Statements																																
Total revenue		1	2	0	0	0	0	0																								
Intercompany investment																																
income			7	9	0	0	0																									
Total revenue and income		1	2	7	9	0	0	0																								
Total costs and expenses			9	0	0	0	0	0																								
Net income			3	7	9	0	0	0																								
Statements of Retained Earnings																																
Retained earnings, beginning																																
of year			5	0	0	0	0	0																								
Net income			3	7	9	0	0	0																								
Subtotal			8	7	9	0	0	0																								
Dividends declared			2	0	0	0	0	0																								
Retained earnings, end of year			6	7	9	0	0	0																								
Balance Sheet																																
Assets																																
Current assets			7	0	0	0	0	0																								
Investment in Mapleleaf																																
Company common stock			2	3	4	0	0	0																								
Plant assets (net)		1	6	0	0	0	0	0																								
Intangible assets (net)			2	4	0	0	0	0																								
Total assets		2	7	7	4	0	0	0																								
Liabilities & Stockholders' Equity																																
Current liabilities			4	0	0	0	0	0																								
Long-term debt			5	0	0	0	0	0																								
Common stock		1	2	0	0	0	0	0																								
Retained earnings			6	7	9	0	0	0																								
Foreign currency translation																																
adjustments	(			5	0	0	0	)																								
Total liabilities & stockholders'																																
equity		2	7	7	4	0	0	0																								

Eagle Corporation and Subsidiary													
Working Paper Elimination													
December 31, 2005													

a.

	Itican Subsidiary							Exchange		U.S. dollars	
	pesos							**rates**			
Income Statement											
Sales	IN	3	8	1	0	0	0				
Costs and expenses:											
Cost of goods sold	IN	3	0	0	0	0	0				
Depreciation expense			1	7	5	0	0				
Selling expenses			1	6	5	0	0				
Other operating expenses			2	3	6	6	7				
Income taxes expense				9	3	3	3				
Total costs and expenses	IN	3	6	7	0	0	0				
Net income	IN		1	4	0	0	0				
Statement of Retained Earnings											
Retained earnings, beginning of year	IN			7	0	0	0				
Net income			1	4	0	0	0				
Retained earnings, end of year	IN		2	1	0	0	0				
Balance Sheet											
Assets											
Cash	IN		1	0	0	0	0				
Trade accounts receivable (net)			3	5	0	0	0				
Inventories			8	3	0	0	0				
Plant assets		1	7	5	0	0	0				
Accumulated depreciation of plant assets		(	7	5	0	0	0)				
Total assets	IN	2	2	8	0	0	0				
Liabilities & Stockholder's Equity											
Trade accounts payable	IN			7	0	0	0				
Long-term debt		1	0	0	0	0	0				
Common stock, 1,000 shares		1	0	0	0	0	0				
Retained earnings			2	1	0	0	0				
Foreign currency translation adjustments											
Total liabilities & stockholder's equity	IN	2	2	8	0	0	0				

b.

		Panamer Corporation			
		Adjusting Entries			
		December 31, 2006			

		U.S. Subsidiary																			
		Adjusting Entry																			
		December 31, 2006																			

c.

Panamer Corporation and Subsidiaries

Working Paper for Consolidated Financial Statements

For Year Ended December 31, 2006

Income Statements	Panamer Corporation	U.S. subsidiary	Itican subsidiary	Eliminations increase (decrease)	Consolidated
Revenue:					
Sales					
Intercompany sales					
Intercompany investment income					
Total revenue					
Costs and expenses and minority interest					
Cost of goods sold					
Intercompany cost of goods sold					
Depreciation expense					
Selling expenses					
Other operating expenses					
Income taxes expenses					
Minority interest in net income of subsidiary					
Total cost and expenses and minority interest					
Net income					
Statements of Retained Earnings					
Retained earnings, beginning of year					
Net income					
Subtotal					
Dividends declared					
Retained earnings, end of year					

Panamer Corporation and Subsidiaries

Working Paper for Consolidated Financial Statements (concluded)

For Year Ended December 31, 2006

	Panamer Corporation	U.S. subsidiary	Itican subsidiary	Eliminations increase (decrease)	Consolidated
Balance Sheet					
Assets					
Cash					
Trade accounts receivable (net)					
Intercompany receivables (payables)					
Inventories					
Investment in U.S. Subsidiary common stock					
Investment in Itican Subsidiary common stock					
Plant assets					
Accumulated depreciation					
Total assets					
Liabilities & Stockholders' Equity					
Trade accounts payable					
Dividends payable					
Long-term debt					
Common stock					
Minority interest in net assets of subsidiary					
Retained earnings					
Foreign currency translation adjustments					
Total liabilities & stockholders' equity					

Panamer Corporation and Subsidiaries
Working Paper Eliminations
December 31, 2006

Panamer Corporation and Subsidiaries					
Working Paper Eliminations (concluded)					
December 31, 2006					

	Operating Segment																														
	Alpha								Beta								Gamma								Delta							

Wabash company
Computations of Segment Profit or Loss for Operating Segments
For Year Ended November 30, 2006

Cregar Company								
Corrected Partial Comparative Income Statements								
For Three Years Ended December 31, 2006								
	2006			2005			2004	

a.

Lang Corporation
Computation of Effective Income Tax Rates
For Year Ended July 31, 2006

	Year ended July 31, 2006			
	First quarter	Second quarter	Third quarter	Fourth quarter
Forecasted or actual pre-tax financial income for year	$ 8 0 0 0 0 0	$ 8 0 0 0 0 0	$ 8 0 0 0 0 0	$ 8 3 0 0 0 0

b.

Lang Corporation

Journal Entries

20 05					
Oct	31				
20 06					
Jan	31				

Bixler Company				
Income Statements				
For Two Years Ended December 31, 2006				
	2006		2005	

a.

		Draco Company		
		Income Statement		
		For Year Ended December 31, 2006		

b.

		Draco Company		
		Journal Entry		
		December 31, 2006		

a.

Principia Corporation and Subsidiaries

Information about Segment Profit or Loss and Segment Assets and Liabilities

For Year Ended December 31, 2006

(amount in thousands)

	Operating Segment				
	Principia	Seattle	Boston	London	Total

b.

Principia Corporation and Subsidiaries

Reconciliation of Operating Segment Totals to consolidated Totals

For Year Ended December 31, 2006

(amount in thousands)

	Revenue	Segment		Assets
		Profit		

a.

Lobeck Company
Partial Income Statement
For Year Ended April 30, 2006

b.

Spratt Company
Journal Entries

20	06					
Mar	31					

c.

Jackson Company
Journal Entries

20	06					
Mar	31					

Re-Org Company

Journal Entries

20	06						
July	24						

a.

Dodge Company
Statement of Affairs
October 31, 2006

Carrying amount	Assets	Current fair value	Estimated amount available	Loss or (gain) on realization
	Assets pledged for fully secured liabilities:			
	Assets pledged for partially secured liabilities:			
	Free assets:			

Carrying amount	Liabilities & Stockholders' Equity		Amount unsecured
	Unsecured liabilities with priority:		
	Fully secured liabilities:		
	Partially secured liabilities:		
	Unsecured liabilities without priority:		

b.

Dodge Company
Estimated Percentage of Claims to be Paid
October 31, 2006

Creditor group	Amount of claim	Amount to be paid	Percentage to be paid

a.	**Robaire Corporation, in Bankruptcy**																											
	Charles Stern, Trustee																											
	Journal Entries																											
20 07																												
Jan 2																												

	Robaire Corporation, in Bankruptcy			
	Charles Stern, Trustee			
	Journal Entries (concluded)			
20 07				

b.	Robaire Corporation, in Bankruptcy			
	Charles Stern, Trustee			
	Statement of Realization and Liquidation			
	For Month Ended January 31, 2007			

c.

				Debit	Credit
		Robaire Corporation, in Bankruptcy			
		Charles Stern, Trustee			
		Trial Balance, January 31, 2007			

a.

		Javits Corporation																										
		Correcting Journal Entries																										
		July 10, 2006																										

b.

Javits Corporation
Statement of Affairs
July 10, 2006

Carrying amount	Assets	Current fair value	Estimated amount available	Loss or (gain) on realization	Carrying amount	Liabilities & Stockholders' Equity		Amount unsecured
	Assets pledged for fully secured liabilities:					Unsecured liabilities with priority:		
						Fully secured liabilities:		
	Assets pledged for partially secured liabilities:					Partially secured liabilities:		
	Free assets:							

Laurel Company
Statement of Affairs
June 30, 2006

Carrying amount	Assets	Current fair value	Estimated amount available	Loss or (gain) on realization	Carrying amount	Liabilities & Stockholders' Equity	Amount unsecured
	Assets pledged for fully secured liabilities:					Unsecured liabilities with priority:	
						Fully secured liabilities:	
	Assets pledged for partially secured liabilities:					Partially secured liabilities:	
	Free assets:					Unsecured liabilities without priority:	

a.		Bilbo Corporation																									
		Journal Entries																									
		April 1, 2006																									
	(1)																										

b.

		Bilbo Corporation			
		Journal Entry (not required)			
		April 30, 2006			

		Bilbo Corporation			
		Balance Sheet			
		April 30, 2006			
		Assets			
		Liabilities & Stockholders' Equity			

Michael Synn, Executor		
Of the Will of Mildred Young, Deceased		
Charge and Discharge Statement		
For Period June 5 through December 31, 2006		
First, as to Principal		

a.

		Mark Castro, Executor																											
		Of the Will of Pablo Garica, Deceased																											
		Journal Entries for 2006																											

Mark Castro, Executor
Of the Will of Pablo Garcia, Deceased
Journal Entries for 2006 (concluded)

b.

Mark Castro, Executor
Of the Will of Pablo Garcia, Deceased
Charge and Discharge Statement
For Period March 1 through December 10, 2006

		First, as to Principal			

c.

	Manuel Montejano Trust			
	Journal Entry			
	December 10, 2006			

Dudley Mann, Executor

Of the Will of Janet Mann, Deceased

Charge and Discharge Statement

For Period May 31, 2002, through July 1, 2007

First, as to Principal

Second, as to Income

Dudley Mann, Executor		
Of the Will of Janet Mann, Deceased		
Charge and Discharge Statement (concluded)		
For Period May 31, 2006, through July 1, 2007		

Richard Cordes, Executor				
Of the Will of Frederick Doheny, Deceased				
Charge and Discharge Statement				
For Period February 1 through December 31, 2006				

First, as to Principal

Second, as to Income

Richard Cordes, Executor		
Of the Will of Frederick Doheny, Deceased		
Charge and Discharge Statement (concluded)		
For Period February 1 through December 31, 2006		

Seaside Hospital

Statement of Activities

For Year Ended June 30, 2006

(amounts in thousands)

		Holley School Quasi-Endowment Fund				
		Journal Entry				
		For Year Ended June 30, 2006				

		Holley School Plant Fund				
		Journal Entries				
		For Year Ended June 30, 2006				

		Holley School Unrestricted Fund				
		Journal Entries				
		For Year Ended June 30, 2006				

Nonprofit Trade Association

Statement of Activities

For Year Ended June 30, 2006

Nonprofit Trade Association

Statement of Financial Position

June 30, 2006

Assets

Liabilities & Net Assets

Suburban Welfare Services

a. (1)

Suburban Welfare Services

Computation of Original Equity Percentages for Investment Pool

July 1, 2005

	Cost	Current fair value	Original equity, %

(2)

Suburban Welfare Services

Computing of Revised Equity Percentages for Investment Pool

January 2, 2006

	Cost	Current fair value	Revised equity, %

b.		Suburban Welfare Services Unrestricted Fund																													
		Journal Entries																													
20	05																															
Dec	31																															
20	06																															
Jan	2																															

a.

Harbor Hospital General Fund
Journal Entries
October, 2006

		Harbor Hospital General Fund			
		Journal Entries (concluded)			
		October, 2006			

b.

		Harbor Hospital Arline E. Walters Annuity Fund			
		Journal Entry			
		October, 2006			

		Harbor Hospital Charles Watson Restricted Fund			
		Journal entry			
		October, 2006			

Wigstaff Foundation
Statement of Cash Flows (indirect method)
For Year Ended June 30, 2006

Net cash provided by operating activities (Exhibit 1)		$266000
Cash flows from investing activities:		
Cash flows from financing activities:		

a.

		Mid-City Sports Club																							
		Journal Entries																							
		For Year Ended June 30, 2006																							
	(1)																								

b.

Mid-City Sports Club		
Statement of Activities		
For Year Ended June 30, 2006		

Mid-City Sports Club		
Statement of Financial Position		
June 30, 2006		
Assets		
Liabilities & Net Assets		

	Unrestricted Fund	Restricted Fund	Endowment Fund
	State University		
	Journal Entries		
	For Year Ended June 30, 2006		
Transaction no. Ledger accounts	dr (cr)	dr (cr)	dr (cr)

State University
Journal Entries (concluded)
For Year Ended June 30, 2006

Transaction		Unrestricted Fund dr (cr)	Restricted Fund dr (cr)	Endowment Fund dr (cr)
no.	Ledger accounts			

		Plant	
	General	Replacement and	Endowment
Transaction	Fund	Expansion Fund	Fund
no. Ledger accounts	dr (cr)	dr (cr)	dr (cr)

Resthaven Hospital
Journal Entries
For Year Ended December 31, 2006

(1)

Transaction		General Fund	Plant Replacement and Expansion Fund	Endowment Fund
no.	Ledger accounts	dr (cr)	dr (cr)	dr (cr)

Resthaven Hospital

Journal Entries (concluded)

For Year Ended December 31, 2006

	Unrestricted Fund		Restricted Fund	
Libra College				
Journal Entries				
For Year Ended June 30, 2006				
Transaction no. Ledger accounts	dr (cr)		dr (cr)	
(1)				

		Libra College																				
		Journal Entries (concluded)																				
		For Year Ended June 30, 2006																				
Transaction			Unrestricted Fund dr (cr)								Restricted Fund dr (cr)											
no.	Ledger accounts																					

		Disadvantaged Children Association																							
		Statement of Activities																							
		For Year Ended June 30, 2006																							

		Disadvantaged Children Association																							
		Statement of Financial Position																							
		June 30, 2006																							
		Assets																							
		Liabilities & Net Assets																							

Weedpatch County General Fund

Statement of Revenues, Expenditures, and Changes in Fund Balance

For Year Ended June 30, 2006

(amounts in thousands)

	Budget	Actual	Variance favorable (unfavorable)

Weedpatch County General Fund

Balance Sheet

June 30, 2006

(amounts in thousands)

		Assets			
		Liabilities & Fund Balance			

City of Lory General Fund

Journal Entries

For Year Ended June 30, 2006

City of Lory General Fund
Journal Entries (concluded)
For Year Ended June 30, 2006

		City of Riverdale General fund		
		Correcting Journal Entries		
		December 31, 2006		
	(1)			

		Canning County General Fund				
		Journal Entries				
		For Year Ended June 30, 2006				
	(1)					

a. (1)

Arden School District General Fund

Statement of Revenues, Expenditures, and Changes in Fund Balance

For Year Ended December 31, 2006

	Budget	Actual	Variance favorable (unfavorable)

(2)

Arden School District General Fund

Balance Sheet

December 31, 2006

Assets		
Liabilities & Fund Balance		

b.

Arden School District General Fund

Closing Entries

December 31, 2006

a.

		Melton School District General Fund				
		Journal Entries				
		For Year Ended June 30, 2006				

b.

Melton School District General Fund
Closing Entries
June 30, 2006

c.

Melton School District General Fund
Post-Closing Trial Balance
June 30, 2006

Name_____Section_____Date_____

Pr. 17–7

City of Romaine General Fund		
Computation of Property Tax Levy Required		
For Year Ending June 30, 2006		

		Town of Tosca General Fund																						
		Journal Entries																						
		For Year Ended June 30, 2006																						

Town of Tosca General Fund					
Journal Entries (concluded)					
For Year Ended June 30, 2006					

City of Douglas General Fund

Journal Entries

For Year Ended June 30, 2006

(1)

City of Douglas General Fund				
Journal Entries (continued)				
For Year Ended June 30, 2006				

		City of Douglas General Fund																					
		Journal Entries (concluded)																					
		For Year Ended June 30, 2006																					

		Ridge City General Capital Assets Account Group								
		Journal Entries								
20	05									
Oct	31									

		Town of Dilbey Capital Projects Fund																										
		Statement of Revenues, Expenditures, and Changes in Fund Balance																										
		For Year Ended June 30, 2006																										

		Town of Dilbey Capital Projects Fund																										
		Balance Sheet																										
		June 30, 2006																										
		Assets																										
		Liabilities & Fund Balance																										

a.

		Town of Logan Town Hall Capital Projects Fund			
		Journal Entries			
		For Year Ended June 30, 2006			

b.

		Town of Logan Special Revenue Fund			
		Journal Entries			
		For Year Ended June 30, 2006			

		Town of Logan Special Revenue Fund				
		Journal Entries (concluded)				
		For Year Ended June 30, 2006				

Webster Village Capital Projects Fund
Journal Entry

20	05																			

Webster Village Debt Service Fund
Journal Entry

20	05																			

Webster Village General Long-Term Debt Account Group
Journal Entry

20	05																			

Webster Village General Capital Assets Account Group
Journal Entries

20	05																			

		Webster Village Special Revenue Fund																						
		Journal Entry																						
20	06																							

Calabash County Gasoline Tax Special Revenue Fund

Journal Entry

20	05						

Calabash County Capital Projects Fund

Journal Entry

20	05						

Calabash County Special Assessment Special Revenue Fund

Journal Entry

20	05						

Calabash County General Fund

Journal Entries

20	05						

		Calabash County General Capital Assets Account Group				
		Journal Entry				
20	05					

City of Arlette General fund				
Journal Entries				
20	05			

City of Arlette General Long-Term Debt Account Group				
Journal Entries				
20	05			

City of Arlette General Long-Term Debt Account Group

Journal Entries (concluded)

20	07				

City of Arlette General Capital Assets Account Group

Journal Entries

20	05				

a.	City of Ordway Library Capital Projects Fund																					
	Journal Entries																						
	For Year Ended June 30, 2007																						
20 06																							

City of Ordway Library Capital Project Fund					
Journal Entries (concluded)					
For Year Ended June 30, 2007					
20	07				

b.

City of Ordway Library Capital Projects Fund			
Balance Sheet			
June 30, 2007			
Assets			
Liabilities & Fund Balance			

City of Wilmont Civic Center Capital Projects Fund				
Journal Entries				
For Year Ended June 30, 2006				
	(1)			

a.

		Angelus School District General Fund				
		Journal Entries				
20	05					

b.

Angelus School District Capital Projects Fund
Journal Entries

20	05					

c.

Angelus School District General Capital Assets Account Group
Journal Entry

20	05					

d.

Angelus School District General Long-Term Debt Account Group
Journal Entry

20	05					

		Kaspar City General Fund			
		Journal Entries			
20	05				

		Kaspar City Enterprise Fund			
		Journal Entry			
20	05				

		Kaspar City General Captial Assets Account Group			
		Journal Entry			
20	05				

		Kaspar City Internal Service Fund			
		Journal Entry			
20	05				

Town of Tolliver Enterprise Fund		
Statement of Revenues, Expenses, and Changes in Net Assets		
For Year Ended June 30, 2006		

Town of Tolliver Enterprise Fund																	
Balance Sheet																	
June 30, 2006																	

Assets																	
Liabilities																	
Net Assets																	

Name_____Section_____Date_____

Account titles	Diggs County Tax Agency Fund dr (cr)	Diggs County General Fund dr (cr)	Evans City General Fund dr (cr)	Hickman Township General Fund dr (cr)

Diggs County, Evans City, and Hickman Township
Journal Entries
For Three Months Ended October 1, 2005

		Town of Northville			
		Journal Entries			
		For Year Ended June 30, 2006			
Transaction no.	Fund or account group	Account titles		Debit	Credit

Town of Northville
Journal Entries (concluded)
For Year Ended June 30, 2006

Transaction no.	Fund or account group	Account titles		Debit	Credit

		City of Cavendish Internal Service Fund		
		Journal Entries		
		For Year Ended June 30, 2006		

Name_____Section_____Date_____

a.

Town of Novis General Fund

Adjusting and Closing Entries

June 30, 2006

Town of Novis General Fund

Adjusting and Closing Entries (concluded)

June 30, 2006

b.

Town of Novis General Fund

Post-Closing Trial Balance

June 30, 2006

c.

Town of Novis General Long-Term Debt Account Group																										
Adjusting Entry																										
June 30, 2006																										

Town of Novis General Capital Assets Account Group																										
Adjusting Entries																										
June 30, 2006																										

Town of Novis Water Utility Enterprise Fund																										
Adjusting Entry																										
June 30, 2006																										

Village of Rosner Enterprise Fund				
Statement of Cash Flows (indirect method)				
For Year Ended June 30, 2006				